Leon Strous · Vinton G. Cerf (Eds.)

Internet of Things

Information Processing in an Increasingly Connected World

First IFIP International Cross-Domain Conference, IFIPIoT 2018
Held at the 24th IFIP World Computer Congress, WCC 2018
Poznan, Poland, September 18–19, 2018
Revised Selected Papers

Editors
Leon Strous
De Nederlandsche Bank
Amsterdam, The Netherlands

Vinton G. Cerf
Google
Reston, VA, USA

https://doi.org/10.1007/978-3-030-15651-0

Preface

Like every new technology, the Internet of Things (IoT) offers opportunities for progress and application for beneficial purposes while at the same time it introduces or increases risks and threats. There are many aspects to be considered when talking about IoT. Consequently the IFIP Domain Committee on IoT organized a working conference with a broad scope. In principle, papers on all aspects related to IoT were solicited. This book contains the revised versions of the papers presented at the first IFIP Internet of Things (IoT) conference that took place in Poznan, Poland, during September 18–19, 2018 as part of the IFIP World Computer Congress (WCC) 2018.

The IoT Program Committee consisted of 55 members who considered 24 submissions for the first edition of this conference. Each paper was on average refereed by three reviewers, using the single-blind review principle. In total, 13 papers were selected for presentation resulting in an acceptance rate of 54%. One accepted paper is not included in this book because it was not presented at the conference. The papers were selected on the basis of originality, quality and relevance to the topic.

The papers range from a technology perspective to a business perspective. Topics include hardware, software and management aspects, process innovation, privacy, power consumption, architecture, applications and a few more. In addition to the refereed papers we also have a paper from the invited speaker Kees van der Klauw who challenged the audience by stating that the IoT is hardly about technology. Finally the draft position paper by IFIP on the IoT is included. The paper investigates what choices can or must be made regarding the various aspects of the IoT. This draft was discussed in a panel session and the outcome of the discussion will be included in the final version.

Looking at this wide range of topics makes us realize that we are just at the infancy of the IoT and that a lot of further research and work are needed. We thank the authors, the Program Committee and the participants for their hard work and contributions and look forward to a continued involvement.

The IFIP World Computer Congress (WCC) 2018 had a number of plenary and special sessions scheduled. We are very pleased to present in this book a few contributions out of those sessions. WCC 2018 had four plenary keynote speakers: Wil van der Aalst, Leslie Valiant, Jan Camenish and Shamika Sirimanne. While all four keynote presentations were recorded on video (see www.wcc2018.org and www.ifip.org) Wil van der Aalst also contributed a paper, addressing the question of responsible data science in a dynamic world. A special day at WCC 2018 was the Enigma day with a live demonstration of a message encryption and decryption. A paper in this book describes the history of how three Poznan University students broke the German Enigma Code and shortened World War Two. The third contribution in this book is a summary of workshops on professionalism and frameworks, a "must be" core topic for professional computer societies and associations. And finally, in an open debate, an emerging question was discussed: Should Artificial Intelligence be more regulated? While this session is also recorded on video, a summary is presented in this book.

We feel that all contributions make the book a rich volume in the IFIP AICT series and we trust that the reader will be inspired by it.

February 2019

Leon Strous
Vinton G. Cerf

IFIP WCC 2018

Information Processing in an Increasingly Connected World: Opportunities and Threats

IFIP WCC 2018 Steering Committee

General Congress Co-chairs

Roman Słowiński — Poznan University of Technology, Poland
Leon Strous — De Nederlandsche Bank, The Netherlands

General Program Co-chairs

Mike Hinchey — Lero-The Irish Software Research Centre, Ireland
Jerzy Nawrocki — Poznan University of Technology, Poland

Publication Chair

Basie von Solms — University of Oxford, UK/University of Johannesburg, South Africa

General Organizing Chairs

Robert Wrembel (Chair) — Poznan University of Technology, Poland
Andrzej Jaszkiewicz (Co-chair) — Poznan University of Technology, Poland

Members

Joanna Józefowska — Poznan University of Technology, Poland
A Min Tjoa — Vienna University of Technology, Austria

IFIPIoT 2018

Internet of Things: Information Processing in an Increasingly Connected World

IFIPIoT Program Committee

Co-chairs

Leon Strous*	De Nederlandsche Bank, The Netherlands
Vinton Cerf	Google, USA

Members (* are also member of the IFIP Domain Committee IoT)

Jose Abdelnour-Nocera	University of West London, UK
Hamideh Afsarmanesh	University of Amsterdam, The Netherlands
Carmelo Ardito*	Università degli Studi di Bari Aldo Moro, Italy
Ioannis Askoxylakis	FORTH-ICS, Greece
Soumya Banerjee	Birla Institute of Technology, Mesra, India
Ezio Bartocci	Vienna University of Technology, Austria
Juergen Becker	Karlsruhe Institute of Technology, Germany
Samia Bouzefrane	CEDRIC, Conservatoire National des Arts et Métier, France
Luis Camarinho-Matos*	Universidade NOVA de Lisboa, Portugal
Augusto Casaca*	INESC, Portugal
Tibor Cinkler*	Budapest University of Technology and Economics, Hungary
Luc Claessen	University of Hasselt, Belgium
Lucio Davide Spano	University of Cagliari, Italy
Jose Neuman De Souza*	Federal University of Ceara, Brazil
Ibrahim Elfadel	Masdar Institute at Khalifa University of Science and Technology, UAE
Gordon Fletcher*	University of Salford, UK
Miria Grisot	University of Oslo, Norway
Gerhard Hancke	City University of Hong Kong, SAR China
Michael Huebner	Brandenburg University of Technology Cottbus, Germany
Katrin Jonsson	Umeå University, Sweden
Joaquim Jorge	INESC, Portugal
Srinivas Katkoori	University of South Florida, Tampa, USA
Bouabdellah Kechar	University of Oran 1 Ahmed Ben Bella, Algeria
Arianit Kurti	RISE Interactive, Research Institutes of Sweden, Sweden
Maryline Laurent	Telecom SudParis, France
Antonio Mana	University of Malaga, Spain
Tiziana Margaria	University of Limerick, Ireland

Konstantinos Markantonakis	Royal Holloway University of London, UK
Peter Marwedel	Technical University of Dortmund, Germany
Maristella Matera	Politecnico di Milano, Italy
Christina Mörtberg*	Linnaeus University, Sweden
Raja Naeem Akram	ISG-SCC, Royal Holloway University of London, UK
Maciej Ogorzalek	Jagiellonian University, Poland
Fabio Paterno*	CNR-ISTI, Italy
Rasmus Pedersen	Copenhagen Business School, Denmark
Simon Perrault	Yale-NUS College, Singapore
Joachim Posegga	University of Passau, Germany
Ricardo Rabelo	Federal University of Santa Catarina, Brazil
Franz Rammig	University of Paderborn, Germany
Kai Rannenberg	Goethe University Frankfurt, Germany
Delphine Reinhardt	Georg-August-Universität Göttingen, Germany
Ricardo Reis*	Universidade Federal do Rio Grande do Sul, Brazil
Carmen Santoro	CNR-ISTI, Italy
Damien Sauveron*	University of Limoges, France
Weiming Shen	National Research Center, Canada
Basie von Solms*	University of Johannesburg, South Africa
Dimitrios Soudris	National Technical University of Athens, Greece
Jean-Yves Tigli	University of Côte d'Azur – UCA, France
Chi Tsui	Hong Kong University of Science and Technology Kowloon, SAR China
Fatih Ugurdag	Ozyegin University Istanbul, Turkey
Eugenio Villar	University of Cantabria, Spain
Janet Wesson	Nelson Mandela University, South Africa
Marco Winckler*	Université Nice Sophia Antipolis, France

Additional Reviewers

Boutheyna Belgacem	University of Passau, Germany
Saifeddine Ben Haj Khalifa	Karlsruhe Institute of Technology, Germany
Akos Grosz	Goethe University Frankfurt, Germany
Javier Hoffmann	Ruhr-University Bochum, Germany
Osvaldo Navarro	Ruhr-University Bochum, Germany
Johannes Pfau	Karlsruhe Institute of Technology, Germany

Contents

WCC 2018 Plenary Contributions: Keynote, Special Sessions

Responsible Data Science in a Dynamic World
The Four Essential Elements of Data Science

Wil M. P. van der Aalst(✉)

Lehrstuhl für Informatik 9, Process and Data Science, RWTH Aachen University, 52056 Aachen, Germany
wvdaalst@pads.rwth-aachen.de
http://vdaalst.com

Abstract. Data science is changing our world in many different ways. Data and the associated data science innovations are changing everything: the way we work, the way we move, the way we interact, the way we care, the way we learn, and the way we socialize. As a result, many professions will cease to exist. For example, today's call centers will disappear just like video rental shops disappeared. At the same time, new jobs, products, services, and opportunities emerge. Hence, it is important to understand the essence of data science. This extended abstract discusses the four essential elements of data science: "water" (availability, magnitude, and different forms of data), "fire" (irresponsible uses of data and threats related to fairness, accuracy, confidentiality, and transparency), "wind" (the way data science can be used to improve processes), and "earth" (the need for data science research and education). Next to providing an original view on data science, the abstract also highlights important next steps to ensure that data will not just change, but also improve our world.

Keywords: Data science · Responsible data science · Process mining · Big data

1 Data Science

This extended abstract is based on a keynote given at the IFIP World Computer Congress (WCC 2018) on 18 September 2018, in Poznan, Poland. The main theme of WCC 2018 was "Information Processing in an Increasingly Connected World: Opportunities and Threats". Data science is the main driver for the changes that create these opportunities and threats. Recent reports [6,7] indicate that many jobs will cease to exist because of advances in machine learning, artificial intelligence, robotics, and other forms of smart automation. These advances are only possible because of both the availability of data and progress in data science.

It is not easy to define data science. The data science pipeline shown in Fig. 1 illustrates the breadth of the discipline. The "infrastructure" part of the pipeline

L. Strous and V. G. Cerf (Eds.): IFIPIoT 2018, IFIP AICT 548, pp. 3–10, 2019.
https://doi.org/10.1007/978-3-030-15651-0_1

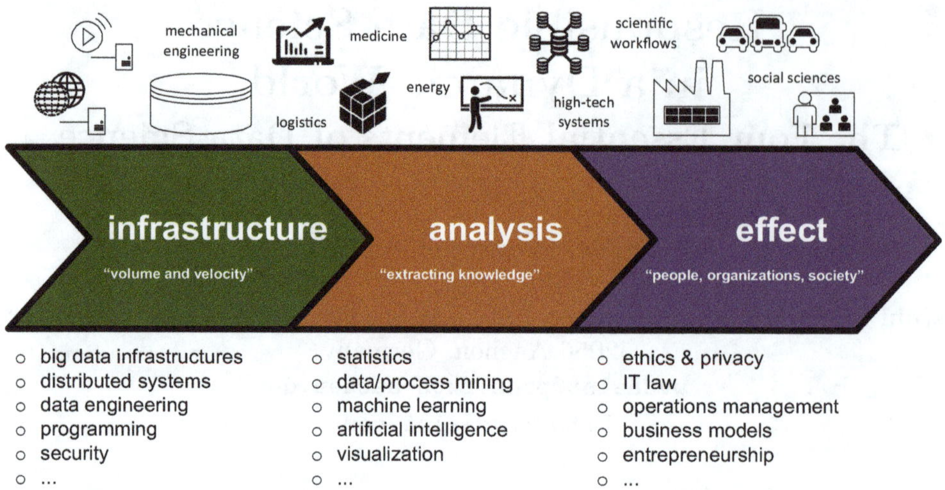

Fig. 1. The data science pipeline showing that different capabilities are needed to turn data into value.

is concerned with the huge volume and incredible velocity of data. Hence, the primary focus is on making things scalable and instant. The "analysis" part of the pipeline is concerned with extracting knowledge. This is about providing answers to known and unknown unknowns.[1] The "effect" part of the pipeline is concerned the impact of data science on people, organizations, and society. Here legal, ethical, and financial aspects come into play.

The uptake of the Internet of Things (IoT) illustrates the pivotal role of data science. More and more devices (light bulbs, clothes, refrigerators, containers, bicycles, etc.) are connected to the internet and produce data. These devices are becoming "smart" by learning from the data collected. The Internet of Things (IoT) depends on the whole data science pipeline shown in Fig. 1. We are (or will be) surrounded by smart devices collecting data and the impact of this cannot be overestimated.

In the remainder, we define the four essential elements of data science. As metaphor we use the classical four elements: "water", "fire", "wind", and "earth". According to the Empedocles, a Greek pre-Socratic philosopher who lived in Sicily in the fifth century B.C., all matter is comprised of these four elements. Other ancient cultures had similar lists, sometimes also composed of more elements (e.g., earth, water, air, fire, and aether) that tried to explain nature and complexity of all matter in terms of simpler substances. Today, we know that this is not the case. However, for data science, we are still in the phase where we are looking for the essential elements. This paper uses "water" as a placeholder for the availability of different forms of data, "fire" as a placeholder for irresponsible uses of data (e.g., threats to fairness, accuracy, confidentiality,

[1] "There are known knowns; there are things we know we know. We also know there are known unknowns; that is to say we know there are some things we do not know. But there are also unknown unknowns – the ones we don't know we don't know." (Donald Rumsfeld, February 12, 2002).

and transparency), "wind" as a placeholder for the way that data science can be used to improve processes, and "earth" as a placeholder for education and research (i.e., the base of data science) underpinning all of this. These four essential elements are discussed in the remaining sections.

2 The "Water" of Data Science

The first essential element of data science ("water") is the data itself. The exponential growth of data is evident. Figure 2 (inspired by the analysis in [9]) shows the rapid developments in terms of *costs* (things are getting exponentially cheaper), *speed* (things are going exponentially faster), and *miniaturization* (things are getting exponentially smaller). This is not limited to *processing* (i.e., CPU and GPU processors), but also applies to *storage* and *communication*. Consider for example the costs of storage. To store one megabyte (MB) of data in the sixties one would need to pay one million euros. Today, one can buy a 10TB harddisk for less than 300 euro, i.e., 0.00003 cents per MB. Another example is the bandwidth efficiency, also called spectral efficiency, which refers to the information rate that can be transmitted over a given bandwidth. It is the net bitrate (useful information rate excluding error-correcting codes) or maximum throughput divided by the bandwidth in hertz of a communication channel or a data link. The spectacular progress of our data handling capabilities illustrated by Fig. 2, explains why data science has become on of the key concerns in any organization. In the sixties, we only had a few "drops of data" whereas today we are facing a "tsunami of data" flooding our society.

Clearly, data science has its roots in statistics, a discipline that developed over four centuries [1]. John Graunt (1620–1674) started to study London's death records around 1660. Based on this he was able to predict the life expectancy of a person at a particular age. Francis Galton (1822–1911) introduced statistical concepts like regression and correlation at the end of the 19th century. Although data science can be seen as a continuation of statistics, the majority of statisticians did not contribute much to recent progress in data science. Most statisticians focused on theoretical results rather than real-world analysis problems. The computational aspects, which are critical for larger data sets, are typically ignored by statisticians. The focus is on generative modeling rather than prediction and dealing with practical challenges related to data quality and size. When the data mining community realized major breakthroughs in the discovery of patterns and relationships (e.g., efficiently learning decision trees and association rules), most statisticians referred to these discovery practices as "data fishing", "data snooping", and "data dredging" to express their dismay [1,4,10].

Put differently; most statisticians were focused on techniques to make reliable statements given a few "drops of data". Such viewpoints turned out to be less effective when dealing with "tsunamis of data".

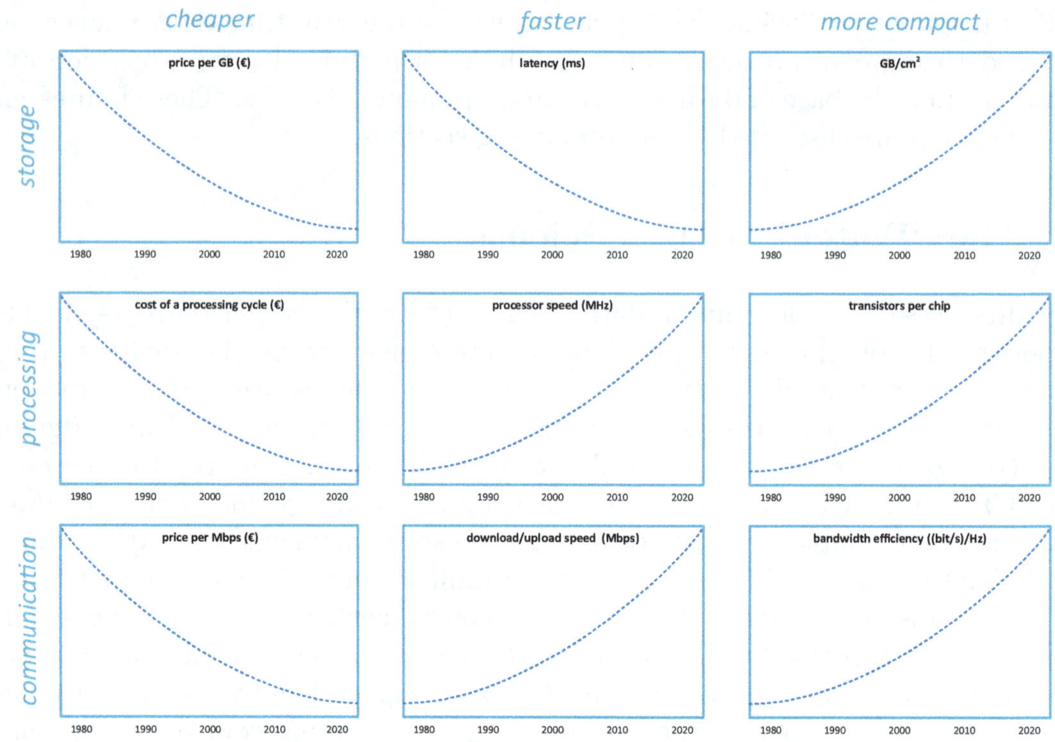

Fig. 2. Moore's law predicts an exponential growth of the number of transistors per chip. This can be generalized to storage and transition and also applies to costs and speed.

3 The "Fire" of Data Science

The second essential element of data science ("fire") refers to the dangers of using data in an irresponsible way. Data abundance combined with powerful data science techniques has the potential to dramatically improve our lives by enabling new services and products, while improving their efficiency and quality. Many of today's scientific discoveries (e.g., in health) are already fueled by developments in statistics, mining, machine learning, artificial intelligence, databases, and visualization. At the same time, there are also great concerns about the use of data. Increasingly, customers, patients, and other stakeholders are concerned about irresponsible data use. Automated data decisions may be unfair or non-transparent. Confidential data may be shared unintentionally or abused by third parties.

From 2015 until 2017, the author led the *Responsible Data Science* (RDS) initiative where the strongest Dutch data science groups joined forces to address problems related to *fairness*, *accuracy*, *confidentiality*, and *transparency* (www.responsibledatascience.org). The goal of RDS is to show that data science techniques, infrastructures and approaches can be made responsible by design. *Responsible Data Science* (RDS) revolves around four main challenges:

- *Data science without prejudice* - How to avoid unfair conclusions even if they are true?

- *Data science without guesswork* - How to answer questions with a guaranteed level of accuracy?
- *Data science that ensures confidentiality* - How to answer questions without revealing secrets?
- *Data science that provides transparency* - How to clarify answers such that they become indisputable?

The term *green data science* was introduced for cutting-edge solutions that enable individuals, organizations and society to benefit from widespread data availability while ensuring *Fairness*, *Accuracy*, *Confidentiality*, and *Transparency* (FACT) [2].

Naïvely one could think that "fire" can be controlled by "water", however this is not the case. When considering RDS, it is better to consider data as "oil" rather than "water". It needs to be controlled and stored carefully.

There is a need for new and positive data science techniques that are responsible (i.e., "green") by design. This cannot be solved by stricter laws. Using the metaphor of "green energy": We should not be against the use of energy ("data"), but address the pollution caused by traditional engines. Fortunately, there are plenty of ideas to make data science green. For example, discrimination-aware data mining [8] can be used to ensure fairness and polymorphic encryption can be used to ensure confidentiality.

4 The "Wind" of Data Science

The third essential element of data science ("wind") is concerned with the way data and processes interact. Storing and processing data is not a goal in itself. Data are there to support processes. The campaign "The best run companies run SAP" illustrates that the purpose of information systems is to ensure that processes run well. Data science can help organizations to be more effective, to provide a better service, to deliver faster, and to do all of this at lower costs. This applies to logistics, production, transport, healthcare, banking, insurance, and government. This also applies to individuals. Data science will increasingly support our personal workflows and take over tasks, or at least support them. Data ("water") can be used to manage and support processes ("wind") through the use of data science technologies.

An emerging technology linking "water" and "wind" is *process mining* [1]. Process mining bridges the gap between traditional model-based process analysis (e.g., simulation and other business process management techniques) and data-centric analysis techniques such as machine learning and data mining. Process mining seeks the confrontation between event data (i.e., observed behavior) and process models (hand-made or discovered automatically) [1]. The process-mining spectrum is broad and includes techniques for process discovery, conformance checking, prediction, and bottleneck analysis. These techniques tend to be very different from mainstream data mining and machine learning techniques which are typically not process-centric.

Consider for example the topic of *Robotic Process Automation* (RPA). RPA is an umbrella term for tools that operate on the user interface of other computer systems in the way a human would do. RPA aims to replace people by automation done in an "outside-in" manner [3]. This differs from the classical "inside-out" approach to improve information systems. Unlike traditional workflow technology, the information system remains unchanged. The robots are replacing humans while leaving the back-end systems intact. RPA is a way to support processes in a more cost-effective manner. However, this requires learning what humans do by observing them. Data science approaches like process mining can be used to learn the behavior of people doing routine tasks. After the desired behavior has been "played in", it can be "played out" to handle new cases in an intelligent manner.

RPA illustrates that data science will lead to new trade-offs between what humans do and what robots do [6,7]. These trade-offs are interesting: How to distribute work between given breakthroughs in data science? Obviously, the question needs to take the "fire" dimension into account.

5 The "Earth" of Data Science

The fourth essential element of data science ("earth") is concerned with the foundations of a data-driven society: *education* and *research*. Education (in every sense of the word) is one of the fundamental factors in the development of data science. Data science education is needed at any level. People need to be aware of the way algorithms make decisions that may influence their lives. Privacy discussions reveal the ignorance of policy makers and end users. Moreover, to remain competitive, countries should invest in data science capabilities. This can only be realized through education. Data science research plays a similar role. On the one hand, it is key for our education. On the other hand, research is needed to address the many technological and societal challenges (e.g., ensuring fairness, accuracy, confidentiality, and transparency).

Currently, eight of the world's ten biggest companies, as measured by market capitalization, are American: Apple, Alphabet (incl. Google), Microsoft, Amazon, Berkshire Hathaway, Facebook, JPMorgan Chase, and Bank of America.[2] The two remaining companies are Chinese: Alibaba and Tencent Holdings. This shows the dominance of a few countries due to investments in IT. Most of the companies are relatively new and emerged through the smart use of data. Amazon and Alibaba are dominating the way we buy products. Google is controlling the way we search. Facebook is controlling the way we socialize. Apple, Alphabet, and Microsoft are controlling the platforms we use (iOS, Android, and Windows). Consider for example Facebook. On the one hand, many people are expressing concerns about the use of data. On the other hand, Facebook has over 2 billion monthly active users that provide personal information in order to use social media. One of the problems of data science is that due to economies

[2] Based on market capitalization data by Bloomberg on 31 March 2018.

of scale "the winner takes it all". This may also apply to education, e.g., on Coursera a few US universities are dominating data science education.

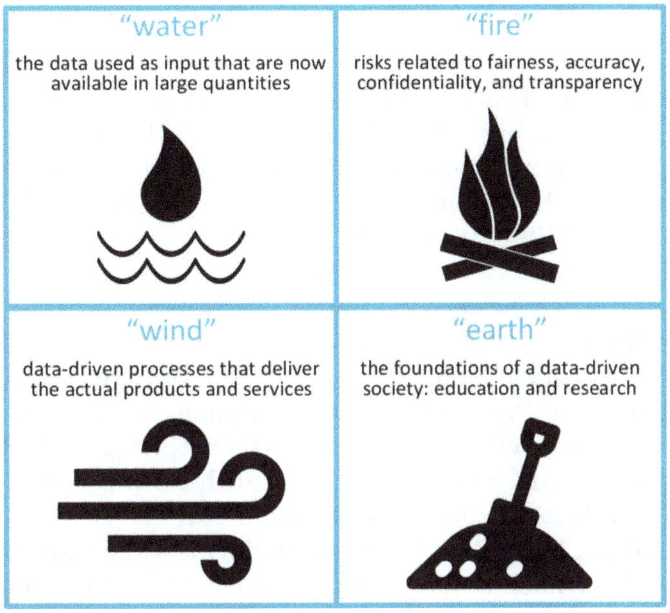

Fig. 3. The "water", "fire", "wind", and "earth" of data science.

Data science literacy and major public investments are needed to address these concerns. This cannot be left to "the market" or solved through half-hearted legislation like the European General Data Protection Regulation (GDPR) [5].

6 Epilogue

This extended abstract aimed to present some of the key messages of the keynote presentation for the IFIP World Computer Congress (WCC 2018). It stresses the importance of data science for people, organizations, and society. Just like computer science emerged as a new discipline from mathematics in the early eighties, we can now witness that the data science discipline is emerging from computer science, statistics, and social sciences.

In this paper, we discussed the four essential elements of data science (see Fig. 3): "water" (availability, magnitude, and different forms of data), "fire" (irresponsible uses of data and threats related to fairness, accuracy, confidentiality, and transparency), "wind" (the way data science can be used to improve processes), and "earth" (the need for data science research and education). By presenting data science in this manner, we hope to get more attention for process-centric forms of data science (e.g., process mining), responsible data science, data science education, and data science research. The dominance of a few companies and countries when it comes to data science is undesirable and requires the attention of politicians and policymakers. The IFIP could and should play an active role in this discussion.

References

1. van der Aalst, W.M.P.: Process Mining: Data Science in Action. Springer, Heidelberg (2016). https://doi.org/10.1007/978-3-662-49851-4_1
2. van der Aalst, W.M.P.: Responsible data science: using event data in a "People Friendly" manner. In: Hammoudi, S., Maciaszek, L.A., Missikoff, M.M., Camp, O., Cordeiro, J. (eds.) ICEIS 2016. LNBIP, vol. 291, pp. 3–28. Springer, Cham (2017). https://doi.org/10.1007/978-3-319-62386-3_1
3. van der Aalst, W.M.P., Bichler, M., Heinzl, A.: Robotic process automation. Bus. Inf. Syst. Eng. **60**(4), 269–272 (2018)
4. Breiman, L.: Statistical modeling: the two cultures. Stat. Sci. **16**(3), 199–231 (2001)
5. European Commission: Proposal for a Regulation of the European Parliament and of the Council on the Protection of Individuals with Regard to the Processing of Personal Data and on the Free Movement of Such Data (General Data Protection Regulation). 9565/15, 2012/0011 (COD), June 2015
6. Frey, C.B., Osborne, M.A.: The future of employment: how susceptible are jobs to computerisation? Technol. Forecast. Soc. Change **114**, 254–280 (2017)
7. Hawksworth, J., Berriman, R., Goel, S.: Will robots really steal our jobs? An international analysis of the potential long term impact of automation. Technical report, PricewaterhouseCoopers (2018)
8. Pedreshi, D., Ruggieri, S., Turini, F.: Discrimination-aware data mining. In: Proceedings of the 14th ACM SIGKDD International Conference on Knowledge Discovery and Data Mining, pp. 560–568. ACM (2008)
9. Brennenraedts, R., Vankan, A., te Velde R., Minne, B., Veldkamp, J., Kaashoek, B.: The impact of ICT on the Dutch economy. Technical report, Dialogic (2014)
10. Tukey, J.W.: The future of data analysis. Ann. Math. Stat. **33**(1), 1–67 (1962)

How Three Poznan University Students Broke the German Enigma Code and Shortened World War Two

Roger G. Johnson(✉)

School of Computer Science, Birkbeck University of London,
Malet Street, London WC1E 7HX, UK
rgj@dcs.bbk.ac.uk

Abstract. The story of the Allied breaking of the German Enigma codes in World War 2 was first published in the 1970s. Even now many of the details, especially concerning the critical work in the 1930s undertaken by gifted and dedicated Polish codebreakers remains largely unknown. Their work is credited with saving the Allies several years work and so shortening the war and saving thousands of lives. The holding of the IFIP World Computer Congress in Poznan, home of the Polish codebreakers, gave an opportunity for their work to be highlighted to an international audience. Talks covering the work of the Polish, British and French codebreakers were given and webcast worldwide. In addition, a encoded Enigma message was sent at the start of the day from Poznan to Bletchley Park in the UK where the volunteers of the Bombe team at The National Museum of Computing successfully confirmed their breaking of the message at the start of the afternoon session.

Keywords: Enigma · Code breaking · World War II · Marian Rejevski · Jerzy Rozycki · Henryk Zygalski · Turing-Welchman Bombe

1 Background

In 1945 General Dwight D Eisenhower (Allied Supreme Commander Europe) wrote to General Stewart Menzies (Head of Bletchley Park in the UK saying that the successful reading of German messages had

> *"saved thousands of British and American lives and, in no small way, contributed to the speed with which the enemy was routed and eventually forced to surrender"*

The story of how the Allied forces broke the German Enigma code during World War 2 has been told many times in recent years usually from a variety of perspectives mostly linked to Bletchley Park in the UK. The critical contribution of the Polish codebreakers remains little known outside Poland and only a limited number of books and papers have been published about their work. The Polish codebreakers repeatedly broke the Enigma code as its security features were steadily enhanced throughout the 1930s. The result was that as war was about to break out in 1939 the Poles were able to give working replica Enigma machines to their French and British allies and to explain how they had successfully broken the German Enigma messages up to that time.

L. Strous and V. G. Cerf (Eds.): IFIPIoT 2018, IFIP AICT 548, pp. 11–20, 2019.
https://doi.org/10.1007/978-3-030-15651-0_2

Without this dramatic gesture it is very unlikely that the British and French would have been able to develop the codebreaking techniques which enabled the British to read German Enigma traffic throughout most of World War 2 at Bletchley Park and also the French until late 1942 at Bletchley Park's French equivalent.

This paper summarises the story of the critical Polish contribution and how it was built on by the French and British, most notably by the British mechanisation of the most time-consuming part of finding the key each day by the building of machines which were named Bombes. The Polish role is well documented in two books, Kozaczuk (1984) first published in Polish in 1979 which focussed primarily on the codebreaking and very recently in (Turing 2018) which recounts the codebreaking exploits but also the lives of the codebreakers during and after this tempestuous period.

The holding of the IFIP World Congress in Poznan in Poland provided an ideal opportunity for IFIP WG 9.7 on the History of Computing to celebrate the work of three talented and heroic Polish mathematics students from the University of Poznan, Marian Rejewski, Jerzy Rozycki and Henryk Zygalski, who trained in Poznan to become codebreakers and whose work ultimately led to the significant shortening of World War 2.

The author is a member of IFIP WG 9.7 and is also the Secretary of the Turing Welchman Bombe Rebuild Trust (TWBRT) which owns the replica Bombe completed in 2007 and is demonstrated every week at The National Museum of Computing (TNMoC) housed in Block H of Bletchley Park in the UK. He arranged for the TWBRT Bombe team to hold one of its occasional roadshow events in which an Enigma message is sent from a remote location to the Bombe Team at TNMoC who then attempt to break the code and send back confirmation of the message being successfully read.

2 Enigma Machine

The origins of the Enigma coding machine were with a commercial coding machine built by a German electrical engineer named Arthur Scherbius. He obtained several patents for his machines starting in 1918. The device evolved into a portable device about the size of a typewriter powered by batteries. Having initially failed to interest the German armed forces in his machine he sold them as commercial coding machines for use by financial institutions such as banks to protect commercially sensitive information being sent by telegraph and other devices. Turing (2018) records that in 1926 both the British and Polish authorities had obtained commercial examples to study while he also notes that, in the same year, German Navy signals using an Enigma machine are noted for the first time.

Following the largely static army operations of the First World War, military strategists developed ideas for future mobile land warfare. However, a critical issue would be to create effective communications for command and control of relatively small frontline military units. In addition, naval commanders, especially with a growing force of submarines, needed secure two-way communications to maintain contact with their forces. What was required was a secure coding machine which, given its presence close to the frontline in mobile warfare, could sooner or later be captured by the enemy without compromising the security of the communications network. This need for portable, secure communications potentially across large distances, was the capability the Enigma machine provided. Figure 1 shows a German army Enigma machine.

Fig. 1. Three wheel Enigma machine

The key features of the Enigma machine were a conventional German keyboard and above it lamps which light each time a key is pressed with the enciphered character corresponding to the key pressed. Above the lamps are the three rotor wheels. Each time a key is depressed the righthand rotor advances one step and after one revolution the adjacent rotor advances one step and similarly with the leftmost rotor. Each rotor has the letters of the alphabet around the rim and every letter is wired to another letter elsewhere on the rotor. Thus a letter “A” typed on the keyboard may emerge from the first rotor as “K” and so on through the other two rotors. The electric current then reaches the plugboard on the front of the machine where 20 of the 26 letters are again wired up in pairs after which it returns through the wheels until it lights up a lamp on the machine. The Army Enigma machine ultimately had five rotors and on any day three would be used in a predefined arrangement of rotors. The result of all these different combinations is to produce over 150 million alternatives. A very comprehensive account of the evolution of the Enigma coding machine is provided in (Perera 2010).

It was this extraordinary number of combinations which several times later in the war led the Germans to conclude, in the face of circumstantial evidence to the contrary such as dramatic increases in submarine losses after the Allied breaking of the naval Enigma, that the Enigma machine had in fact not been broken but that there was an alternative explanation, such as espionage or allied technological advances, for significant German setbacks.

It is worth noting that other military powers, including Britain, also adopted coding machines which made use of rotors. It was fundamentally a good approach to automated enciphering of messages in an electro-mechanical era.

3 Poland and Germany

The inter-war Polish state was a creation of the Versailles Peace treaty. It was situated between Germany and Russia and the Polish authorities trusted neither. In the turmoil following the Russian revolution, the Polish government regarded the German state of the later 1920s as a bigger potential threat than the Soviet Union. Also Soviet codes were still using First World war techniques and so liable to successful attack.

Initial attempts to break German Enigma messages using the commercially available Enigma machine failed. Obviously the machine had been modified. Any attack on the machine would need trained cryptographers and so a special course was run at the University of Poznan which was in a part of Poland which had formerly been part of Germany and hence had many fluent German speakers. In 1929 20 students were recruited to the course. Further attempts at breaking into Enigma still yielded nothing until in 1932 the French recruited a spy, Hans-Thilo Schmidt, who worked as a civilian in the German Army's cryptography unit. To fund an extravagant life style he needed money and proceeded to sell large numbers of photographs of secret files relating to the work of the cryptographic unit to the French.

Unfortunately without a German military Enigma machine the French realised that the photographs of the operating instructions were of no immediate value. The British when offered the photographs came to the same conclusion. The French then approached the Poles who expressed more interest but asked for more information. Gradually through the first half of 1932 the French obtained more and more material from Hans-Thilo Schmidt until finally, in August 1932, they obtained an encrypted message together with the original text. With the other secret material already obtained, it now appeared that it might be possible to reverse engineer the Enigma machine, in particular the wiring of the rotors.

The first recruit to the Polish Cypher Bureau from the Poznan course was Marian Rejewski. Initially he worked on Enigma in the evening after his colleagues in the Cypher Bureau had gone home. Later on it became a full time but still secret project. Month by month he gradually worked out the wiring inside the machine. While for their part the French continued to supply more secret intelligence from Hans-Thilo Schmidt. The final problem to be overcome, once the wiring of the Enigma machine had been worked out was to determine a way to find which rotors were being used, in what order they had been placed into the machine and the starting position for each of the rotors. Marian Rejewski noticed that each message began with the starting position sent twice.

Fig. 2. Marian Rejevski, Jerzy Rozycki, Henryk Zygalski

Marian Rejevski was now joined by two more graduates of the Poznan course. They were Jerzy Rozycki and Henryk Zygalski (Fig. 2). From the stolen operating instructions they knew that the Germans sent the starting position twice at the start of each message and they realised that during the encipherment almost certainly only the righthand wheel turned while the others remained stationery. Studying the patterns enabled them to devise simple lookup methods to find the arrangement of the rotors and also some of the plugboard settings. Further they realised that what they needed was a working copy of an Enigma machine. Starting with an old commercial machine as a model, the Poles constructed in utmost secrecy a small number of machines functionally the same as the then current German Enigma machine complete with correctly wired rotors and a plugboard.

The procedures used by the Germans continued to evolve. Gradually rotor orders were changed more frequently until in October 1936 they were changed daily. Sloppy operating practices were eliminated and more cables were used on the plugboard. A major change took place as war clouds gathered in 1938 when the Germans introduced two new rotors, making five in total, and changed their operating procedure to use a different initial wheel position for each message. Each time the Poles responded with new techniques to re-establish the setup of the machine so that messages could be successfully read.

4 Sharing with Britain and France

By 1938 both the British and French cryptographers had looked at approaches to breaking the Enigma messages but had made little progress with the latest German versions of the machine. They had only succeeded in breaking into simpler versions of Enigma used in the Spanish Civil War and also the less advanced Italian system.

The Munich crisis of 1938 caused both to examine their readiness for war which led to a substantial exchange of information about Enigma. The French knew from the intelligence they had supplied to the Poles that the Poles had probably made some progress but the British appear to have been unaware of the possible significance of the Polish work. However, the major changes by the German in late 1938 had stretched the

Polish resources close to breaking point. Their productivity in breaking into Enigma had dwindled dramatically.

In December 1938 the French proposed holding a three way conference in Paris between France, Britain and Poland at which the French hoped to find out what progress each had made. The meeting, held in January 1939, went badly with each party revealing only very limited amounts of information. However, it was clear to each party that the others were serious in their commitment to break into Enigma and so contacts were maintained through the spring and summer of 1939.

The next meeting was to be truly momentous but neither the British or French knew in advance. At the end of June 1939 the Poles, knowing through Enigma and other intelligence that Germany was preparing to invade Poland, invited the British and the French to Warsaw for a meeting. Thus it was in late July 1939 Alastair Denniston, Head of Bletchley Park and Dilly Knox, Britain's leading cryptographer and their principal expert on Enigma travelled across Nazi Germany by train to Poland. The French were represented by Gustav Bertrand, Denniston's opposite number and his deputy, Henri Braquenie. The Poles sent their trio of Rejewski, Rozycki and Zygalski together with their boss, Maksymilian Ciezki.

On the day following their arrival they were driven to the Poles' secret intelligence HQ at Pyry on the outskirts of Warsaw. To the amazement of the French and British the Poles announced almost immediately that they had broken Enigma some years earlier. The Poles showed them a variety of devices which they used to help determine each day's Enigma settings. Discussions continued next day as the Poles revealed more of their methods for breaking the code. However, without doubt, the highpoint was the offer by the Poles to donate to both the French and the British one of their precious working replica Enigma machines. The two machines left Poland by diplomatic bag for Paris and so, probably unnoticed by fellow travellers, Stewart Menzies, the Deputy Head of the British Secret Intelligence Service greeted Gustav Bertrand, the Head of the French Codebreakers as he arrived at Victoria Station in August 1939 with a large wooden box containing the priceless Enigma machine donated to the British.

At this point Alan Turing enters the story. He had been working part time on the Enigma problem at Cambridge since 1938 but had not made much progress. Following the Pyry meeting, Knox had shared with Turing all the information that the Poles had provided, including their mechanical devices for finding the key of the day. Very rapidly Turing conceived of an electro-mechanical machine to search for feasible solutions for the rotor starting positions based on a technique of guessing what the often stylised clear text of the German Enigma message might be. This specification for a machine was handed to BTM, the UK's leading punched card equipment manufacturer who were closely tied to IBM based in the USA, to turn into a physical reality.

A clear and full account of what became known as the Turing Welchman Bombe and how it was used is given in (Turing 2014).

5 After the Polish Invasion

On September 1st 1939 Germany invaded Poland and by the end of the month Polish resistance had collapsed. Poland was divided into three with large parts being assimilated by Germany in the west and the Soviet Union in the east with a small central area under the control of the Polish General Government. The Poles had planned for an invasion and destroyed evidence of their Enigma codebreaking work. It was vital that the codebreakers got away and so travelling by train and lorry they fled to Romania where they went first to the British Embassy who did not appreciate their significance and asked them to return the following day after the staff had contacted London. However, if they had been caught by the Romanian secret police they would probably be handed over to the Gestapo. Consequently, the Poles moved on immediately to the French Embassy who recognised their links with the French Secret Service and assisted them to reach France where they were met at the border by a representative sent by Gustav Bertrand. Knox and Denniston were not amused to find that the French had now got all the key Polish Enigma experts.

There followed a period of cooperation between Bletchley Park and the French codebreakers now established in the Chateau de Vignolles near Paris. The two groups were linked by a secure landline and from early 1940 there were daily races to find the Enigma key of the day. However, this period was not to last long. Early in May 1940 the German Army attacked the French and British forces in the West and on June 25th an armistice was signed between Germany and France. This divided France into two main areas – Occupied France in the north and "Free France" in the south with its government based in the small spa town of Vichy. From there, the Vichy government ran both Vichy France and also the whole of the worldwide French colonial empire.

In the anticipation that there might be an underground resistance movement within Vichy France, the armistice permitted the Vichy government to maintain a small codebreaking capability to track them down although they were expressly forbidden from intercepting German messages. Bertrand's group, including the Poles, moved to form this group now relocated to a small chateau outside Uzes near Nimes in southern France. The group now continued to intercept message traffic including German Enigma messages. Intelligence obtained, depending on its contents, could be passed to the Vichy authorities or to other groups. Bertrand's group built up a network of links across north Africa and Portugal supplying intelligence directly and through intermediaries to the British as well as De Gaulle's Free French and the Polish Government in exile in London and received equipment, finance and other benefits in exchange.

Assorted codebreakers travelled between the chateau at Uzes and north Africa to meet with other units working there. One of these trips ended in disaster when in January 1942 Jerzy Rozycki was drowned, when the ship on which travelling back to France from Algiers foundered in heavy seas with a substantial loss of life.

North Africa was in a very fluid state with many loose loyalties. In some places, such as Tangier, which had an international zone, officials as well as agents from many of the warring powers rubbed shoulders throughout the conflict. Fascinating insights into this period are to be found in (Pidgeon 2008) which includes material on North Africa.

In November 1942, German and Italian forces took over Vichy France. The German authorities and their Vichy collaborators were closing in on the radio transmissions from the chateau. It was decided that the Poles should leave. The British concluded that the Poles were too numerous to be flown out. The other alternatives were to attempt an evacuation by sea, or overland via Switzerland or Spain. However the route into Switzerland was now effectively closed. Attempts to evacuate by sea proved too dangerous. Consequently in early January 1943 groups of Polish codebreakers began to travel across France towards the Pyrenees and the Spanish border. Marian Rejewski and Henryk Zygalski managed with some difficulty to cross the Spanish border together. In common with most undocumented entrants into Spain they were jailed by the Spanish authorities. However, as the German and Italian armies suffered reverses the attitude of the Spanish authorities softened. Finally, starting in April 1943 the prison camps were gradually emptied. Marian Rejewski and Henryk Zygalski were finally released and by stages travelled via Portugal and Gibraltar to the UK. Having regained their freedom they were once again part of the Polish armed forces. They were attached to a team based near Hemel Hempstead which worked on Russian codes for the remainder of the war.

When peace returned to Europe in May 1945, Marian Rejewski and Henryk Zygalski both faced a difficult choice, whether to return to Poland or to find a new home. Marian Rejewski had a wife and two small children in Poland and so he decided to return to his homeland. Returnees were often regarded with suspicion by the new communist authorities in Poland. Although his career as an accountant was interfered with by the authorities due to suspicions about his wartime work he survived to be honoured by Poland prior to his death in 1980 for his services to the defeat of Germany as the Polish political environment evolved. Henryk Zygalski in contrast had met a British girl during his wartime work in the UK. He became a British citizen and settled down to an academic career in the UK ultimately as a member of staff of the Mathematics Department of the University of Surrey. He remained in contact with Marian Rejewski until his death in 1978.

6 Celebration at WCC 2018

At the IFIP World Congress in Poznan in Poland IFIP WG 9.7 on the History of Computing held a stream on computing in eastern Europe. One of the most significant events of World War 2 was the breaking of the German Enigma codes. As noted earlier, the contribution of the British codebreakers has been widely described but the work of the Poles has been largely unacknowledged.

The Congress provided an opportunity to put right this omission. The day celebrated the work of three talented and heroic Polish mathematics students from the University of Poznan, Marian Rejewski, Jerzy Rozycki and Henryk Zygalski, who trained in Poznan to become codebreakers and whose work ultimately led to the significant shortening of World War 2. The event attracted significant media interest including TV and radio in both Poland and the UK. The event was also webcast and is currently available online (YouTube 2018).

The one day Bombe stream comprised three lectures and a Bombe Roadshow challenge under the title of "Enigma Live", The opening talk was by Sir John Dermot Turing who asked the question "Did Alan Turing see an Enigma machine at Bletchley Park?". The second two talks were by Prof Marek Grajek from Poland. He spoke on the work of the Polish Codebreakers and secondly the proposed Poznan Enigma Centre one of whose main aims will be to promote the interest of young people in cryptography and computing.

Fig. 3. Turing Welchman Bombe used to break the Poznan message

The Bombe Roadshow was a challenge to decode an Enigma message using the Turing Welchman Bombe in the UK. This is a fully authentic replica of the machine originally designed by Alan Turing, enhanced by Gordon Welchman and built by BTM (Fig. 3). It is regularly demonstrated at The National Museum of Computing housed in Block H at Bletchley Park in the UK by the Bombe team of volunteers. The Bombe's function was to find feasible wheel positions which is a critical and time consuming procedure in finding the key of the day. This process is fully explained in (Turing 2014).

The plan for the event was to send, as an email attachment, an encrypted message with its clear equivalent (or "crib") followed by another encrypted message whose contents were unknown to the Bombe team. Due to a minor technical fault limiting the Bombe's operating speed it was necessary to send the crib message ahead of the event. Otherwise the day ran to plan and a successful break was made in the early afternoon when the decrypted message was sent to Poznan from the UK.

References

Kozaczuk, W.: Enigma. Arms and Armour Press (1984). ISBN 0 85368 640 8

Perera, T.: Inside Enigma. Radio Society of Great Britain (2010). ISBN 978 1 90508 664 1

Pidgeon, G.: The Secret Communications War – The Story of MI6 Communication 1939–1945. Arundel Books (2008). ISBN 978 0 95605 152 3

Turing, D.: Demystifying the Bombe. The History Press (2014). ISBN 978 1 84165 566 6

Turing, D.: X, Y and Z – The Real Story of How Enigma was Broken. The History Press (2018). ISBN 978 0 75098 782 0

Turing, D., Grajek, M.: Enigma Live webcast – eight talked including talks. Chaired by Roger G. Johnson. http://wcc2018.org/Enigma-live. Accessed 1 Jan 2019

Professionalism and Frameworks

Moira de Roche(✉)

Chair IFIP IP3, Johannesburg, South Africa
mderoche@ipthree.org

Abstract. In two sessions the International Professional Practice Partnership (IP3) of IFIP addressed a number of frameworks that provide definitions of ICT competences and typical profiles. These frameworks contribute to establishing an ICT profession that consists of competent and responsible professionals who can demonstrate the necessary skills and competences.

Keywords: Professionalism · Competences · Skills frameworks · Certification · e-CF · SFIA · ACS cyber security framework

1 Professionalism and IP3

1.1 The Importance of ICT Professionalism

Information and communication technologies (ICT) impact almost every facet of personal and business life. Such technologies are key drivers of innovation and of both economic and social progress, making enormous contributions to prosperity and to the creation of a more open world, enabling pluralism, freedom of expression, and allowing people and organisations to share their culture, interests and undertakings worldwide.

Such powerful technologies, and their application, must be driven by competent and reliable professionals who can demonstrate the necessary competences (including knowledge), integrity, responsibility and accountability, and public obligation.

Recognising that ICT is now a global industry, the ICT profession must also be global. It must have clear international standards that accommodate cultural differences in the regulation of professions, which is enhanced by strengthened competence requirements.

1.2 International Professional Practice Partnership – IP3

Through IP3, the International Professional Practice Partnership [1], IFIP established a global partnership that promotes professionalism. By doing so it strengthens the ICT profession and contributes to the development of strong international economies by creating an infrastructure that will:

- encourage and support the development of both ICT practitioners and employer organizations;
- give recognition to those who meet and maintain the required standards for knowledge, experience, competence and integrity; and

L. Strous and V. G. Cerf (Eds.): IFIPIoT 2018, IFIP AICT 548, pp. 21–27, 2019.
https://doi.org/10.1007/978-3-030-15651-0_3

- define international standards of professionalism in ICT.

IP3 defines and maintains global standards for ICT and recognises and certifies professionalism. Frameworks underpin the accreditation process, and their use is essential to the maintenance of professional standards at any IT Society or body that is certified.

To carry out its' mission, IP3 works closely with partners who share a commitment to creating a sound global ICT profession. IP3 encourages employing organisations, governments, commercial enterprises and IFIP member societies to join in this partnership through their membership.

IP3 in 2016 launched iDOCED, the IFIP Duty of Care for Everything Digital campaign which promotes trust in ICT, and the duty of care that everyone should have in the digital world. Duty of care goes hand in hand with professionalism, as trustworthiness is an essential element.

2 Professionalism and Frameworks

A number of frameworks has been developed that provide definitions of ICT competences and typical profiles. These initiatives are characterised by an open and inclusive approach, and accredit valuable qualification elements, either national, regional or global. In two workshops at the IFIP World Computer Congress (WCC) 2018 an overview was provided of some frameworks in use, as well as the practical implementations of the frameworks.

2.1 e-CF Overview

[2]: "The European e-Competence Framework (e-CF) provides a reference of 40 competences as applied at the Information and Communication Technology (ICT) workplace, using a common language for competences, skills, knowledge and proficiency levels that can be understood across Europe. The European e-Competence Framework provides a common language to describe the competences including skills and knowledge requirements of ICT professionals, professions and organisations at five proficiency levels, and is designed to meet the needs of individuals, businesses and other organisations in public and private sectors."

Cleary [3], Deputy Chief Executive of the Irish Computer Society and former chair of the e-CF workshop, explained the state of the ICT profession in Europe, focussing on maturing the profession, with a short-term aim of a fully professionalised sector. The profession must be committed to a relevant body of knowledge, with standardised competences, a commitment to continuous professional development and a clear code of ethics. Progress has been made in achieving these goals.

e-CF is now a European standard (EN 16234-1, April 2016), and work is underway to establish a standardised Body of Knowledge (BoK), education and certification, and a code of professional ethics. There is a standardised set of 30 ICT professional role profiles, which are fully incorporated into the EC ICT Rolling Plan for ICT Standardisation.

2.2 SFIA Overview

[4]: "The Skills Framework for the Information Age (SFIA) describes skills and competencies required by professionals in roles involved in information and communication technologies, digital transformation and software engineering. It provides a framework consisting of professional skills on one axis and seven levels of responsibility on the other. It describes the professional skills at various levels of competence and it describes the levels of responsibility, in terms of generic attributes of autonomy, influence, complexity, knowledge and business skills."

Seward [5], General Manager of the SFIA Foundation, (Skills Framework for the Information Age), explained the history of SFIA and how the framework is used in the Skills and Competency Management Cycle. A useful description of the structure of the framework was included, which comprises: six categories; 17 subcategories; 102 skills names with associated skills descriptions; and 388 skills level descriptors in the professional skills component. There are seven levels of responsibility, five generic attributes, and 35 attribute level descriptors in the behaviours and knowledge component.

SFIA is developed by industry and business for use by industry and business in the real world. At its heart is experience. A practitioner has a skill or competence because of the experience of practicing the skill in a real-world situation.

2.3 e-CF in an Academic Environment

Bolanowski [6], representing the Faculty of Electrical and Computer Engineering Rzeszow University of Technology and the Polish Information Processing Society IT Competence Council, considered the e-CF in an Academic setting.

An overview was provided of the typical University of Technology graduate, and considerations of the employers' needs. The university explored "Who is the modern IT Specialist?". They needed to consider the legal issues ruling university education in Poland. The e-CF was examined considering the point of views of all stakeholders: the student, the university and the employer. Questions to be answered were: What are the possibilities of implementing the e-CF in the university environment in relation to the needs of the job market; How can the students use the e-CF to build and develop their careers; and What are the difficulties associated with the implementation of the e-CF in the university environment?

The technical competences and business/soft competences, required by the job market, were explored. The issue is complicated by the lack of a definition for an IT specialist. Common definitions and terminology are required, and it is hoped that the e-CF will provide at least part of the solution.

From a students' perspective e-CF helps in organizing the requirements of the job market, it creates a common terminology dictionary, it helps to determine competences and it can help in career planning. For teachers it allows to periodically verify the content of the educational module and to focus not only on technical skills. It may also help to internationalize the education process.

For employers it can improve communication between companies, students and universities, it can help to organize the employment structure. It might also allow a company to prepare internship programs and to actively participate in the educational process. An additional benefit may be a reduction in the costs of the recruitment process.

2.4 ACS Cyber-Security Framework Overview

This framework, developed by the Australian Computer Society (ACS) as the basis for an extension of the ACS professional certifications scheme and adopted by IP3, was presented by Wong [7], IFIP IP3 Director, and Immediate Past President of ACS.

The following points were covered: Cybersecurity, Privacy and Technological challenges – what are Organisations and Governments seeking; How can we align Business and Organisational priorities with those of security professionals; The Professionalisation of Cybersecurity and Privacy practitioners; Challenges & key issues – is EU GDPR transforming the landscape; What are the repercussions of doing nothing?

The Duty of Care that is requisite for governments was examined, and the rationale illustrated. This includes: Measures relating to the confidentiality, availability and integrity of information that is processed, stored and communicated by electronic or similar means; The implications for government perspectives on cyber law, cyber policy both local and international, how issues and attacks are communicated, offensive cyber security, the cyber economy, cyber intelligence and forensics. Furthermore, there is a global shortage of Cyber-Security professionals, which runs into millions.

Cyber Security, Privacy and Technological challenges include: Definitions of ‘Cyber security’ still unclear; There is a strong demand for Cyber security practitioners but understanding of ‘professionalism’ not explicit; Pseudo Professional Standards proliferate; Cyber security and privacy issues are now mainstream in the boardroom. These challenges together with urging from government, resulted in the development of the Cyber Security frameworks. These are “specialisms” which are in addition to the standard IP3 Technologist (IP3T) and IP3 Professional (IP3P) certifications. In response to this, the frameworks were developed in Australia by the ACS. They are designed to provide a level of Assurance and Trust, and to address the growing shortage of cyber security expertise. The frameworks and related certifications will raise professional standards for cyber security specialists and highlight the Duty of Care for cyber security professionals.

3 Frameworks Implementation

The second workshop included sessions which explored the practical implementation of the frameworks. Ruoff [8], KNVI (Netherlands) explored the usage of the new e-CF profiles and role documents in different settings. She provided an overview of the Professional ICT workforce in the EU, as at 2016. The purpose of the e-CF is to provide a shared language which can be used to address the Skills gap. She provided information about the building blocks of the Framework and went on to explore these in detail. She demonstrated the mapping of the e-CF to SFIA. To tie it all together, she shared several use cases:

- Job profiles for information security 2.0, PvIBQIS
- Supplier Management: KPN consulting IT-CMF –e-CF
- Data Science, EU-Edison project, University of Amsterdam
- E-CF© NEXT, profile tool/assessment of EXIN
- Rake-Shape, blockchain f.e. UWV, LRWA.

Tony Parry, IITPSA, explained how SFA is used for membership grading. He explained that IITPSA uses SFIA as a standardised approach, that is consistent, fair and aligns to IP3 and the South African Qualifications Authority requirements. It is used for: the Professional Designation (PMIITPSA) which is IP3 accredited and SAQA registered; peer reviews; Critical Skills Assessments (foreign worker work permit requirement). The philosophy is "Assessing each case on its merits".

Dębski [9], PTI-IT Competence Council, Ministry of Digital Affairs examined how the e-CF can be used in the education system for ICT Professionals. The e-CF should be considered in Computer Science Education for high school and vocational school students, as the foundation of the creation of the future ICT Professionals, as well as their development. Having discussed the skills requirements with all stakeholders, they were very pleased to discover the e-CF. Using the e-CF and its 40 competences helped to speed up the work of developing curricula. They took the competence framework, went through its 40 competences and on this base we actually created a common language. The power of the e-CF is that it relates to real life and real labor market.

Wong [10] provided insights of the Cyber Security Framework in Action. He examined the situation around the world, especially the effects of GDPR. The biggest threat is the sever shortage of skills in the Cyber Security space globally, citing examples showing the estimates of 1.8 million people. The EU is leading the world in legislating to protect and provide access to personal data with its EU General Data Protection Regulation (GDPR), which replaced the 1995 Data Protection Directive in May 25, 2018. The implications are far-reaching, affecting with an establishment in the EU or that offer goods and services to business or citizens of the EU, or that monitor the behaviour of individuals in the EU may need to comply. There are significant penalties for non-compliance with fines up to €2million, or 4% of global turnover. GDPR specifies job designations related to compliance officers, and the requisite skills for those in these roles. The ACS developed the Cyber Security Framework:

- Designed to provide a level of Assurance, Trust and to address the growing shortage of cyber security expertise.
- Launched by Australian Minister Assisting the Prime Minister for Cyber Security, the Hon Dan Tehan in Canberra in Sept 2017.
- Adopted by IFIP IP3 as a new specialism certification for member societies around the world.
- ACS support for the implementation of the Australian International Cyber Engagement Strategy announced by the Hon Julie Bishop MP, Minister for Foreign Affairs in October 2017.
- Raise professional standards for cyber security specialists.
- Highlight the Duty of Care for cyber security professionals.

Reflecting the multi-disciplinary nature of Cyber Security, flexibility is built into the certification for Technologists (SFIA Level 3) and Professionals (SFIA Level 5). Professionals who have achieved the Cyber Security Professional certification come from the aviation, banking and finance, audit and risk, consulting, and healthcare industries.

Adrian Schofield, Chair IP3 Standards and Accreditation Committee, explained how frameworks are used to ensure the trust aspect of accreditation (video presentation). Framework ensure that levels are benchmarked – irrespective of the framework used the skills levels and competencies are at a similar level.

4 Follow Up

At the end of the workshop, the speakers and audience considered how it can be ensured that all frameworks are mapped to each other, and the work that needs to be done to realise this goal. We accept that more than one framework is being utilised but encourage new entrants to use something that already exists, rather than create a new framework. Having too many frameworks causes confusion and it duplicates work. Mapping and customisation are better options.

An IP3 task force has been created to develop a project plan to carry out this work in collaboration with all key players. It is hoped that this project will be funded. IP3 call for all interested parties to join us in this work to ensure that the process is inclusive and representative. Contact mderoche@ipthree.org for more.

References

1. IFIP IP3. https://www.ipthree.org/
2. http://www.ecompetences.eu/. Accessed 18 Jan 2019
3. Cleary, M.: https://www.ipthree.org/wp-content/uploads/Mary-Cleary-e-CF-and-TC-428.pdf
4. https://www.sfia-online.org/en. Accessed 18 Jan 2019
5. Seward, I.: https://www.ipthree.org/wp-content/uploads/SFIA-Overview-Ian-Seward.pdf
6. Bolanowski, M.: https://www.ipthree.org/wp-content/uploads/MB-Frameworks-in-an-Academic-setting.pdf
7. Wong, A.: https://www.ipthree.org/wp-content/uploads/Cyber-security-Framework-overview-Anthony-Wong.pdf
8. Ruoff, L.: https://www.ipthree.org/wp-content/uploads/eCF-Implementation-Liesbeth-Ruoff.pdf
9. Dębski, B.: https://www.ipthree.org/wp-content/uploads/e-CF-Education-System-B.Debski.pdf
10. Wong, A.: https://www.ipthree.org/wp-content/uploads/Cyber-Security-specialism-framework-in-action-Anthony-Wong.pdf

Should Artificial Intelligence Be More Regulated?

Panel Discussion

Leon Strous(✉)

De Nederlandsche Bank, Westeinde 1, 1017 ZN Amsterdam, The Netherlands
strous@iae.nl

Abstract. Artificial Intelligence (AI) can and does bring immense benefits in all sorts of areas. But it also introduces (new) risks. Is more regulation needed? In order to answer this question arguments pro and con were presented by four panel members and discussed and challenged by the audience. Many issues were raised, ethical principles, the obstacles that make it hard to draft good legislation. We don't want to stifle innovation or deny society the benefits of these technologies by excessive regulation. A distinction is made between science (research) and the application of AI technologies. Comparisons with other sectors and technologies are made to see whether parallels can be drawn.

Keywords: Artificial Intelligence · AI · Regulation · Ethics · Ethical principles · Liability · AI science · AI applications

1 Introduction

Many discussions are taking place at the moment about Artificial Intelligence (AI), about ways AI may benefit mankind and about risks of AI. Autonomous cars, automated trust assignment to individuals, and autonomous weapons are only a few examples how AI can change our life. Some people warn us that AI can be even more dangerous than nuclear power. On the other hand it seems impossible and undesirable to stop development of AI and its applications. Thus, the question arises what should be the role of governments. Should AI be more regulated with respect to research and/or its usage? This question was addressed at WCC 2018 in a panel discussion with four panel members:

Ulrich Furbach, University Koblenz-Landau, Germany,
Eunika Mercier-Laurent, Lyon III University, France,
Chris Rees, British Computer Society, UK and
Jerzy Stefanowski, Poznan University of Technology, Poland.

An audience of 40 participants actively engaged in the discussion. The session was recorded on video [1].

L. Strous and V. G. Cerf (Eds.): IFIPIoT 2018, IFIP AICT 548, pp. 28–34, 2019.
https://doi.org/10.1007/978-3-030-15651-0_4

2 Arguments Pro and Con

To start the debate, two panel members presented arguments in favor of more regulation and two members presented arguments against more regulation.

Arguments in Favour of (more) Regulation
AI can and does bring immense benefits in all sorts of areas: in cancer diagnosis, mind diseases, caring of elderly, and many more will follow such as autonomous vehicles. We don't want to stifle innovation or deny society the benefits of these technologies by excessive regulation. Any regulation should be risk based. If the risk is low, regulation should be avoided. If it is high, the application should be regulated. That's how it is in the non-AI world and the AI world should be no different. Further we have to recognize that drafting regulations for new and fast developing technologies such as AI is difficult. There is a risk of building assumptions and language in the regulation that don't stand the test of time.

Our starting point is ethics. The implementation of AI systems, including of AI driven robotics, poses a number of ethical challenges. A non-exhaustive list includes:

- reliability and safety of complex systems,
- bias in systems and bias in the data,
- black box systems that cannot explain or justify their decisions,
- the allocation of responsibility for failure,
- malicious use of AI and lethal autonomous weapon systems,
- the destruction of jobs by AI,
- the protection of privacy.

The question is: where can we rely on the ethical actions of developers and users of AI and where is this clearly not adequate and therefore regulation is necessary. Some of the applications of AI are in domains that are already regulated and have a long history of regulation, medicine and finance are two obvious examples. But the existing regulations may not cover the application of AI. These regulations may need to be enhanced to prevent harm to patients or unfair financial practices. Autonomous cars should not be allowed to go on the road until there is an agreed allocation of responsibility and therefore liability for harm. You need a third party insurance that covers the driver. But in an autonomous car there is no driver. So who is responsible/liable: the manufacturer of the car, the manufacturer of failing components, the car salesperson, the owner of the car? And what if the car is hacked? Or if software updates have not been installed? There is no doubt that existing regulations do not cover autonomous cars and that this is needed.

Many people have already asked for a ban on autonomous lethal weapons, comparable to nuclear and chemical and biological weapons. While controlling adherence to such a ban may be difficult and sometimes such weapons are used nevertheless, laws and regulations have a powerful effect on the public opinion.

Economists predict a growth in jobs due to AI, but only in the long term. In the short term jobs will be lost. Regulation may be needed to provide funding for retraining employees for a new job.

AI can be used to de-anonymize personal data that has been anonymized. GDPR may already be a good step in the right direction restoring the control over personal data to the owner instead of the company. However the protection in the GDPR against AI based use of personal data is weak and needs strengthening.

Machine learning and AI systems are complex systems. In a number of application areas we should think about regulation. Consider machine learning and AI systems as a product and therefore regulation is focused on the application of AI, on the product. In the medical domain we see systems that can make prognoses and by doing that impact people's health. It is important that the system can not make errors. It is the task of the producer/vendor to take care of that. Compare it with the process to get a new drug (medicine) accepted. Strict procedures and tests take place before the new drug is allowed to be put on the market. Producers of AI should provide assurance that their product is working correctly and this should be enforced through regulation. Regulation does not always have to be laws, it also can be community agreed rules and processes or evaluation and certification. Another element concerns the question whether an AI system should be able to explain the decision it took. For some domains and applications this may not be necessary, for others it is, think about legal decisions (e.g. AI supported court cases). It should be mandatory for such systems to be able to explain. That may not be easy, when is an explanation clear enough, what is the context.

Another issue is intellectual property rights. Advanced systems can write poems and stories or compose music. Who owns this and benefits from the profits this might generate? Regulation may be needed to clarify such rights.

Arguments Against (more) Regulation

Regulation of AI may be undesirable and extremely difficult if not impossible. A number of questions support that position:

- Regulation may work in a normal ethical society but how can we regulate a society that is composed of robots and humans.
- If regulation is used to prevent machines from doing "something foolish", who decides what is foolish?
- We live in a business driven world. What will happen if we try to regulate the market giants? They will move to countries without regulation.
- If you look at military use of AI, that is big business with powerful people behind it. Extremely difficult to regulate.
- How will regulation be effective in data protection if people are willing to provide their data voluntarily to companies.
- What about regulation and the creativity of the researcher. Efforts to regulate this without proper understanding how researchers work may lead to disasters.
- How to regulate a robot from learning. How to say to a robot what he can and what he should not learn.

If regulation is needed, it could be considered to not only look at legal regulations but also at initiatives about principles. An example of these are the Asilomar AI Principles. Industry giants and experts such as Elon Musk and Stephen Hawking have advocated for humane and "safe" robotics. Along with hundreds of researchers and experts in the fields, they have proposed 23 "guiding principles" that will ensure the development of AI for the benefit of mankind [2, 3].

Although one might in principle be pro regulation of certain aspects of AI system, it simply seems to be impossible. The problem is we don't know what it is, an AI system. AI is not a monolithic system, it is in other systems, it is in our cars, in our search engines, in our shopping cart. AI is a functionality of existing systems. It is completely impossible to control the development of these techniques and also it is impossible to control its use. Other areas that have been regulated also show this. Two examples from the weapons industry. Nuclear weapons, we all know how difficult it is in certain parts of the world to control the development of nuclear weapons. It is a highly political issue. The other example is chemical weapons. They are banned and nevertheless used. It is impossible to control the use of technology and it is impossible to control the development of technology. We also should not want this because technology is a driving force of our society. We want to learn more. We shouldn't stop science or regulate science. There may be some exceptions with respect to ethical issues. We don't know exactly what to regulate and how to regulate it. The United Nations does not succeed in getting a letter signed by all countries about the goal of a ban on lethal autonomous weapons. Some countries have major interests in such an industry or other arguments for not signing it.

Another example concerns autonomous cars. Where liability and insurance issues might be regulated there are also ethical issues. The German government drafted a report saying that an autonomous car should never be able to face an ethical dilemma situation. That is impossible, it would be similar to saying that human drivers should never face an ethical dilemma. Furthermore the report argues that algorithms should be checked and that self-adapting systems should not be applied in autonomous cars. That is also strange, an autonomous car should learn by driving and adapt. It is also unimaginable that a human driver would be forbidden to learn from mistakes.

In a distant past when cars were just introduced, there was a rule in the UK that in front of a car there should be someone walking with a red flag to warn people. Perhaps we should use a red flag to warn (or better: make people aware) that you are dealing with an AI system. A Blade Runner situation where it is difficult to distinguish humans from machines should be avoided. Regulation might be helpful for that.

3 Summary of the Debate

During the debate the arguments pro and con were both challenged and supported and some new issues were raised. This chapter provides a selection of the main topics discussed. Sometimes in a Q&A format, sometimes just as additional remarks.

AI tools, systems, technology could/should be regulated as human beings are also regulated. What about AI as a scientific discipline, should that be regulated as well? In a sense this is already regulated in the same way as other scientific disciplines like medicine and genetics. When applying for research funding for instance the request has to be judged on many aspects including ethical issues. What should not be regulated are the goals to pursue with research.

A comparison with the regulation of the Internet can be made. We now realize that we were too late thinking about regulation of the Internet when the Internet was created and that makes it difficult to repair it now. Maybe it is also due to the way scientists think. The benefits prevail, especially in areas where AI can assist professionals such as medical doctors who are already overburdened to take over part of the routine work. And focusing on the benefits, the risk of abuse of technology that is created with the best of intentions might be overlooked.

Regulations should be in place in certain areas but an additional question is who will be responsible for those regulations. If it is the lawmakers do they know enough about the topic to draft good regulations. A lot of poor law is written because of insufficient knowledge of the subject matter. Society/lawmakers lag behind with respect to technological developments. We as professionals at the forefront of these developments are better placed to judge where these developments might lead and what might be an appropriate societal safeguard long before the lawmakers can make those decisions. This means that we as an IT community have an obligation to engage with legislators to support them in drafting decent legislation. We should at least make an effort to be involved.

The issue was raised that a request for funding of scientific research usually has to pass via ethical committees, because funds are tax payers money. That is not the case for research and product development done by industry. AI as technology may perhaps not face ethical questions but the applications do. Is the current ethical oversight (for academic funding) sufficient? During many years of AI research ethical questions never popped up, we researched nice technology. Because there were no real-life applications. Now this is changing for instance with autonomous cars. And that introduces also the question of impact of the application. The impact of an application is often not or rarely assessed before selling or using it.

An interesting perspective was mentioned from a small and medium sized enterprise point of view. When you develop a new product, regulation in the beginning is an obstacle and difficult. However, it can also mean a benefit if you can advertise that your product meets certain regulations. And the competition has to keep up with that. Also good for consumers who can see that a product meets certain requirements as laid down in regulations.

Regulation in the globalized world is difficult. It is not enough to have regulations in a country or a region. However, so far regulation on a global scale, for instance via UN, is not successful. If we want to regulate a borderless development such as AI, we need to do that on a global scale otherwise it is meaningless. The statement that regulation will only work if it is on a global scale was challenged. Take for example the argument that companies will go to a country that is not regulated. That will not help them because they can maybe produce the product in such a country but if they want to sell it in a country that has regulation, it will not be able to do so unless it complies with the regulation. GDPR is a good example. US companies have to comply with GDPR if they want to do business in the EU. It can work well even if it is jurisdiction based.

Another talk at WCC about shifting identities triggered an issue of importance to AI. Identities touch a multidisciplinary field. Regulating this part of science also means that we need to be very clear where we want to go, what we want to be in the future. It was mentioned that perhaps a link can be made to the work on consciousness.

Psychologists and philosophers are trying to find out what does it mean for humans to have consciousness. As developers of AI we are working on AI systems that have a kind of consciousness. A German philosopher Metzinger argues that we should never try to bring consciousness into an artificial system because then we would be able to bring harm to them and we are not allowed to do harm to other human beings.

It is our duty as IT professionals to explain AI to people. We should be able to understand how algorithms work. And to explain the choices that have been made in designing the algorithm and the effects the algorithm may have.

4 Conclusions and Follow up

While there was not a complete agreement on everything and the outcome of the discussion was not fully conclusive, in general a broad consensus could be noted on a number of issues.

Artificial Intelligence is a broad term that includes science, technology, applications and products. AI can bring benefits but it also can introduce (new) risks. The answer to the question "should it be (more) regulated" depends on a variety of aspects, it can't be a yes or no. Consider things case by case. The term regulation is not precise, it can mean a law but it can also mean mutually agreed rules and procedures.

We do not have clear easy answers but we should make efforts and increase awareness. We should debate and work on documents to indicate critical points. We cannot control everything. You should know who you are talking to. Difficult, challenging but not a reason for not trying.

It is important as professionals to engage in discussions like this. We as an IT community have an obligation to engage with legislators to support them in drafting decent legislation.

We should develop methodologies to certify AI products. There is a role for IFIP and other professional societies to think about ways about how to define workflows for approving AI based products.

April 25th 2018 the European Commission issued a Communication COM (218) on Artificial Intelligence for Europe [4]. This Communication sets out a European initiative on AI, which aims to ensure an appropriate ethical and legal framework. The Commission will (selective quotes):

- *set a framework for stakeholders and experts to develop draft AI ethics guidelines, with due regard to fundamental rights;*
- *issue a guidance document on the interpretation of the Product Liability Directive in light of technological developments. This will seek to ensure legal clarity for consumers and producers in case of defective products;*
- *publish a report on the broader implications for, potential gaps in and orientations for, the liability and safety frameworks for AI, Internet of Things and robotics;*
- *support research in the development of explainable AI and implement a pilot project proposed by the European Parliament on Algorithmic Awareness Building, to gather a solid evidence-base and support the design of policy responses to the challenges brought by automated decision-making, including biases and discrimination.*

This Communication addresses precisely the issues raised in the discussion. It also invites stakeholders to participate in the efforts. Let's contribute to these and other efforts in the world. There is a need and an opportunity for us as IT professionals to pick up the challenge and to continue the discussion. There is momentum now, let's not waste the opportunity. We don't want to observe in ten years' time that we again missed the boat (after the Internet). We also have to research some fundamental questions, where do we want to go with regulation, where do we want to go with applications, who do we want to be. This is an appeal to all participants and readers who are interested in continuing this debate in a search for guidance. If you want to get involved, let me know. Send an e-mail to the address at the start of the paper.

References

1. WCC 2018 session should AI be more regulated? Video recording. http://www.wcc2018.org/movs/oxford_debate_rf27.mp4. Accessed 21 Jan 2019
2. 23 AI principles, news article. https://www.natureworldnews.com/articles/35633/20170215/23-principles-ai-stephen-hawking-elon-musk-experts-pitch-rules.htm. Accessed 21 Jan 2019
3. 23 AI principles, Future of Life. https://futureoflife.org/ai-principles/. Accessed 21 Jan 2019
4. Artificial Intelligence for Europe, EC Communication COM (2018) 237, 25 April 2018. https://ec.europa.eu/digital-single-market/en/news/communication-artificial-intelligence-europe. Accessed 21 Jan 2019

IFIPIoT 2018 Invited Papers: Keynote, Panel Discussion

The Internet of Things is Hardly About Technology

Kees van der Klauw[1,2(✉)]

[1] Alliance for Internet of Things Innovation, Brussels, Belgium
chair@aioti.eu
[2] InnoAdds, High Tech Campus 27, Eindhoven, Netherlands
kees.van.der.klauw@innoadds.com
http://www.aioti.eu, http://www.innoadds.com

Abstract. Most definitions of the Internet of Things (IoT) take a technology perspective, referring to connected devices exchanging data with each other and with higher levels, establishing autonomously operating systems. From a business perspective, IoT can be regarded as a business transformation, driving commoditization or even threatening conventional businesses, providing opportunities for product and process improvements and opening perspectives for services business or entirely new businesses based on data acquired by IoT. While the development of the Internet of Things resembles in many aspects the characteristics of for example semiconductor and IT platforms, there are some essential differences, mainly in scale and scope, that make the kickstart of a successful IoT more complex. This paper addresses key elements of a successful deployment of IoT and also key roles for IT professionals in IoT.

Keywords: Internet of Things · IoT · Platforms · Open innovation · Ecosystems · Digitization

1 Introduction

Most definitions of the Internet of Things (IoT) take a technology perspective, referring to connected devices exchanging data with each other and with higher levels, establishing autonomously operating systems. Such definition easily fits in with other technological developments that are driving the digitisation of our world. Sensing, ubiquitous communication networks, information systems, data analytics, artificial intelligence, robotics, edge and cloud computing are all linked to the development of IoT, either as an enabler or leveraging IoT for new applications.

From a business perspective, IoT can be regarded as a business transformation, driving commoditization or even threatening conventional businesses, providing opportunities for product and process improvements and opening perspectives for services business or entirely new businesses based on data acquired by IoT. New economic powers and regions will emerge, others will lose relevance.

There is no doubt that IoT will be a driver of socio-economic change like the industrial revolution was. Our society will increasingly be run by autonomous systems, self-learning robots will assist people not only in manufacturing, but also in their daily

L. Strous and V. G. Cerf (Eds.): IFIPIoT 2018, IFIP AICT 548, pp. 37–49, 2019.
https://doi.org/10.1007/978-3-030-15651-0_5

life. Resource management (energy, food, water) will be based on IoT, combining data from numerous sensors and actuators and systems in the field, providing real time insight and steering optimized flows. Curative healthcare will be replaced by a continuum with preventive monitoring, highly automated treatments and home care. Systems of systems will autonomously run operations in energy, mobility, cities, buildings, industry…

Jobs will disappear while other jobs are created. Education will change to life-long learning while new creative fulfilment of free time will be required. And since the speed of change is fast, people will feel uncertain, distrusting new technologies.

Don't worry about the definition of IoT. IoT is all of it and it is about time that we take an integral, holistic approach while 'separating concerns' to make it work for all.

2 A Short History of the Future: Enabling Platforms

Already in the 80-ies have we seen the need for such 'separation of concerns' approach in the electronics industry, although predominantly in the technology area. Socio economic considerations were lagging, as usual.

In the 80-ies the electronics industry was predominantly analog and the design, manufacturing & application required (scarce) deep and wide knowledge. Chip application engineers, designers and technologists were very much from the same origin and closely working together.

But once IC technology was mastered, one could massively apply transistors as switches and a digital technology platform was established. While one breed of engineers worried about making a good transistor switch and replicating them hundred thousand times without flaw, a new generation of engineers that never had seen a transistor was enabled with tools to create complex computing circuits with those large numbers of transistors, not requiring deep transistor and technology knowledge but using instead simulation models ('digital twins'). Separation of concerns.

This created a whole new framework of knowledge and associated professions, but it also bifurcated IC business in fab and fabless companies, all enabled by digital technology platforms.

This bifurcation has repeated several times, all driven by the same principle of establishing a platform that enabled the development of new knowledge, professions and business on it, separating concerns from the layers below.

Integrated Circuit Designers started using standard building blocks and those building blocks were combined in standard IC's such as, microprocessors, microcontrollers and communication chips. Again establishing a digital platform enabling a new breed of engineers to run away with them building programmable computers, communication networks and automation and control systems.

Those systems needed standard SW operating systems and standard application software packages in order to have them deployed massively and a new platform layer, this time in SW was established, based on the same economy of scale as Moore's Law driving the bottom of the pyramid. Large software stacks have high creation and maintenance cost and therefore application toolsets enabled a new breed of SW application engineers to deploy and configure those standard software packages in many domains. This role is largely filled in by many small and medium enterprises.

While this development has disrupted businesses, it has created enormous economic value overall. It has been a strong driver of 'Moore's Law' in the sense that it created the economic justification for the technological advancements in IC technology and on higher levels in SW. Without platformisation, the market would not have developed and Moore's Law and SW growth would have been stagnating because of lacking returns.

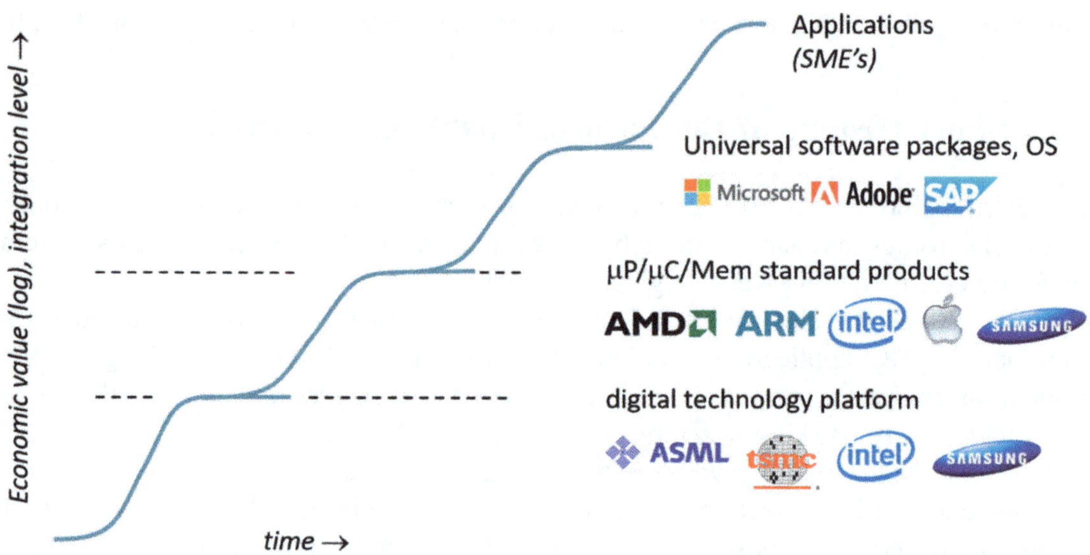

Fig. 1. Schematic representation of technology platforms developed over time in the IC/ICT domain enabling higher integration layers and economic value. Some key players on various levels are illustrated (non-exhaustive)

Figure 1 expresses this stacking of platforms over time, while the overall value exponentially grows with each layer. This is also reflected in the number of jobs that is anticipated in the software industry vs. the hardware industry, being orders of magnitude larger. Particularly in the SW application industry have many smaller companies developed that are configuring and customizing implementations of standard software packages such as ERP systems and databases. This being the case, the economic value is still enabled by the hardware industry.

The rapid development of digital platforms has posed a dilemma for many companies active as they had to decide on their position in this developing value chain. IC manufacturers had to consider focusing on technology or design (separating concerns), or both. Generic SW companies (ERP, OS, DB) had to decide whether to support all its implementations or focus on one of the two. And life is very different above and below:

- Very different perspectives;
- Very different lifecycles;
- Very different competencies required;
- Very different economics (business control points).

But the choice that companies had was enabled by a 'common interface' in terms of language, protocols, simulation models… 'digital twins', creating a strong interdependency (Fig. 2).

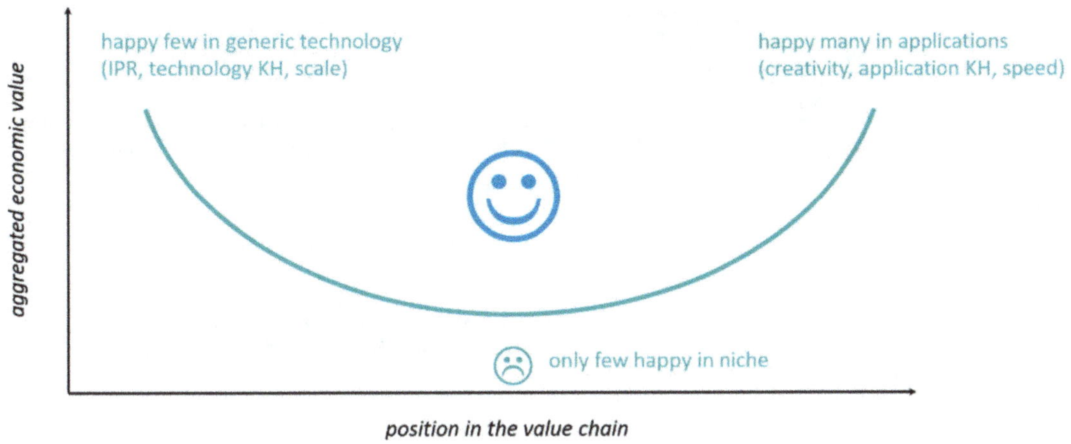

Fig. 2. The smile curve, picking your place in the value chain. In general the economic model on the left side is fueled by high volume, high investments and on the right side by lower volume, high diversity. The number of players on the left side is substantially lower than on the right side, leaving room only for niche players with customized technology in the center.

Already in the 90's was the so-called 'smile curve' introduced to express the dilemma of positioning oneself in the value chain. The vertical axis reflects the economic value that a company may create and the horizontal axis the (upward) movement in the value chain. As stated earlier, the total value of all companies is substantially larger on the right hand side but this value is created by many more application companies. There is only room for fewer players on the left hand side where the rules of the game are in general scale and high investments. The center reflects that you can't be both and there is only room for niche players with relatively low impact. That does not imply that representatives of the same (vertically integrated) conglomerates can show up on the left and the right… They can, but within those companies they will be very different animals requiring dedicated management and business controls.

3 The Internet of Things: Some Things are Repeats of History

Like the stacked platform picture that one can draw for the IT technology and applications ecosystem, one can create such picture the Internet of Things (Fig. 3). Clearly the IC technology stack is deeply embedded in the first layer of this IoT ecosystem, creating intelligent devices that are able to communicate. They represent (embedded) systems on their own.

Figure 3 does not aim to depict a standard way of looking at the IoT but one could recognize a few layers of the OSI model in it. The main thing is that it represents a very strong way of 'separating concerns' as the various layers have so much specialism in technology, business models, competencies and culture that one could regard it as different worlds that somehow are intimately dependent on each other.

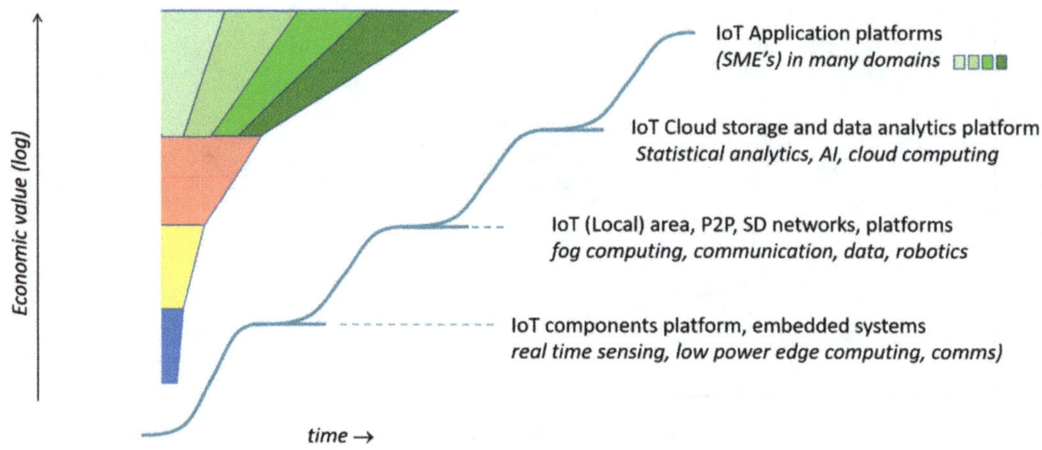

Fig. 3. Schematic representation of some key platform layers in the development of Internet of Things. The economic justification of enabling (lower) layers comes from many applications in various domains, each requiring expert knowledge

The picture also represents different architectural choices when it comes to data processing, that can be executed in end-nodes of the IoT (edge computing), in intermediate nodes, often representing local area networks and servers (fog computing) and central information processing often in the cloud. Hybrid forms are the most likely candidates for a solid implementation of IoT as the non-functional characteristics of centralized and decentralized systems are very different. We will go a bit deeper in this in the next sections.

The higher one gets in this picture, and the higher up in the value chain, the more diversification is taking place and knowledge of the application domain becomes essential. While this was already the case in IT for e.g. bookkeeping, for CAD, for control systems, it is taken to an extreme in IoT. IoT will be much more pervasive in society and one cannot create meaningful IoT applications without a solid understanding of the socio economic impact of it. This is where technology push ends.

Only by enabling an ecosystem that is deeply involved in applications in real life can a scale be created to justify the investments in the underlying layers such as communication networks and software systems. The key question is whether we are on track to create such ecosystem.

4 The Internet of Things: Some Things are Different

While the development of the Internet of Things resembles in many aspects the characteristics of the semiconductor and IT platforms as discussed in Sect. 2, there are some essential differences, mainly in scale and scope, that make the kickstart of a successful IoT more complex.

First of all has the investment scale gone up, for example in communication infrastructures. While the investment in 2G communication networks could be justified by just mobile phone traffic and 3G networks by increased data use on smart phones, future networks will be based on serving trillions of IoT devices in many different application domains with different requirements that all have the be developed.

But the same holds for platform developments in e.g. smart mobility or smart cities. They will require large investments that can only be earned back with many different application use cases. There is no single use case anymore that justifies the investment. This brings a higher level of uncertainty, that has to be countered by a strongly orchestrated approach for which we see 3 variants in today's world:

- Orchestration by governments;
- Orchestration by powerful (vertically integrated) companies;
- By collaborative platforms and ecosystems.

Secondly, IoT technology requirements differ from general Internet requirements that all require dedicated developments. Some of the most obvious ones are:

- Very low standby and communication power consumption in devices;
- Flexible bandwidth allocation (from very low to high);
- Very low cost per node serving extremely large numbers of nodes;
- Flexible and programmable communication layers (P2P, local, central);
- Extremely low latency for several applications;
- Extremely high reliability and resilience for several applications;
- Strong security and privacy requirements;
- … several other non-functional elements such as sustainability.

Serving some of these requirements will require fundamental changes in the architecture of next generation internet.

Thirdly, the higher one gets in the value chain, the wider the scope that needs to be orchestrated/managed and deep involvement of application domain specialist beyond technology will be crucial for IoT, more than it was for ICT development:

- A very wide range of application domains such as Smart Cities, Homes/Living, Healthcare, Farming, Energy, Mobility, Water Management, Industry… and more to come;
- Many technologies in HW, SW, Communications, Systems Engineering, Robotics, Sensing, Data Analytics, Hypercomputing, User Experience… and all non-functional requirements such as security and privacy;
- Legal and liability aspects;
- Socio-economic and human aspects;
- Education and training;
- Use case development.

The overall orchestration in scope, complexity and uncertainty of all these elements and the establishment of platforms that allow a 'separation of concerns' is probably the largest challenge for the development Internet of Things in Europe, more than the individual developments in technologies.

5 Key Elements for a Successful Deployment of IoT

The key issue with IoT is not technology, but the fact that

applications and platforms are insufficiently established…
because supporting platforms are insufficiently established…
because their justification by applications is insufficiently established

This is depicted in Figs. 4 and 5. Figure 4 represents the idealized stack of 'smile curves' of players in the components and IoT devices domain, the networks domain, the data domain and the application domain. As stated before, this is not necessarily the only way of breaking down the IoT value chain, but it illustrates that matter. The value is increasing exponentially along the chain and within each domain, one has to pick is position, require a high degree of focus and specialization.

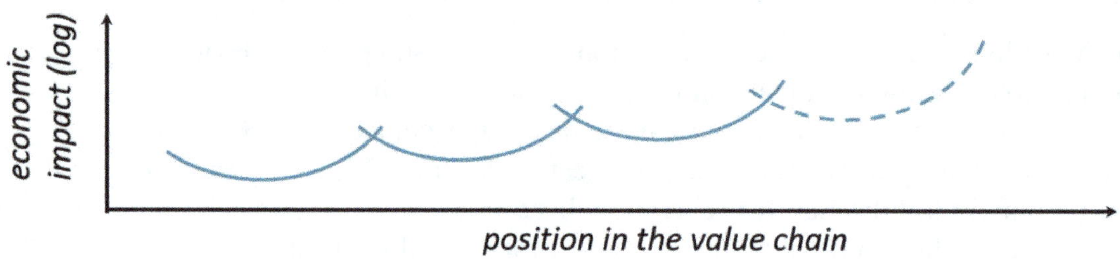

Fig. 4. The idealized stack of smile curves for an IoT value chain. Common interfaces and well connected platforms establish a high economic impact

This 'ideal' situation is emerging in ecosystems driven by government in China or by very strong platform companies in US. Note that the left hand part of the value chain does not require strong orchestration as industry platforms have very much established itself, but the challenge starts already at next generation communication networks.

However, a more realistic picture today which holds for Europe is depicted in Fig. 5. Not being driving by a central government powers or by large platform players, there is a lack of established data and application platforms, orchestrated and managed standard interfaces and in essence a lack of common goals. Even though individual expertise and goals of companies may differ, they require a common goal in IoT platform developments to be successful for their individual successes. Without such platforms, their individual value creation will become obstructed.

Not having a central governmental power for orchestration, nor extremely powerful platform companies established in Europe, the question to companies in this ecosystem is therefore very much: *Do you bet on your monopolistic do-it-yourself power or on your collaborative power for IoT?*

The only alternative way forward in establishing the required ecosystem seems to be the creation of *collaboration platforms*, uniting individual players around the common interest. The establishment of such platforms in Europe first of all assumes a sense of urgency in European industry that no single company/organisation can manage the whole stack on its own related to:

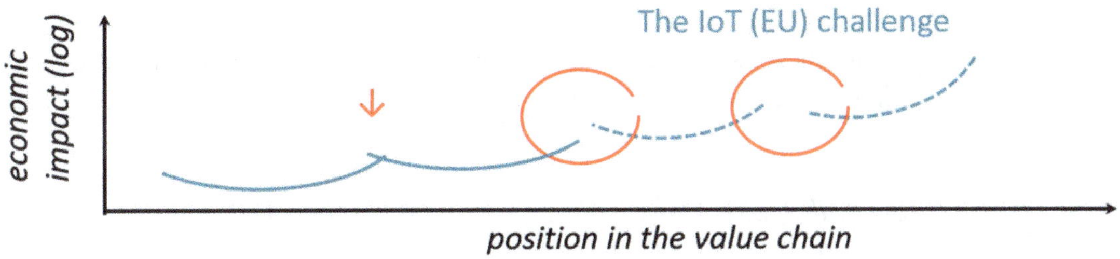

Fig. 5. A representation of today's ecosystem in EU Internet of Things, with data and application platforms and their orchestrated interfaces lacking, making the application value creation speculative and also reducing the economic value of lower layers

- Investments required and need to focus for economy of scale
- Knowledge and competency scope required for different parts
- Culture required for different parts

and a willingness to work together in an open innovation ecosystem that:

- Separates concerns ('mind your own business') building on strengths;
- Shares the common elements that don't differentiate the one company from the other (protocols, standard functions, infrastructures, architectures);
- Creates a large degree of interoperability.

Such ecosystem, although much more difficult to establish than alternatives that work under singular top-down control, can even prove to be more stable and attractive in the longer term because of:

- Involvement of a wider group of stakeholders, leading to higher acceptance and trust by society and governments;
- Better attention to non-functional aspects of IoT, in particular security, privacy, portability, resilience, flexibility;
- Faster development of use-cases, particularly when SME's and creatives gain access to these platforms. Their applications can greatly contribute to the justification of platforms whereas the creation and maintenance of platforms generally requires the skills and scale of larger companies.

And so, the key issue with IoT development in Europe is not technology, but a lack of:

- Collaboration between industrial players;
- Collaboration across functional silos;
- Understanding that economic justification of IoT infrastructures comes from multiple use cases in multiple domains, requiring an integrated approach.

It is not just the creation of platforms that needs a justification from many use cases in many domains, but very much the maintenance of such platforms, requiring a 24/7/365 high performance in the operational management of cities, homes, healthcare, energy, mobility etc.

Since the economic justification for any platform comes from *collectives* of applications, another key element in the deployment of IoT is the selection of those applications or use cases. This comes with a great deal of uncertainty that can only be managed by applying large scale experimentation in real scale environments. The mindset for the linked development of platforms and applications should therefore be:

Many applications will fail, get used to it!
Several applications will be successful, count on it!

Unlike technology development that usually takes place in laboratories, the development of uses cases takes needs to take place in cities, homes, healthcare ecosystems etc., involving:

- A real world environment
- Early involvement of end-users and key stakeholders beyond technology
- Expectation management (including non-functional aspects)
- The notion that early failure on any aspect is valuable learning

Governments have an important role to play in facilitating such real-world experimentation, e.g. by using innovative procurement procedures instead of traditional buying of upfront specified solutions against lowest cost.

Particularly the involvement of societal stakeholders in this experimentation is crucial in order to get valuable feedback on implementations but also to gain trust and address critical concerns in society regarding the impact of IoT applications and new technology that could hamper a successful deployment of IoT, even though technology works perfectly. In that sense should experimentation include e.g. legal and social aspects.

Lack of trust is considered the largest inhibitor of IoT deployment and lack of trust is strongly related to the non-functional aspects of IoT such as privacy and security. Trust is perception that cannot always be addressed by technology. Education and involvement of people in the development of IoT is essential and new knowledge and insights will be developed that in the end could pay off for Europe running a human centric socially embedded IoT.

The Internet of Things development is largely a self-fulfilling prophecy creating higher value for all, provided we:

- Create a collaborative platform in many aspects beyond technology
- Involve a wide range of (societal) stakeholder in an early stage
- Are prepared to experiment, fail and learn
- Are prepared to enable higher value creation before re-distributing it.

6 Key Roles for IT Professionals in IoT

From the sections above, one may anticipate also large changes in certain professions, particularly the ones that operate on interfaces of different disciplines or across different domains and in applications. Other, more specialised professions will not fundamentally change even though underlying technologies will evolve.

Professionals at the end of the chain, in applications, will be increasingly confronted with the enormous opportunities of IoT. This is already happening in e.g. Smart Farming, where the new generation of farmers is strongly involved with the latest technologies in sensing, data analytics and automated growing control in e.g. city farming. In many other domains will the traditional craftsmen become users of intelligent systems, robotics and data that will on the one hand replace many of their traditional work and on the other hand enable them to do ground breaking new things. This is a large part of the social transformation.

Many more IT professionals will be required that operate on interfaces, bringing a wide scope of knowledge and experience or able to link with application domain specialist, talking 'farmers language' with IoT farmers, 'transporters language' with IoT transporters etc. Several universities and colleges have already recognised this need and started educational programs for:

- T-profile Engineers, 'platformers' integrating many functional and non-functional aspects of platforms with strong IT components (communications, data, embedded systems). Typically these professionals need strong architecting and platform management skills;
- Π-profile Engineers, linking with other disciplines (legal, social) and/or engaging with application domains, requiring non-technical skills and application knowledge.

These profiles are schematically depicted in Fig. 6. I-profiles these days form the majority of ICT profiles, focusing on dedicated subjects and specialism in the ICT landscape. But there is a limitation to what a single mind can do in this increasingly complex world of systems. It is unlikely that 'I can do it all' and increasingly we need T- and Π-profile Engineers integrating vertically and horizontally.

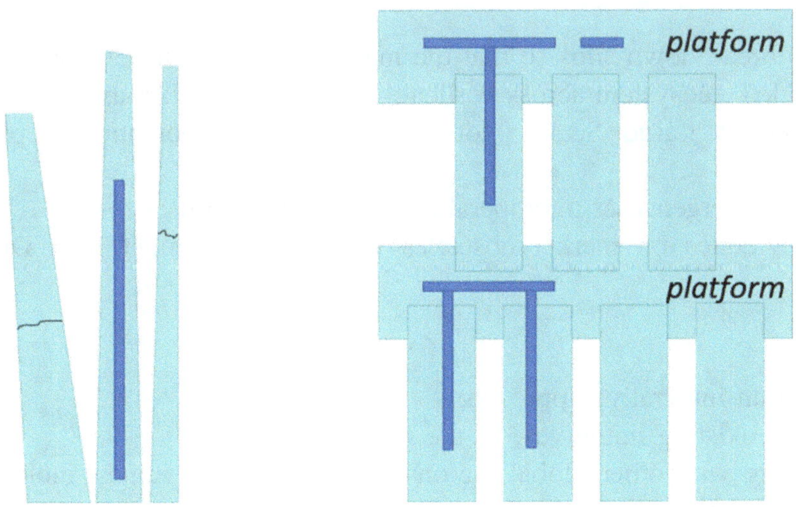

Fig. 6. Schematic representation of competency profiles, applicable to ICT professionals. I-profiles represent 'do it yourself' end-to-end professionals from the early days and the many specialist that today operate in a specific expertise field. Increasingly, platform integration profiles (T-shape) and cross-domain integration profiles (∏-shape) are required to build the IoT.

It requires the development and maintenance of technical and non-technical skills to be successful in:

- Solving societal challenges
- Addressing non-functional system aspects crucial for trust
  - Educating and involving society
  - Providing end users with options and personal data ownership
- Managing convergence on application level
  - Internet, IoT, mobile, IIoT, OT, data analytics, systems of systems, SDN
  - Cybersecurity
  - Cloud-, fog-, edge-computing and their distribution
  - Real-time, mission critical SW for specific application domains
  - VR, AR, robotics, digital twins, BIM…
- Interoperability and portability of functions and data
- Designing and deploying distributed Systems Architectures

But this also provides many development opportunities for IT professionals and an increase of jobs.

7 The Alliance for Internet of Things Innovation (AIOTI)

The Alliance for Internet of Things Innovation (www.aioti.eu) was kickstarted in 2015 and formally established in 2017 with the aim to address the cross functional and integration aspects of building a successful IoT. It is a member driven organisation with representatives from industry (large and small), academia and society that:

- Is at the forefront of IoT adoption, able to identify what is required to drive this adoption;
- Strives to break down silos so that the market for IoT can develop;
- Develops loT ecosystem across vertical silos including start-ups and SMEs;
- Contributes to Large Scale Pilots to foster experimentation, replication and deployment;
- Supports convergence & interoperability of loT standards;
- Gathers evidence on market obstacles for loT deployment in a Digital Single Market.

by

- Promoting an integrative approach;
- Leveraging existing initiatives, be the missing link;
- Co-operating with other global regions while European values, including privacy and consumer protection, are maintained.

AIOTI embraces diversity, expressing the different views of interest group along the value chain. AIOTI is leveraging a structure of horizontal working groups, addressing common elements in technology research, ecosystems, standards and policies with an implementation driven approach in vertical working groups. This is depicted in Fig. 7.

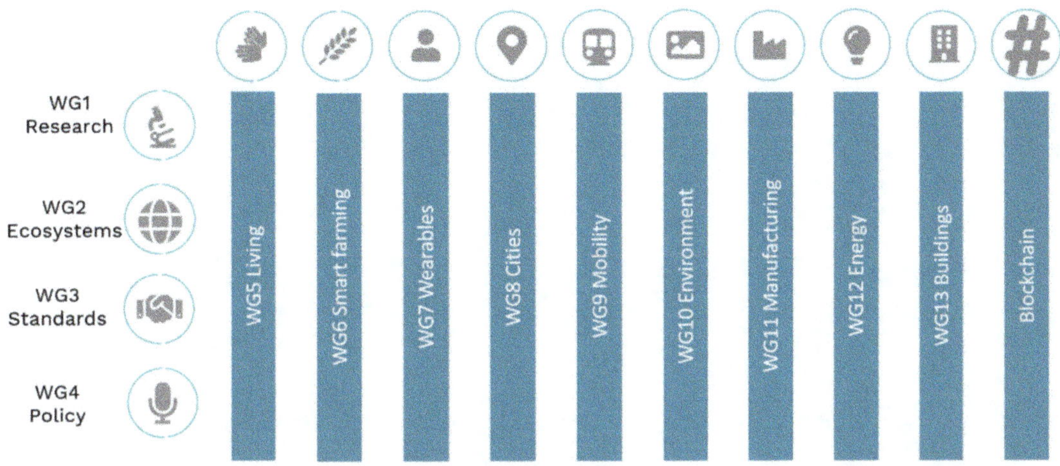

Fig. 7. Working structure of the Alliance for Internet of Things Innovation (2018), combining horizontal and vertical working groups (WG)

8 Conclusions

We have taken an integral perspective on the development of IoT, beyond technology and clearly the Internet of Things holds many *promises*. But just as much as the promises, the development of IoT has many *challenges* requiring a new approach involving:

- Creating platforms by a strong collaborative approach beyond technology;
- Socio-economic aspects in a Human Centric IoT;
- The education and involvement of end-users;
- Privacy, security, resilience… and many more non-functional aspects;
- Critical architectural choices;
- Real scale experimentation.

Those elements and technical elements should be addressed in an integrated approach, on the one hand leveraging specialist companies and individuals, separating concerns, but linking them in an overall approach. The Alliance for Internet of Things Innovation promotes and drives such approach.

Interesting and responsible opportunities emerge for IT professionals, playing key roles in architecture and platform integration and in linking application domain specialists and end-users.

IoT: Do We Have a Choice?

Draft IFIP Position Paper

Leon Strous(✉) and IFIP Domain Committee on IoT

Amsterdam, The Netherlands
strous@iae.nl

Abstract. Many experts and organizations are addressing the Internet of Things (IoT) in policy statements, papers and conferences. There are many aspects to be considered when talking about IoT. The International Federation for Information Processing (IFIP) contributes to the discussion by investigating what choices can or must be made regarding these various aspects. And by addressing the question what choices various stakeholders should have. This draft version of the position paper was discussed at the IFIP IoT working conference on 18-09-2018 and in the IFIP General Assembly on 23-09-2018. The outcome of these discussions will be processed in the final version of the position paper.

Keywords: Position paper · Choices · IoT dimensions · IoT lifecycle

1 Introduction

IoT is hot. Many experts and organizations are addressing the topic in policy statements, papers and conferences. There are many aspects to be looked at when talking about IoT. IFIP wants to contribute to the discussion by investigating what choices can or must be made regarding these various aspects. And by addressing the question what choices various stakeholders should have. This paper briefly lists the aspects and dimensions of the IoT. Then IFIP's position on some major questions and choices is presented. It concludes with an overview of (possible) contributions that are already made or can be made by IFIP and its member societies and by ICT professionals in general to the open questions.

This draft version of the position paper was discussed at the IFIP IoT working conference on 18-09-2018 and in the IFIP General Assembly on 23-09-2018. The outcome of these discussions will be processed in the final version of the position paper.

2 Definition

More than one definition of the IoT exists. For the essence of this paper the definition is not the most important element. It was therefore decided to neither choose one from the list nor create one of our own to guide the discussion. A few examples of definitions are

L. Strous and V. G. Cerf (Eds.): IFIPIoT 2018, IFIP AICT 548, pp. 50–56, 2019.
https://doi.org/10.1007/978-3-030-15651-0_6

added in an annex at the end of the paper. It is important to note however that while the IoT can be seen as a global infrastructure several vertical domains for distinct applications can be defined.

3 Aspects and Dimensions

3.1 Opportunities Versus Threats

Like every new technology also the Internet of Things offers opportunities for progress and application for beneficial purposes while at the same time it introduces or increases risks and threats. When addressing choices about various aspects, both sides will be considered.

3.2 Dimensions

As mentioned in the introduction, there are many aspects to be looked at when talking about IoT and discussing what choices can or must be made regarding these various aspects. In the current literature, many lists of aspects are a mixture of types of aspects. In an attempt to structure this, a three-dimensional model is proposed. The three dimensions would distinguish choices to be made:

- by whom (individuals and organizations)
- during which phase of the lifecycle of an IoT application
- about which issues.

By Whom

Choices are to be made by individuals and by organizations. An individual can be in the role of ICT professional developing IoT infrastructure or IoT applications or in the role of a user of IoT. Organizations can be in the role of user, of ICT industry developing IoT hardware and software or of authorities/regulators responsible for policies, standardization, legislation and other types of regulation.

Phases of an IoT lifecycle

Many lifecycle phases of products, systems and applications can be found in literature. Generally speaking the following phases can also be distinguished for an IoT application:

- Analysis/design;
- Development/production;
- Operation/maintenance;
- Disposition.

Issues

The broad spectrum of issues to be considered includes:

- Technical issues
- Legal issues (including liability)

- Ethical issues
- Education, training, awareness
- Usability and accessibility issues/freedom of choice and personalization issues
- Environmental issues
- Privacy issues
- Risks, Security, Resilience
- Impact on persons and society
- Professionalism/duty of care.

4 IFIP's Position on Major Questions and Choices

This position paper is not a series of positions on the technologies in the Internet of Things but it is a series of statements about choices that can be made and/or should be made and that should be enabled by technologies and/or policies. As a federation of societies of ICT professionals, for our positions we take the perspective of a human centred IoT: *"A human centred IoT would imply an environment where IoT will empower people and not transform them into hostages of technology"* [1].

The most elementary choice is the question "can I choose not to use an IoT?". The answer to this question is not straightforward for all cases. There may be arguments e.g. for national security or environmental reasons to limit the choices. In the following paragraphs this and a number of other questions will be addressed. In each paragraph IFIP's position on a variety of aspects is presented and substantiated.

The paragraphs are following the dimension "By whom" (see Sect. 3.2).

4.1 ICT Professional

I. **IFIP's position is that an ICT professional should have sufficient professional and ethical competencies to make the right choices when designing, developing, implementing, operating or managing software/hardware as part of an Internet of Things that is able to offer choices to its' users.**

Having sufficient professional and ethical competencies is a general requirement for ICT professionals. However, in an IoT environment this is especially important because users may not be aware of the fact that choices are, could or should be possible. Users also may not be in a position to demand choices or to influence the usage of collected data. Therefore, the professionals should see to it that such choices are embedded and offered. The constraint of course is that also an ICT professional may not be in a position to decide upon the design etcetera. This means that a condition for making this work is to have professional and ethical competencies not only embedded in the codes of ethics of societies of professionals but also in companies' policies. And to have a work environment that is supportive of putting these policies into practice.

II. **IFIP's position is that ICT professionals have a choice to educate/inform users on both the potential benefits and the risks of the Internet of Things the users are confronted with.**

Users should be informed about the benefits and risks of Internet of Things applications they use. If the owner/developer of such applications does not (sufficiently) inform the users, ICT professionals have a choice, maybe even a duty, to do this, for instance via research papers and publications. In order to be able to do this, there should be no legal liability when publishing such results.

4.2 User

Both individuals and organizations can be in the role of user.

III. **IFIP's position is that users at least must have a choice to switch off the connection/not use the smart part of smart devices. In other words, users should have an opt in or opt out choice.**

IV. **IFIP's position is that it supports the possibility to empower users in such a way that they can control and personalize the behaviour of smart objects and associated applications through appropriate design tools even if they do not have programming knowledge.**

For example, if a smart meter gives the energy company full insight in the user's energy consumption, the user should have the option to not provide this information. This means that policies/regulations/legislations should allow for this and also the technology/devices should make this possible. Users should be aware of the consequences of both the opt in and opt out choice.

There may be applications or circumstances where it is not possible or desirable to give users an opt in or opt out choice, for instance in cases where national security is at stake. When this is the case, it should be clearly explained to users.

V. **IFIP's position is that users should inform themselves about the various aspects (benefits/risks) of the devices that are connected in the IoT they are using.**

While ICT professionals and ICT industry have a choice, or actually an obligation, to educate/inform users, these users have a choice, or also perhaps an obligation, to inform themselves. This can be by simply reading the information provided or asking for information if that is not provided. A condition to help users is the availability of "a set of the right questions".

VI. **IFIP's position is that involving users in the design/development of IoT (application) should be encouraged.**

Users are not only passive users but are also often people who possess knowledge and can contribute in the design/development of IoT. Having a say – if possible, in the design process – would be one way to make them more active.

4.3 ICT Industry

VII. **IFIP's position is that the ICT industry providing IoT applications should inform users about the benefits and potential risks.**

This should not be a choice but an obligation. It has to be clear for users for which purposes data are collected. A mechanism needs to be in place to assure the security and protection of such collected data and providers should inform users about these mechanisms. It should also be made clear what the consequences of either choice (opt in or opt out) are.

VIII. **IFIP's position is that the ICT industry should not develop IoT applications that provide data that can be used without the owners of the data knowing about the use or consenting to it. The ICT industry has a choice not to do this.**

Owners of data, both personal data or data that can be linked to persons in an indirect way, should know who is doing what with their data and they should have the right to give consent for such usage. This may not be possible in all cases but that should then also be clear.

4.4 Authority/Regulator

IX. **IFIP's position is that policymakers/regulators should take into account the interests of users when regulating the use of (personal) data (including data that can be linked to a person in an indirect way e.g. via home, car, etc.).**

Policymakers/regulators have a choice to balance the interests of various stakeholders in the applications and their data. It is important that policies and regulations provide the conditions for the choices that users and providers can or should be able to make.

5 Possible Actions

IFIP, it's member societies and their members can contribute to solve the "choice problems" addressed in the previous chapter. What can be done:

- Check/promote the presence of the professional and ethical competencies issue, for example in codes of ethics of professional societies and in companies' HR policies.
- Provide a "set of the right questions".
- Promote the position statements to the professionals, users, industry and authorities.
- Research the benefits and risks of the various Internet of Things applications.
- Increase research of those aspects that are insufficiently addressed and/or that are gaining more and more importance. Examples could be: (1) With the increasing number of IoT devices will there be energy to run all of them? IoT is requesting the production of low power devices, that means the use of optimisation techniques, and the direction is to have dedicated devices to each need or function. (2) With the increasing number of IoT applications, ethical (privacy, surveillance etc.) and

security issues are becoming more and more important due to the use, design and implementation of such applications.

6 Annex. Sample Definitions

ITU [2]

"Internet of Things (IoT): A global infrastructure for the information society, enabling advanced services by interconnecting physical and virtual things based on existing and evolving interoperable information and communication technologies.

Thing: an object of the physical world or the information world, which is capable of being identified and integrated into communication networks.

Device: a piece of equipment with the mandatory capability of communication and the optional capabilities of sensing, actuation, data capture, data storage, and data processing."

Wikipedia [3]

"The **Internet of Things** (**IoT**) is the inter-networking of physical devices (also referred to as "thing", "object", "connected devices" or "smart devices") such as vehicles, buildings, and other items embedded with electronics, software, sensors, actuators, and network connectivity which enable these objects to collect and exchange data. The IoT allows objects and their environments to be sensed or controlled remotely across existing network infrastructure, creating opportunities for more direct integration of the physical world into computer-based systems, and resulting in improved efficiency, accuracy and economic benefit in addition to reduced human intervention. When IoT is augmented with sensors and actuators, the technology becomes an instance of the more general class of cyber-physical systems, which also encompasses technologies such as smart grids, virtual power plants, smart homes, intelligent transportation and smart cities. Each thing is uniquely identifiable through its embedded computing system but is able to interoperate within the existing Internet infrastructure."

Gubbi et al. [4]

"The worldwide network of interconnected objects uniquely addressable based on standard communication protocols." and "Our definition of the Internet of Things for smart environments is: Interconnection of sensing and actuating devices providing the ability to share information across platforms through a unified framework, developing a common operating picture for enabling innovative applications. This is achieved by seamless ubiquitous sensing, data analytics and information representation with Cloud computing as the unifying framework."

References

1. EC Staff working document "Advancing the Internet of Things in Europe", April 2016. https://ec.europa.eu/digital-single-market/en/news/staff-working-document-advancing-internet-things-europe
2. ITU Recommendation Y.4000/Y.2060 - Overview of the Internet of things. https://www.itu.int/rec/T-REC-Y.2060-201206-I
3. https://en.wikipedia.org/wiki/Internet_of_things. Accessed 14 Aug 2017, 21:22 Amsterdam, (Slightly Adjusted)
4. Gubbi, J., Buyya, R., Marusic, S., Palaniswami, M.: Internet of Things (IoT): a vision, architectural elements, and future directions. Future Gener. Comput. Syst. **29**(7), 1645–1660 (2013)

IFIPIoT 2018 Refereed Papers

The Outcomes of the Implementation of Internet of Things: A Public Value Perspective

Ott Velsberg(✉)

Department of Informatics, Umeå University, Umeå, Sweden
ott.velsberg@umu.se

Abstract. In recent years, Internet of Things (IoT) has gained presence in all areas of life. Whilst private sector is the forerunner in the adoption of these devices, public sector usage has been lagging. With the rise of smart initiatives, public organizations are increasingly implementing IoT. The necessity to know in which areas of public sector IoT has been implemented and what public value has been derived, has gained importance as reporting of the cost efficiency and benefits of these initiatives has gained attention. This paper seeks to determine the importance of IoT in the public sector from the perspective of public value. IoT implementation in Estonian municipalities was studied to provide concrete data on the use of IoT. Next to efficiency, which is a known goal of IT implementation, the research findings suggest that while IoT has generated public value, there has been a shift in value creation with other outcomes such as effectiveness, transparency and collaboration gaining increased presence. While IoT shows great promise for public value creation, more research is needed to study how public sector can leverage these devices to harvest more benefits than the simple automatization of work processes.

Keywords: Public values · Public sector · Value creation · Internet of Things

1 Introduction

The term Internet of Things (IoT) has attracted considerable attention in academics, industry and public sector, and is envisioned as a global network of machines and devices that can interact with each other [23]. The IoT has been regarded as one of the most important areas of future technology [23] and to be at the core of the fourth industrial revolution [19]. The European Commission envisions IoT as an indispensable component towards the digitisation of our society and economy [8]. It is forecasted that the market value of IoT in the EU will exceed one trillion euros by 2020 [7], and by 2025 the yearly global economic impact of IoT is estimated to be between 3 trillion to 9 trillion euros, accounting close to 11% of the world economy [25].

Research indicates that by 2020, close to 26% of all IoT solutions will be consumed by public sector [12]. A high rate of expenditure can be predicted, as national and local governments have been voracious consumers of information technologies (IT) in the past [29]. However, recent studies indicate that close to 60% of IoT initiatives stall at the Proof of Concept stage and 75% of completed IoT projects fail to produce value

L. Strous and V. G. Cerf (Eds.): IFIPIoT 2018, IFIP AICT 548, pp. 59–75, 2019.
https://doi.org/10.1007/978-3-030-15651-0_7

[16]. With regards to this, it becomes questionable whether the value created from IoT overweighs the financial risks taken by the public sector.

Creating public value has been a key focus in digitizing public sector organizations. If the public sector continues to invest in IoT, our innate logic tells us that it must create public value. Agarwal and Lucas [1] argued that to contribute to the IS field it is fundamental to demonstrate the value of IT. Following the same argumentation, it is crucial to demonstrate the public value of IoT. However, to date, the research on IoT and public value creation has been scarce.

The aim of this research is to offer a contribution regarding the public value created by IoT, asking: What public value does IoT create in the public sector? The study offers a glimpse on the main values created by IoT, based on an extensive qualitative study on 46 municipalities in Estonia. The paper briefly introduces the concept of public value and IoT, including an overview of IoT implementation in the public sector.

The paper is structured as follows. First, the theoretical basis is set by introducing the concept of public value. Next, the concept of IoT and its role in public sector will be introduced. In the following parts, the research design and findings are presented. This will be followed by a discussion of findings and a conclusion.

2 Theoretical Background

This section introduces the concept of public value, which is regarded as one of the main reasons for public sector innovation. The following section introduces the concept of IoT and discuss its importance in generating public value.

2.1 Public Value Perspective

Public entities such as governments, municipalities and county councils are constantly seeking to address contemporary challenges and opportunities through utilizing emerging technologies [29]. While there are many motivators for adopting IT solutions, a primary goal of IT initiatives is to create and deliver public value [18]. Public value focuses on governmentally produced benefits that serve the interests of stakeholders both inside and outside the public organization [14]. The creation of public value entails balancing competing public interests through emphasizing collective preferences and expectations of government, citizens and other stakeholders who consume the services [5, 27]. Consequently, public sector bases its decisions to implement IT on the expected benefits and conflicting demands of various stakeholders [30].

It is widely acknowledged that IT creates public value. A successful IT implementation is believed to drastically change how governmental organizations operate, bringing forth substantial organizational, technical, business and societal benefits [10, 20]. IT-based value manifests itself both in terms of economic values e.g. operational efficiency, and non-economic values e.g. trust in government and sustainability [29]. For the associated stakeholders, e.g. citizens, users, public administrators and politicians, the public value can manifest differently, e.g. administrative personnel and managers from public sector might place high value on accountability, c.f. [10], while citizens might value accessibility to governmental information [38]. Harrison et al. [14] divided public value into seven categories, namely:

1. Economic – impacts on current or future income, asset values, liabilities, entitlements, or other aspects of wealth or risks to any of the above.
2. Political – impacts on a person's or group's influence on government actions or policy, or their role in political affairs, influence in political parties or prospects for public office.
3. Social – impacts on family or community relationships, social mobility, status, and identity.
4. Strategic – impacts on person's or group's economic or political advantage or opportunities, goals, and resources for innovation or planning.
5. Quality of life – impacts on individual and household health, security, satisfaction, and general well-being.
6. Ideological – impacts on beliefs, moral or ethical commitments, alignment of government actions/policies or social outcomes with beliefs, or moral or ethical positions.
7. Stewardship – impacts on the public's view of government officials as faithful steward.

The incorporation of public value in the discussion of public sector investment in IT is especially relevant as it allows to monitor the outcome of government investment and understand the relationship between IT and public value delivery [36]. Understanding the relationship between IT and public value creation can assist public organizations in the pursuit of suitable use of technology to benefit society and secure the cost efficiency of public value creation [3].

2.2 Role of the Internet of Things

The IoT has rapidly gained presence and is sometimes regarded as the most disruptive phase of the Internet revolution [2, 34]. IoT is ubiquitous by nature and is present in different almost identical concepts, such as "Internet of Everything", "ubiquitous computing", "pervasive computing" and "ambient intelligence", whereas the differences between the terms are of academic nature [9]. IoT is a general term used for objects interconnected through networks, that encompass processing and sensor capabilities, allowing the devices to transmit recorded information from the outside environment. IoT allows information, resources, "things", e.g. sensors, beacons, actuators, mobile phones etc., to interact with each other and cooperate with their smart components to reach common goals [15]. Realizing the value of IoT requires integration of IT infrastructures and information services - such as RFID tags, wireless broadband and geographic information systems [33]. Sensory data must be gathered from distributed smart objects and be transmitted using a communication infrastructure, which can encompass both wired and wireless communication technologies [32]. IoT allows to link real-life objects with the virtual world - providing anytime, anyplace connectivity for anything [34].

These capabilities can be applied to everyday objects, thus affecting all areas of life [9]. IoT will change the way we collect, analyse, and respond to data, creating opportunities for individuals, governments, and businesses to develop new business models and forms of interaction that take advantage of ubiquitous computing power embedded in objects [13]. While the majority of IoT initiatives have been implemented in the private sector, studies have indicated that the importance of IoT in public sector is increasing [4, 12]. This is driven by the rapid development of IT, and expanding efforts by national and local governments to change how they operate. Local governments are increasingly turning towards new information systems, often utilizing IoT, to develop livable, economically sustainable and efficient living environments. IoT is implemented in various settings from cities to rural areas. Utilizing IoT devices allows local governments to monitor and take immediate action on almost every aspect of urban and rural space, and provide citizens with relevant information and services [33, 35]. Among others, IoT can be used to create new and enhance existing services, improve efficiency and effectiveness of internal management and service delivery, and foster collaboration with different stakeholders [9, 22]. Due to the dynamic nature of public sector, the requirements for IoT devices can vary significantly. The IoT devices that can swiftly and accurately transmit information can be crucial for winter road maintenance, while speed would not be a requirement for water consumption monitoring.

In the context of public sector, IoT has the potential to improve several areas, including: healthcare, education, utilities, infrastructure, buildings, environment and culture. With regards to this, IoT becomes pivotal in streamlining governmental processes and engaging citizens in all areas of local governance. However, to date, little is known on how IoT generates public value. Consequently, there also lacks knowledge on how local governments could benefit from implementing IoT.

3 Public Value Framework

For the study in hand, it was considered suitable to use the six public value generating mechanisms proposed by Harrison et al. [14] to understand what public value IoT creates in public sector (See Table 1). Harrison et al. [14] created the set of value generators to specify how public value is created, i.e. which government action lead to the creation of public value. For analysis, the six public value mechanisms proposed by Harrison et al. [14] were used for guidance. To investigate the relationship between IoT and public value generating mechanisms, a public value framework was created to assess the IoT initiatives and to distinguish between the outcomes (See Table 1). Based on Nam and Pardo [28] the evaluation dimensions were presented from the external view (interactions with citizens, private companies and other relevant non-governmental actors) and from the internal view (interactions within the local government). Identifying and measuring the public value of IoT is complicated as different stakeholders may have different attitudes on what is regarded a successful outcome of an IT initiative [37]. As a result, public value creation was studied from the perspective of public organizations. Similarly to this study, most research on IT value studies the outcome of past IT investments through a post hoc analysis [21]. As the study is concerned with how IoT solutions add value to local governments and public, broader economic factors are not considered unless they directly relate to governmental or public impact.

Table 1. Public value framework.

Dimensions	Management (internal view)	Service delivery (external view)
Efficiency	Concentrates on the internal managerial efficiency in terms of obtaining increased outputs, workloads, activities, processes and goal attainment	Concentrates on the efficiency of producing and delivering services
Effectiveness	Concentrates on the quality of internal management	Concentrates on the quality of services delivered
Intrinsic enhancements	Concentrates on the changing environment or circumstances for governmental stakeholders	Concentrates on the changing environment or circumstances for non-governmental parties
Transparency	Concentrates on the access of information or processes inside the local government	Concentrates on the external access to information and processes regarding service provision and delivery
Participation	Concentrates on the frequency and intensity of direct involvement of internal stakeholders in decision making or operation of government	Concentrates on the frequency and intensity of direct involvement of external stakeholders in decision making or operation of government
Collaboration	Concentrates on the improvement of collaboration inside the local government in terms of sharing responsibility or authority for governmental processes and actions	Concentrates on the collaboration between governmental and non-governmental parties in terms of sharing responsibility or authority for governmental processes and actions

4 Research Design

To understand how IoT creates public value, a qualitative study was carried out on the use of IoT in Estonian municipalities. The following section provides information on the research domain, data collection and analysis.

4.1 Data Collection

To paint a thorough picture of the use of IoT in public sector, the research concentrated on the use of IoT in Estonian municipalities. The data was collected between March and December 2017 through semi-structured interviews and supporting documentation reviews.

The research participants were found by first contacting all 202 municipalities in Estonia via e-mail regarding the use of IoT in public sector, the municipalities that had implemented IoT solutions were included to the study and the municipalities who were in the planning phase of IoT implementation or who had not implemented IoT solutions were excluded. Thus, ex ante descriptions of the predicted outcome of IoT were not included in the study. In total 81 municipalities replied, of whom 46 were included in the study. From those 46 municipalities, 67 participants were contacted and interviewed regarding the implemented IoT solutions. In some municipalities, more than one public official was interviewed due to a lack of involvement of the interviewee with other IoT solutions.

The interviews were conducted in person where possible, and over the phone in other circumstances. An interview guide was used to determine the course of the interviews, which included open-ended questions that allowed to include topics that were not predetermined by the interview guide. The type of questions in the interview guide included the type of solutions implemented, the outcomes of the solutions, collaboration with other stakeholders, the role of IoT, measurement techniques for the outcomes etc. In Table 2 an overview of the interview questions is presented. The interview guides were iteratively changed, according to the research conducted prior to the interviews - publicly available information on each municipality was gathered to determine the type of solutions introduced.

Table 2. Overview of interview questions.

Interview question examples:
What IoT solutions have been implemented?
What has been the guiding principle behind the deployment of IoT?
What benefits has the IoT brought?
How has the IoT affected municipal processes?
How do you verify the integrity of the collected data?
Why did the municipality decide to use the devices?
Would it be financially beneficial for other municipalities to use these devices?

The interviews lasted between 20 and 120 min, with an average of 57 min. All interviews were audio recorded and later transcribed. The participants had been using IoT solutions from five months to five years - providing enough time to realize the value of IoT initiatives [24]. A summary of all interviews will be presented in Table 3.

Table 3. Summary of interviews.

Public sector representatives	Total number of respondents
Chief information officer	7
Environmental and municipal advisor	3
Head of economics department	9
Head of public administrative unit	4
Head of road maintenance	1
Head of utilities	7
Municipal mayor	14
Municipal vice-mayor	22

Supporting documentation such as procurement documents, public documents, and technical files were collected from governmental databases and online sources, e.g. municipal websites and from technology providers. Technical documentation was attained on both the system and the device where possible. Procurement documents which allowed to better understand the reasons and granularities of the implementation of any device were studied where possible. Public documents used included governmental reports, public statements etc. Secondary data sources were used to prepare for interviews, map government priorities etc. A summary of all additional procedures for data collection are presented in Table 4.

Table 4. Summary of data collection.

Supporting documentation	
Procurement documents	118
Public documents	173
Technical documents	131

4.2 Data Analysis

To analyse the data, the recommended procedures for qualitative research were followed to guide through the three steps of coding [6, 26]. During the first round of coding an initial coding scheme was developed. As the research was concerned with identifying what public value IoT generates, the coding scheme was based on public value framework (See Table 1). During the second round of coding, examples of IoT generated public value were identified. As the study focused on how IoT has generated public value for the municipalities, the perspective of citizens and other stakeholders were considered through municipal perspective. The different dimensions were recorded altogether 2644 times. From the mentioned segments, 1481 concentrated on the external view. The remaining segments were divided between the internal dimensions. A summary of coded segments can be seen in Table 5.

Table 5. Summary of coded segments.

Dimensions	Management (internal view)	Service delivery (external view)
Efficiency	431	339
Effectiveness	298	405
Intrinsic enhancements	67	74
Transparency	113	301
Participation	143	185
Collaboration	111	177
Total	1163	1481

The third round of coding compared previously coded segments to summarize shared features and variance within and across research sites. Multiple data sources allowed to compare, contrast and triangulate data [26]. ATLAS.ti was used throughout the study for data analysis. Findings are presented in the following section.

5 Empirical Analysis

In recent years, IoT has gained traction in public discourse as IoT solutions are increasingly implemented. This research concentrates on the use of IoT in Estonian municipalities - studying the public value created by these solutions.

5.1 Mapping the Estonian IoT Solutions

IoT solutions can be implemented for virtually any purpose, however the study identified some core areas in which the implementation of IoT was more common, namely buildings and transportation. In total, 158 IoT solutions were implemented, from those, the study identified 30 different IoT solution types. Table 6 will present an overview of the implemented solutions and the number of municipalities that implemented those.

Table 6. Summary of IoT solutions.

Area	Number of solutions (percentage of all solutions)	Overview of the solutions	Examples (number of solutions)
Buildings	29 (18.3%)	Systems that include simple motion sensors to regulate lightning to more complex systems that regulate window canopies depending on lightning and temperature	Heating system (9); Smart lightning (10); Ventilation system (8); Window canopies (2)
Infrastructure	21 (13.3%)	Systems that include simple motion sensors to turn on and regulate lightning, to more complex systems that regulate lightning depending on vehicle speed and depending on public transportation movement. Pothole identification system allows to identify and map the condition of roads	Pothole identification system (1); Intelligent lightning (20)
Healthcare	2 (1.3%)	Sensors collecting physical vitals and transmitting them to healthcare professionals and public officials. Allows to notify of emergencies	SOS-bracelets (2)
Security	19 (12%)	Vehicle surveillance systems collect, analyze and transmit information on	Smoke detectors (3);

(*continued*)

Table 6. *(continued)*

Area	Number of solutions (percentage of all solutions)	Overview of the solutions	Examples (number of solutions)
		vehicles. Smoke detectors and surveillance systems allow remote access and improved detection	Surveillance system (7); Vehicle surveillance system (9)
Transportation	49 (31%)	Connected buses and fleet telematics allow remote monitoring of location, performance and behavior of vehicles Remote passenger validation system allows to validate passengers and track their movements Traffic and pedestrian/cyclist counter allows to count the number of individuals and various other elements, e.g. their speed and whether they wear bicycle helmets Smart parking allows to track and visualize the available parking spaces	Connected buses (5); Fleet telematics (34); Pedestrian/cyclist counter (2); Remote passenger validation system (1); Self-driving buses (1); Smart bicycle parking (3); Traffic counter (3)
Utilities	23 (14.6%)	Array of sensors that allow to improve the processes and automate the monitoring and maintenance of utility systems, e.g. geothermal systems, garbage transfer stations and wastewater treatment plants. Smart meters allow to collect and analyze water consumption and automate various processes, e.g. billing and detection of leakage	Biomass heating systems (5); Garbage transfer station (1); Garbage bins (2); Geothermal systems (6); Water meters (5); Water plant (2); Wastewater treatment plant (2)
Weather and environmental monitoring	15 (9.5%)	Array of sensors that collect and analyze environmental information, such as water and air quality, temperature and constituents. The system alerts when these values exceed a set threshold	Air quality sensors (3); Noise sensors (1); Pavement sensors (1); Snow monitoring (3); Water monitoring (3); Weather Stations (4)

Table 7. Number of solutions with identified public value.

Dimensions	Number of solutions		Total number of solutions
	Management (internal view)	Service delivery (external view)	
Efficiency	68	36	75
Effectiveness	64	53	94
Intrinsic enhancements	16	7	19
Transparency	28	64	67
Participation	24	17	32
Collaboration	38	42	45

Table 7 presents a summary of solutions where public value was identified. A solution could simultaneously provide public value in many dimensions, for example there were 75 solutions which generated efficiency, from those solutions, 68 produced public value for management and 36 solutions produced public value in service delivery.

The following part presents how IoT impacted the six public value mechanisms, drawing on specific IoT implementation examples for illustration, see Table 6.

5.2 Efficiency

The study identified that 64.5% of solutions (102 solutions) had efficiency as their primary desired outcome. From all solutions, 47.5% of solutions (75 solutions) identified efficiency as an achieved outcome. While reducing costs was the main consideration during the procurement, it was difficult for municipalities to isolate the effects and measure the outcome. Consequently, improvements in efficiency were visible in terms of productivity, most commonly through reduced time and improved communication. The devices allowed municipal employees to work everywhere at any time without physically being present. This allowed to get a better and timelier overview of work processes, coordinate and reduce the workload. The devices allowed to verify whether service contractors and systems worked as needed. Through automatic analyzation it was possible to identify deviations that would have otherwise remained unnoticed. Even though IoT in some instances increased the hourly rate of work, the number of hours spent decreased. For instance, the fleet telematics enabled maintenance managers to re-route optimal vehicles, better maintain roads, and reduce the time vehicles were standing idle. Commonly implemented solutions included fleet telematics which helped to resolve disputes among stakeholders and reduced strain on municipalities to provide timely information to citizens. At the forefront of cost cutting were solutions related to energy consumption reduction, however the use of motion and CO_2 sensors were difficult to utilize to their fullest potential due to the human element which interfered with the automatization, i.e. people opened windows instead of allowing the ventilation system to operate independently. To counter the human element, various approaches were taken, from employee training to changes in the physical environment, i.e. making it impossible to open windows. Still, cost efficiency remained difficult to achieve and often even harder to measure due to the changing environmental elements, e.g. changing weather conditions made it hard to compare changes on yearly basis.

5.3 Effectiveness

Improved effectiveness was the most commonly achieved outcome from the use of IoT, identified as an achieved outcome in 59.5% of solutions (94 solutions). Although the implementation of IoT systems commonly had a goal to gain efficiency, especially in financial terms, most highly valued outcomes identified by the municipalities were derived from improved effectiveness. The devices allowed public officials to reduce unnecessary work (avoid personal interaction, provide easier access to information, allow for increased control, and offer convenience), and improve decision making and work outcomes (services could be personalized and provided in timely manner, investments were more targeted). Data provided by the sensors allowed to evaluate the work of devices, e.g. heating systems and private contractors, e.g. garbage disposal providers. In case of deviations, municipalities were notified of the changes. This allowed to improve the quality of service delivery and through that reduce costs as it took less time to achieve the intended outcome. Controversially, the devices often proved to be more efficient in identifying the shortcomings in effectiveness rather than aiding in improving them. For example, the pothole identifying system allowed to map the problematic roads, however the information did not necessarily lead to improvements as the processes surrounding the road management were not improved to reflect the capabilities of the data generated by IoT. As an example, a municipality used the system to identify potholes, but made no changes to organizational operation and road management strategy.

5.4 Intrinsic Enhancements

Intrinsic enhancements were identified as the least important outcome from the use of IoT, only identified in 12% of solutions (19 solutions) as an achieved outcome. In majority of cases intrinsic enhancements were not considered during the implementation, but rather emerged as unexpected outcomes during the use of the devices. Intrinsic enhancements considered here, i.e. less redundant work practices regarding communication, were by nature silent outcomes, as they were experienced by all, but the highest improvements would be expected at service level and for consumers, but not necessarily by service providers - in this case municipalities. This in turn contributed to the low priority of intrinsic enhancements.

5.5 Transparency

Improved transparency was identified as an achieved goal of IoT in 42.4% of solutions (67 solutions). IoT allowed municipalities and their employees to defend their decision making, overcome false accusations (reduce the impact of political loyalty), and helped to avoid unethical and unlawful actions, i.e. provide equal treatment for all stakeholders and protect individual rights. Through making information available for the public, municipalities could reduce their workload, make more calculated decisions, foster trust and accountability, and receive valuable feedback on their services. When citizens demanded information, the public official could rely on IoT generated data to provide up-to-date information. Municipalities could further control whether service contractors worked in an agreed upon amount and according to contracts - helping to contribute to reliability and stability of service provision. This allowed to avoid conflicts between the municipality and the service contractors, paved the way towards a trusting relationship and enhanced cooperation. However, transparency remained the most controversial outcome of IoT implementation, as improvements in transparency generated countless unforeseen difficulties that resulted in reversing the improved work practices to the previous mode of operation. To illustrate, citizens started to ambush winter road maintenance vehicles when the information of the vehicle movement was made available online. This resulted in an overall stigma for improvements in transparency, as failures in municipal management could have given a political disadvantage in upcoming elections, or provided a competitive advantage for neighboring municipalities.

5.6 Participation

Improved participation was identified as an outcome of IoT implementation in 20.3% of solutions (32 solutions). Improved participation was never the primary intent of IoT implementation, however municipalities experienced improved participation both from local government and from external stakeholders. From the improvements in the dimension of participation, 24 solutions identified improvements on an internal level, improvements on an external level were visible in 17 solutions. However, silos existed whereby internal actors from different departments were not invested in the improvement of government operation even if capabilities to support it were created. Circumstances where internal stakeholders were involved consisted of instances where the system directly affected them in terms of their private or working life. While external stakeholders were more highly interested in decision making and in the operation of government, it was generally not welcomed by the government officials. Instead the generated data was used to support the sole decisions of managers involved with the IoT implementation, leaving out the external actors - mistrust and uncooperative behaviors remained wide-spread.

5.7 Collaboration

Improved collaboration was identified as an achieved outcome in 28.5% of solutions (45 solutions). Collaboration was wide-spread both internally and externally. However, in majority of cases, collaboration was required for IoT implementation, but not necessarily fostered it. For instance, vehicle surveillance systems required police involvement due to the data protection acts. Collaboration was often present before the implementation of IoT, however IoT greatly enhanced the level of involvement and supported influx of more relevant information. For instance, when municipalities noticed that the quality of work was consistently worse for some drivers, e.g. garbage removal, they notified the private contractors, which allowed to improve the service delivery. Due to the availability of information, collaboration emerged between public officials and private contractors. For instance, when a technician previously had to be present to fix a biomass heating system, then following IoT implementation public officials took increasingly care of the maintenance. Similarly, when there were problems with private contractors' work, public officials directly contacted the people responsible. IoT provided capabilities that made municipalities adopt a more active role in service delivery. Indeed, municipalities had started to consider providing services without public-private collaboration. For instance, in winter road maintenance IoT created a situation where the public official became more actively invested in the maintenance than the private maintenance manager. Citizens on the other hand were involved in government operation through actively evaluating the available information, notifying of shortcomings. When services did not meet citizen expectations or citizens needed a custom service, they contacted for improvements. While citizens were involved, their participation in the governance was not wide-spread. With regards to this, citizens had limited impact, i.e. did not contribute, on the functioning of government.

6 Discussion

Previous research indicates that efficiency is typically the primary goal of IT initiatives [11], which also holds proof here. However, the findings suggest that public organizations are increasingly focusing their attention on other dimensions besides efficiency, most commonly on effectiveness and transparency. This goes against the typical notion of IoT which is mainly articulated in terms of economic value [31]. Municipalities included in the study often considered other dimensions as the most sought after, neglecting efficiency as an important outcome even if an element of efficiency, e.g. time or cost, was stated as the primary implementation goal. By contrast other elements, most notably effectiveness and transparency, were increasingly derived as outcomes of these government initiatives. With regards to this, IoT allows to create public value beyond efficiency.

The findings suggest that while collaboration, transparency and participation generated public value, they should not be viewed as an administrative goal [14]. The opposing needs of stakeholders could create disturbances that could negatively affect the effectiveness and efficiency of public organizations. Harrison et al. [14] argued that transparency, participation and collaboration should be viewed as means toward desirable ends. The findings of this study suggest that without clear goal, public organizations should refrain from making information publically available. Controlled secrecy in some instances could prove more beneficial for deriving public value. For instance, available information was used to interfere with service provision and how the system operated, e.g. stopping winter road maintenance vehicles or opening windows to regulate temperature. Hence, each case should be closely evaluated to determine whether external and/or internal actors should be engaged in the operation of government. While it is easier to continue in secrecy, transparency and collaboration had a strong effect on achieving public values from other dimensions, e.g. effectiveness and efficiency, which otherwise were not achieved. Thus, government initiatives should be directed to stakeholders that allow to achieve the optimum public value.

The study illustrates that while some solutions are more beneficial than others, deriving public value from IoT initiatives requires public organizations to use the generated data to change how they operate. While the most substantial changes require IoT technology, management and policy changes make the biggest difference in the derived outcome of IoT. Using smart garbage bins or fleet telematics without changing how public organizations operate brought forward positive changes, but substantial benefits, required a change in management and policy. Public organizations had to change how they operate through using the devices and generated data in a unique way. For instance, they could continue to use fleet telematics for surveillance of vehicles, however when incorporating the generated data in investments, decision making or fostering closer collaboration with private organizations, the most substantial benefits occurred. As a result, the findings suggest that most public organizations are handling post-implementation phase of IoT inadequately, most notably regarding what to do with the produced data.

The research indicates that public organizations are not evaluating the outcome of IoT implementation. Throughout the study, rather few organizations had performed a formal evaluation of an IoT initiative. Similarly, the study by Jones and Hughes [17] identified that public organizations tended to rely on an assessment whether the technology works, rather than considering the social impact or value of the technology. If the outcome was evaluated, it was done through the prism of efficiency in an abstract manner. Without the formal assessment, it becomes difficult for public organizations to demonstrate the public value of IoT. Relying on abstract measurement systems, such as the number of complaints by citizens, could be a viable predictor of the success of an initiative, but it neglects the more substantial outcomes the technology could produce. There thus remains a need to explore how IoT created public value can be measured and is measured by public organizations. As the previous findings suggest, other aspects besides efficiency are gaining traction in IoT generated public value, the study concludes that the analysis of IoT should also consider other value generators besides efficiency when evaluating the solution. Evaluation and presentation of the different forms of public value generated by IoT could allow public organizations to avoid public scrutiny and improve the utilization of IoT. Especially, as many IoT projects were sealed off from external stakeholders due to the fear of criticism and political harm.

7 Conclusion

To conclude, IoT has the capability to create public value and the intended public value dimensions have widened from the goal of improved efficiency. There has been a shift in value creation with other goals and outcomes such as effectiveness, transparency and collaboration gaining increased presence. Furthermore, the data suggest that the evaluation of IoT remains largely insufficient, and is mostly done abstractly or through financial metrics alone, which inhibits capturing the full potential of IoT. Public value derivation cannot rest on the implementation of IoT solutions alone, but must include improvements in management and policy according to the ample data generated by the devices.

Finally, there are limitations to be acknowledged. First, the research studied public value through the perspective of public organizations, however public values are rarely identical for stakeholders. Thus, additional research is required to study public value from the perspective of stakeholders like citizens and private organizations. Secondly, evaluating public value is never an easy task and more longitudinal studies could offer further in-depth understanding of public value created by IoT.

References

1. Agarwal, R., Lucas, H.C.: The information systems identity crisis: focusing on high-visibility and high-impact research. MIS Q. **29**(3), 381–398 (2005)
2. Atzori, L., Iera, A., Morabito, G.: The internet of things: a survey. Comput. Netw. **54**(15), 2787–2805 (2010)
3. Bannister, F., Connolly, R.: The trouble with transparency: a critical review of openness in e-government. Policy Internet **3**(1), 1–30 (2011)
4. Bradley, J., Reberger, C., Dixit, A., Gupta, V.: Internet of everything: a $4.6 trillion public-sector opportunity. Cisco (2013)
5. Cordella, A., Bonina, C.M.: A public value perspective for ICT enabled public sector reforms: a theoretical reflection. Gov. Inf. Q. **29**(4), 512–520 (2012)
6. Eisenhardt, K.M.: Building theories from case study research. Acad. Manag. Rev. **14**(4), 532–550 (1989)
7. European Commission: Definition of a research and innovation policy leveraging cloud computing and IoT combination. Digital Single Market (2015)
8. European Commission: The Internet of Things. https://ec.europa.eu/digital-single-market/en/policies/internet-things. Accessed 01 Feb 2018
9. Friedewald, M., Raabe, O.: Ubiquitous computing: an overview of technology impacts. Telemat. Inform. **28**(2), 55–65 (2011)
10. Gil-Garcia, J.R., Chengalur-Smith, I., Duchessi, P.: Collaborative e-Government: impediments and benefits of information-sharing projects in the public sector. Eur. J. Inf. Syst. **16** (2), 121–133 (2007)
11. Gil-Garcia, J.R., Zhang, J., Puron-Cid, G.: Conceptualizing smartness in government: an integrative and multi-dimensional view. Gov. Inf. Q. **33**(3), 524–534 (2016)
12. GrowthEnabler: Market Pulse Report, Internet of Things (IoT) (2017)
13. Gubbi, J., Buyya, R., Marusic, S., Palaniswami, M.: Internet of things (IoT): a vision, architectural elements, and future directions. Future Gener. Comput. Syst. **29**(7), 1645–1660 (2013)
14. Harrison, T.M., et al.: Open government and e-government: democratic challenges from a public value perspective. Inf. Polity **17**(2), 83–97 (2012)
15. Hermann, M., Pentek, T., Otto, B.: Design principles for Industrie 4.0 scenarios. In: The Proceedings of the 49th Hawaii International Conference on System Sciences, Koloa, HI, USA (2016)
16. Johansen, C., Culp, B., Mora, M.: Cisco survey reveals close to three-fourths of IoT projects are failing, Cisco (2017)
17. Jones, S., Hughes, J.: Understanding IS evaluation as a complex social process: a case study of UK local authority. Eur. J. Inf. Syst. **10**(4), 189–203 (2001)

18. Jørgensen, T.B., Bozeman, B.: Public values: an inventory. Adm. Soc. **39**(3), 354–381 (2007)
19. Kagermann, H., Wahlster, W., Helbig, J.: Recommendations for implementing the strategic initiative Industrie 4.0. (2013)
20. Krishnamurthy, R., Desouza, K.C.: Tony Parham: fostering innovation DNA in the commonwealth of Massachusetts (2014)
21. Kohli, R., Grover, V.: Business value of IT: an essay on expanding research directions to keep up with the times. J. Assoc. Inf. Syst. **9**(2), 23–39 (2008)
22. Lee, J., Lee, H.: Developing and validating a citizen-centric typology for smart city services. Gov. Inf. Q. **31**(1), 93–105 (2014)
23. Lee, J., Lee, H.: The Internet of Things (IoT): applications, investments, and challenges for enterprises. Bus. Horiz. **58**(4), 431–440 (2015)
24. Marchand, D.A., Kettinger, W.J., Rollins, J.D.: Information orientation: people, technology and the bottom line. Sloan Manag. Rev. **41**(4), 69–80 (2000)
25. McKinsey: The Internet of Things: Mapping the Value Beyond the Hype. McKinsey Global Institute (2015)
26. Miles, M.B., Huberman, A.M., Saldana, J.: Qualitative Data Analysis: A Methods Sourcebook, 3rd edn. SAGE Publications, Thousand Oaks (2014)
27. Moore, M.H.: Creating Public Value: Strategic Management in Government. Harvard University Press, Cambridge (1995)
28. Nam, T., Pardo, T.A.: The changing face of a city government: a case study of Philly311. Gov. Inf. Q. **31**(1), 1–9 (2014)
29. Pang, M.S., Lee, G., DeLone, W.H.: IT resources, organizational capabilities, and value creation in public-sector organizations: a public-value management perspective. J. Inf. Technol. **29**(3), 187–205 (2014)
30. Pereira, G.V., Macadar, M.A., Luciano, E.M., Testa, M.G.: Delivering public value through open government data initiatives in a Smart City context. Inf. Syst. Front. **19**(2), 213–229 (2016)
31. Prasopoulou, E.: A half-moon on my skin: a memoir on life with an activity tracker. Eur. J. Inf. Syst. **26**(3), 287–297 (2017)
32. Singha, D., Tripathi, G., Jara, A.J.: A survey of Internet-of-Things: future vision, architecture, challenges and services. In: Proceedings on 2014 IEEE World Forum on Internet of Things (WF-IoT) (2014)
33. Shin, D.-H.: Ubiquitous city: urban technologies, urban infrastructure and urban informatics. J. Inf. Sci. **35**(5), 515–526 (2009)
34. Sundmaeker, H., Guillemin, P., Friess, P., Woelfflé, S.: Vision and challenges for realising the Internet of Things. Eur. Comm. **3**, 34–36 (2010)
35. Zanella, A., Bui, N., Castellani, A., Vangelista, L., Zorzi, M.: Internet of Things for smart cities. IEEE Internet Things J. **1**(1), 22–32 (2014)
36. Zhang, J., Puron-Cid, G., Gil-Garcia, J.R.: Creating public value through open government: perspectives, experiences and applications. Inf. Polity **20**(2), 97–101 (2015)
37. Teo, T., Srivastava, S., Jiang, L.: Trust and electronic government success: an empirical study. J. Manag. Inf. Syst. **25**(3), 99–131 (2008)
38. Vicente, P., Lourdes, T., Royo, S.: Are ICTs improving transparency and accountability in the EU regional and local governments? An empirical study. Publ. Adm. **85**(2), 449–472 (2007)

Strategies for Reducing Power Consumption and Increasing Reliability in IoT

Ricardo Reis(✉)

Instituto de Informática – Universidade Federal do Rio Grande do Sul (UFRGS), Caixa Postal 15.064, 91501-970 Porto Alegre, RS, Brazil
reis@inf.ufrgs.br

Abstract. The Internet of Things (IoT) demands new challenges in the design of computing and electronics components. One of the challenges is the power reduction of this expanding network of connected devices, where the majority is permanently connected. In a large set of applications, another significant issue is reliability, especially on critical areas as health and transport. This paper shows an overview of design strategies that we have developed to reduce power consumption and to increase reliability in circuits that are components of the IoT, as the reduction of the number of transistors in IoT devices, using optimisation techniques and the physical design of circuits tolerant to radiation effects.

Keywords: Internet-of-Things · Optimization · Physical design · Fault tolerance · Radiation effects · Nanoelectronics

1 Introduction

The growing number of connected devices in the Internet of Things (IoT) is one of the reasons for the ever increasing increase in the number of transistors produced annually in the world. Figure 1, based on (SIA 2005), shows the number of transistors manufactured annually in the world, year by year. This impressive growth is due to 3 main factors: the increasing number of transistors integrated into a chip, the growing number of products that include embedded chips and the increasing number of manufactured copies of each product. The manufacturing cost of a transistor is relatively cheap. In (The Economist 2010) a comparison is presented between the cost of a grain of rice and the cost of a transistor. The price of a rice grain can be equivalent to the manufacturing cost of more than 125,000 transistors. This would indicate that there is no need to optimise the number of transistors in a design, since the cost of them is relatively small. But the cost of energy required for the operation of a transistor is increasing a lot. We also have to consider that a high-power consumption can reduce the lifetime of a system, as well as increase the effects of variability that can cause an integrated system to malfunction and/or also reduce its useful life. With the increasing connection of electronic and computational devices on the Internet, that is, in the Internet of Things, power consumption problems tend to get worse, and a lot. How much Power Plants we will need to cope with the IoT/IoE (Internet of Everything) world? This is a major issue.

L. Strous and V. G. Cerf (Eds.): IFIPIoT 2018, IFIP AICT 548, pp. 76–88, 2019.
https://doi.org/10.1007/978-3-030-15651-0_8

So, an essential keyword on the Internet of Things is **optimisation**, especially the optimisation of power consumption, which must be addressed at all levels of abstraction in the design flow of a computer or electronic system. The total power optimisation is a summation of the optimisation done at each level of design abstraction. So, sustainable computing requires optimisation at all design levels of a computer or electronic system design.

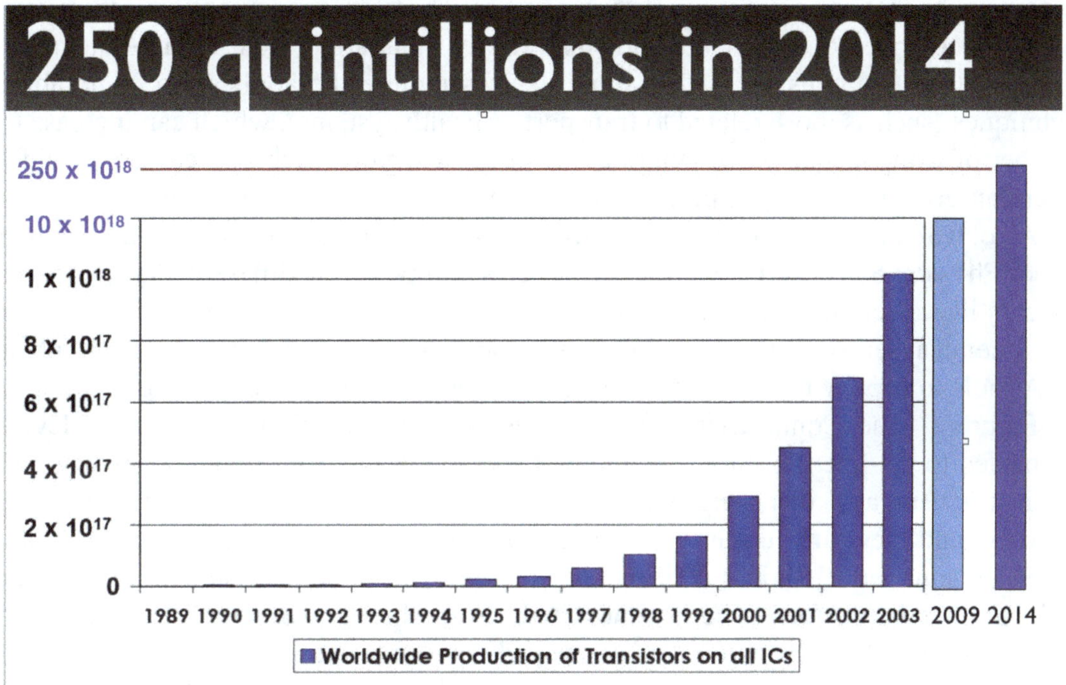

Fig. 1. Number of transistors produced annually in the world (adapted from SIA 2005)

2 Internet of Things

The term Internet of Things has already given rise to several other associated terms, such as the Internet of Health (IoH), Internet of People (IoP) and the Internet of Everything (IoE). In fact, the latter term becomes the most comprehensive, but each one of the others has some specific characteristics. When talking about the Internet of Health, which includes real-time monitoring of a person's clinical conditions, as well as chips injected in a person, the issue of reliability is a key one. And reliability is also related to power consumption in most cases. High power consumption can reduce the lifetime of a system. When it comes to the Internet of People, the issue of people's security and privacy is of great relevance. But in all cases, the importance of optimising energy consumption is growing more and more.

When considering optimisation, it means that integrated systems must increasingly be dedicated to the intended application to optimise the number of components, that means the number of transistors. Another important strategy for optimisation is the hardware and software codesign, where one can manage the compromise between performance, consumption, and reliability.

Devices connected to the Internet of Things (or the Internet of Everything), can have very different complexities. If it is analysed the complexity considering the number of components, we can find small devices with few transistors and large devices with billions of transistors. Of course, large devices will consume much more power, but we have to consider that most devices on the Internet of Things are devices with a low number of transistors. But, because they are found in large quantities, they can represent a total consumption more important than the consumption of the so-called large devices that are present in a lower number. Therefore, consumption optimisation must be performed on both large and small devices that are present in large quantities. Another aspect to consider is that some devices require the application of reliability techniques (such as those related to transport or health systems), which can increase the number of components, while other devices are not critical, such as a camera or video, where an error in viewing a pixel of an image does not cause significant problems.

Also, we can expect that many systems connected to the Internet of Everything will be Cyber Physical Systems (CPS), that are systems composed by different classes of components like electronic elements, mechanical elements, optical elements, physical sensors, chemical sensors, organic components, and many others. So, it is needed to obtain EDA tools to cope with the design of CPS composed of all these classes of devices.

Figure 2 (The Connectivist 2014) shows an estimate of the number of devices connected to the Internet since 1992 when they were about 1 million devices. By 2020 when it is estimated that there will be more than 50 billion devices connected in the network, and there are currently around 35 billion connected devices. In (IHS Markit 2018) the number of devices connected to the network in 2018 is shown by industrial and commercial sectors, where almost half is in the area of communication. The significant growth in the number of connected devices to the Internet has naturally led to a considerable increase in the energy consumed in the Internet of Things. For how long will we have the energy to meet this growing demand? Therefore, it is necessary to use techniques to minimise the energy consumption of each connected device in the Internet of Things.

The Internet of Health (IoH) is a significant way to increase the life of human beings but also to improve life quality. Some of the examples of devices to be connected to the IoH are: Glasses that can advise eye correction; Toothbrush that can find cavities and breath issues; Razor that identify acne; Pacemakers that broadcast data to cardiologist; Underwearables that can provide early detection of cancer and other anomalies; Combs that can scan for fungus and hair loss; Earphones that does measurement of hearing, analysis of emotional level; Watches able to measure parameters like blood pressure, heart rate and others.

In critical areas such as the design of implanted devices (chips) in humans (Fig. 3), the reliability of the implanted systems is obviously critical. Some of the techniques used are based on the triplication of circuits and the temporal analysis of the propagation of a signal. Previously, the design of fault-tolerant circuits, to cope with radiation effects, was mainly in circuits that were sent to space. With the reduction of the value of the supply voltage of integrated circuits, nowadays the integrated circuits for use at ground level are also sensitive to errors caused by the radiation incident on the earth. Therefore, in critical areas such as implanted chips in humans, it is necessary to implement radiation effects tolerance techniques (Velazco et al. 2007). Also, critical

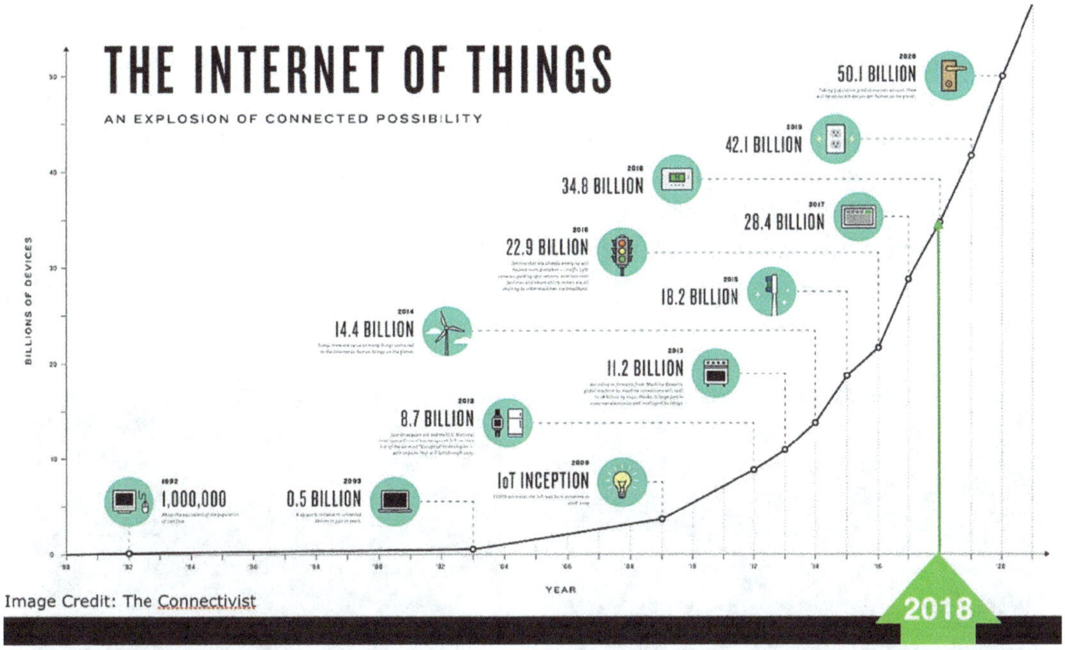

Fig. 2. Number of devices connected on the Internet (adapted from The Connectivist 2014)

systems used on the Internet of Health should be tolerant to any kind of noise (internal or external to the human body). They also must have a larger lifetime as possible, for obvious reasons and also should cope with environmental variability.

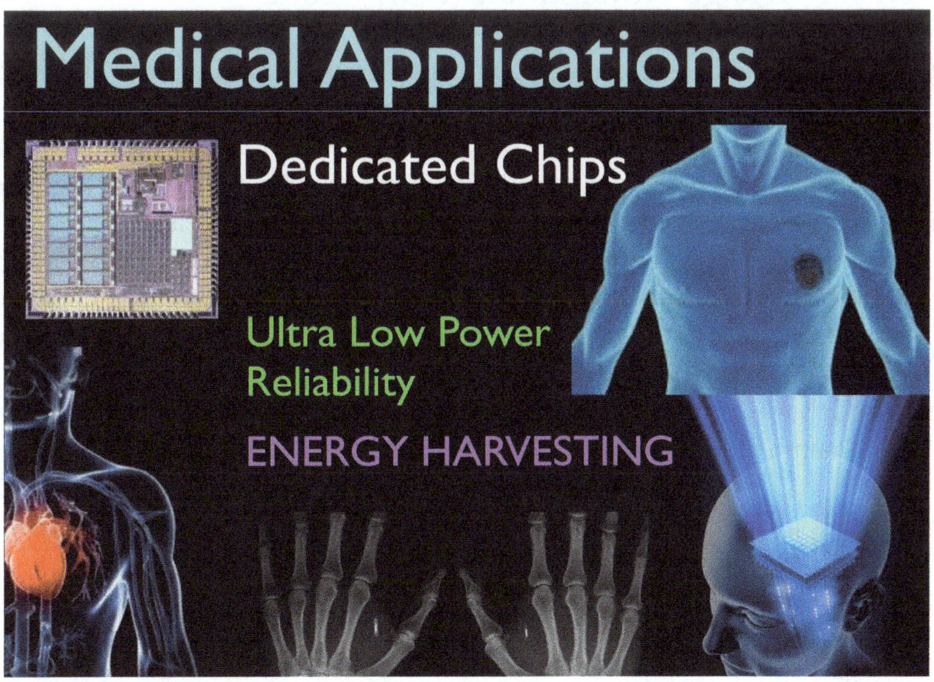

Fig. 3. The implantation of Chip Systems in humans demands reliability and ultra-low consumption

Also, there is the effect of "ageing", that is, the ageing of the circuit, which is more eminent in nanometric technologies (Vasquez et al. 2012). One of the most important effects is known as NBTI (Negative Bias Temperature Instability) that alters the threshold voltage of the PMOS transistors, degrading the operation of the transistor. Another effect that causes failures in circuits throughout their life is the effect of electromigration, which can cause short circuits or rupture of connections (Fig. 4). In order to increase the lifetime of the chips, it is necessary to use physical design techniques that reduce the probability of electromigration (Posser et al. 2016, 2017).

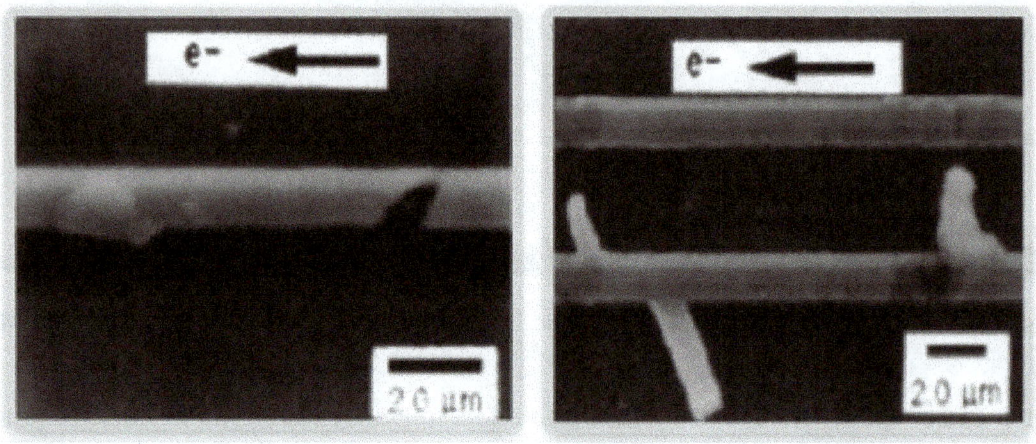

Fig. 4. Exemplo of a Void (open circuit) and hillock (short circuit) (Geden 2011).

3 Electronic Design Automation (EDA) Tools

The use of EDA tools is essential for optimising energy consumption and increasing reliability, as the design flow has a large set of steps as well the number of components of a cheap can reach billions off transistors. In Fig. 5 we can see the floorplan of an integrated circuit, where the hotter colours show regions (hot spots) with higher energy consumption, indicating that in some points there is a significant concentration of power consumption. One way to deal with the problem is to modify the placement of the logic cells in the circuit to distribute the cells with the highest energy consumption over the entire circuit area. But this must be done without compromising the area, wirelengh and operating frequency specifications (much depends on the routing). Another way is to decrease the number of transistors, since the static consumption is related to the number of transistors (Reis 2011A).

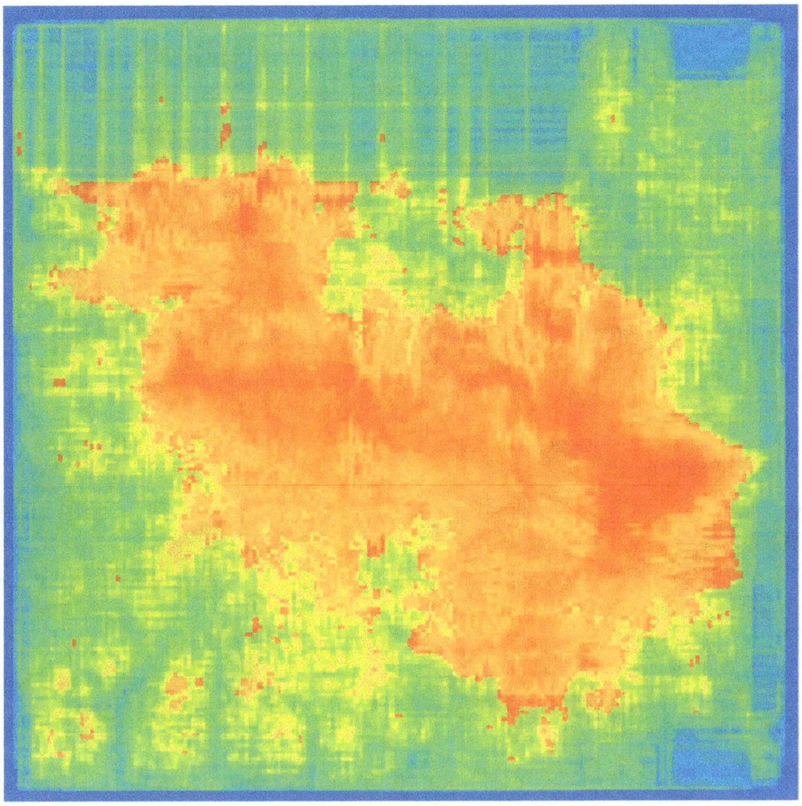

Fig. 5. View of the consumption density on a chip

4 Power Consumption Reduction by Reducing the Number of Transistors

The reduction of the power consumption of a System on a Chip (SoC) is a function of a sum of techniques and strategies of design applied in different levels of abstraction in the design flow of an integrated system (Reis 2010). The summation of the gains is that it will set the total gain in power reduction. When we deal with the physical synthesis of a system on a chip, one technique is the optimisation of the number of components, that is, the number of transistors. In Fig. 6 (Reis 2011A) we can observe two solutions for the implementation of the same equation. The first solution makes use of 4 basic logic gates (3 NOR 2-input ports and one CMOS inverter), using a total of 14 transistors. The second solution makes use of only one logic gate, which performs the same function but with only 8 transistors. That is, the second solution, having a reduction in the number of transistors, will also have a proportionally smaller static power consumption. Furthermore, in the example of Fig. 6, we can see that the first solution also has 3 connections between the basic gates (and therefore even vias and contacts) that are eliminated in the second option with only one logic gate.

This elimination of connections is increasingly important because it decreases the number of connections to be implemented using the different metal layers. The decrease in the number of connections decreases the density of connections and, therefore, increases the routability of the circuit and also contributes to reduce the average length of the connections, which implies in a reduction of the delay. In modern technologies, the delay in connections is so or more significant than the delay in the switching of logic gates. A greater spacing between the connections also contributes to an increase of reliability, due, for example, to the reduction of the possibility of electromigration, as already mentioned above.

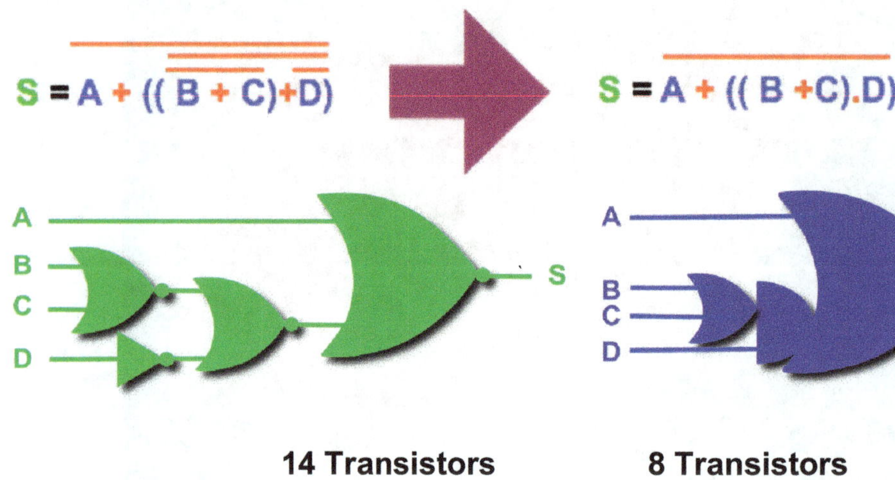

Fig. 6. Two options for the implementation of the same function (Reis 2011A)

The reduction of the number of transistors depends on the use of efficient Electronic Design Automation (EDA) tools that transform the logical equations of a system so that in addition to mapping equations in CMOS gates, make optimum use of complex logic gates. In (Conceição et al. 2017) we present a tool to reduce the number of transistors in a circuit through the fusion of networks of transistors that present fanout equal to 1. Also, it is fundamental the use of an automatic synthesis tool that can perform the automatic layout of any logical function. There is no use to achieve a logical optimisation if it is necessary to map (transform) the equations according to the logic gates available in a traditional cell library [which have few functions, in general, no more than 100 functions], as is still done when using traditional EDA systems. This mapping step is called technology mapping, and it represents a step of deoptimization. With this aim, we have developed automatic layout synthesis tools such as ASTRAN (Ziesemer and Reis 2015) (Fig. 7), which allows automatic generation of the layout of any network of transistors (Reis 2011A, B).

Another technique to reduce consumption is through the sizing of the transistors. Modern integrated circuit manufacturing technologies show a significant increase in static power consumption that is often greater than dynamic power consumption. One way to mitigate power consumption, especially the static one, is to carry out a sizing of transistors to optimise power consumption (Posser 2011). In (Reimann et al. 2016) significant decreases in consumption are obtained through the use of automatic transistor sizing tools. This is also called cell selection, where the cells are selected from a cell library. In this case, cell selection means the selection of cells with a specific size and Vth (threshold voltage). In traditional cell libraries, one function has in general 3 sizings (one for less area, one for less power, and one for less delay) and 3 Vth (threshold voltage).

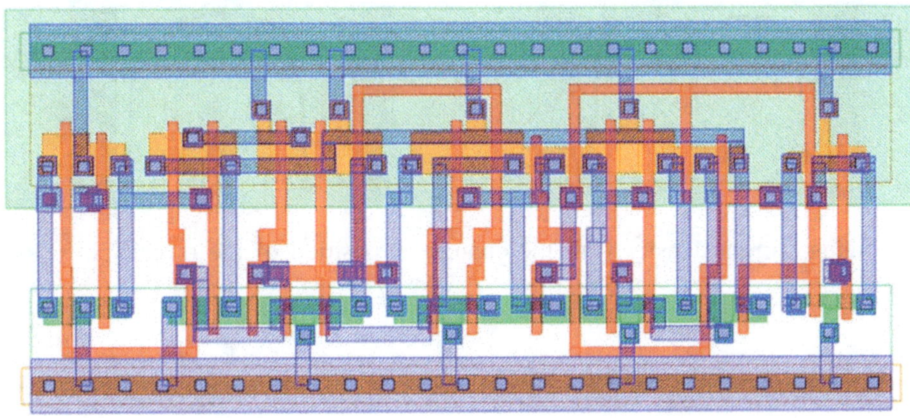

Fig. 7. Transistor network layout generated automatically (Ziesemer and Reis 2015)

5 Reliability

As in the reduction of power consumption, in the design of critical systems, it is needed to use techniques to increase reliability at different levels of design abstraction. At the architectural level, a very applied method is the redundancy of modules, especially triple module redundancy (TMR) (Kastensmidt et al. 2006). Another is the temporal redundancy (Nicolaidis 1999) where a signal traverses two paths, one with higher delay and another one with less delay. The difference of delay must be longer than the duration of a transient. Comparing the signal after traversing the two paths indicates whether there has been a transient propagation or not. At the physical level, we can apply different techniques to reduce or avoid problems such as electromigration (Posser et al. 2016, 2017). In the example of Fig. 8, the position of the output pin in the centre (point 4) increases the lifetime of the circuit because it allows reducing the maximum density of current in the segments of the metal layer.

In (Velazco et al. 2007) it is presented a series of works aimed at mitigating the effects of radiation on integrated circuits. In (Kastensmidt et al. 2006; Neuberger et al. 2014; Gennaro et al. 2017; Aguiar et al. 2016; Lazzari et al. 2011) we present some of the results that our research group has obtained in the development of techniques aiming the design tolerant to faults due to transients, as the effects due to radiation.

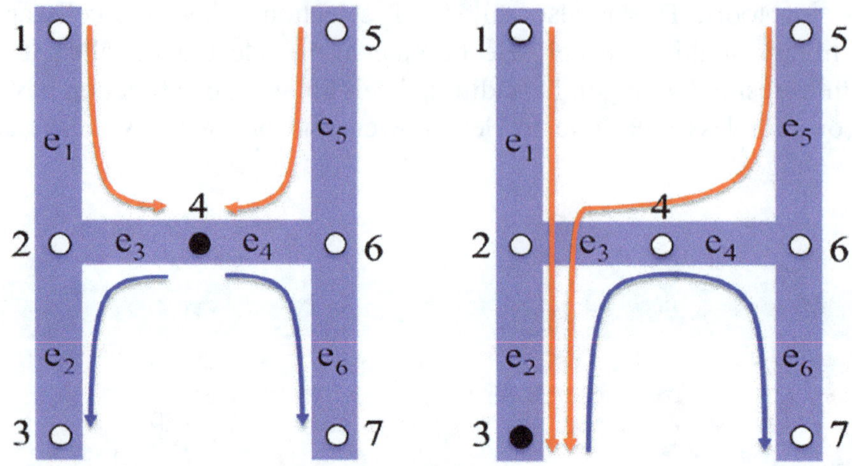

Fig. 8. Changing current density with the change of position of the output pin (Posser et al. 2016, 2017)

6 Hardware Accelerators

The evolution of computer architectures, that today means, the evolution of microprocessor architectures has been very significant. In the 1970s, one marketing argument from microprocessor producers was the number of instructions that the microprocessor could execute as well as the clock frequency of the microprocessor. In the last decades, there has been a change of paradigm, discontinuing the race for the increase of the clock frequency, because the increment of the clock means an increase of the dynamic consumption. Instead, there was an increase in the number of cores (CPUs) aiming at increasing performance. Initially with homogeneous cores and later with heterogeneous cores.

Currently, we can find chips with multiple CPUs and several GPUs (as can be seen in Fig. 9 (Shao 2016) showing the floorplan of the A8 microprocessor (from Apple). In this same figure, it can be observed that about half of the area is occupied with hardware accelerators, which are modules dedicated to the execution of a specific function. For example, an encryption module placed next to the output/input pins and which will encode the output data and decode the received data. So, the execution of this function will be faster, because it is done by a dedicated module (that means smaller) and with only the needed number of components to perform that function. It also will consume less power.

A more important fact is that the use of hardware accelerators leads to greater energy efficiency (allowing more sustainable computing), mainly due to the reduction in the number of components used to perform a function. At any given time, only the hardware accelerators in use at that time are being powered. So, the hardware accelerators that are not in use are disconnected from the power supply. This strategy is also known as “Dark Silicon”. We can even predict architectures consisting essentially of hardware accelerators, with only one or two small CPUs to manage these hardware accelerators.

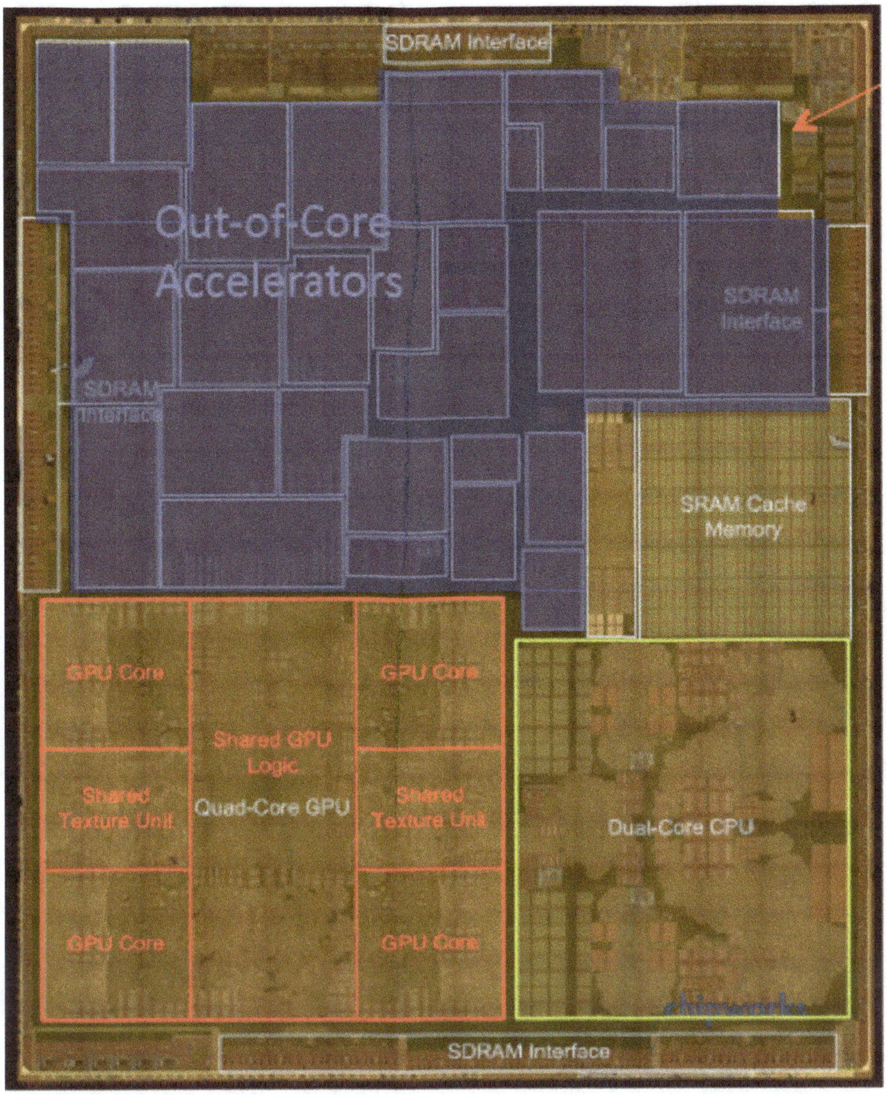

Fig. 9. Apple 8 floorplan with 29 hardware accelerators (AnandTech 2014; Shao 2016)

The introduction of an NPU in A11 is another element characterising the heterogeneity of the SoC (chip system). And we can expect increasingly heterogeneous architectures, with dedicated modules for different operations to be performed by a SoC. In Fig. 10 (Techinsights 2017) the floorplan of the Apple A11 microprocessor is presented, where one of the modules is an NPU (Neural Processing Unit). NPU is mostly dedicated to facial recognition (Techinsights 2017), processing machine learning tasks more efficiently, consuming less energy than CPUs do. The CPUs occupy about 15% of the area of the chip and 6 GPUs occupy about 20% of the area. Most of the area is filled with the hardware accelerators. That is, it is growing in the architecture of Apple microprocessors the use of hardware accelerators.

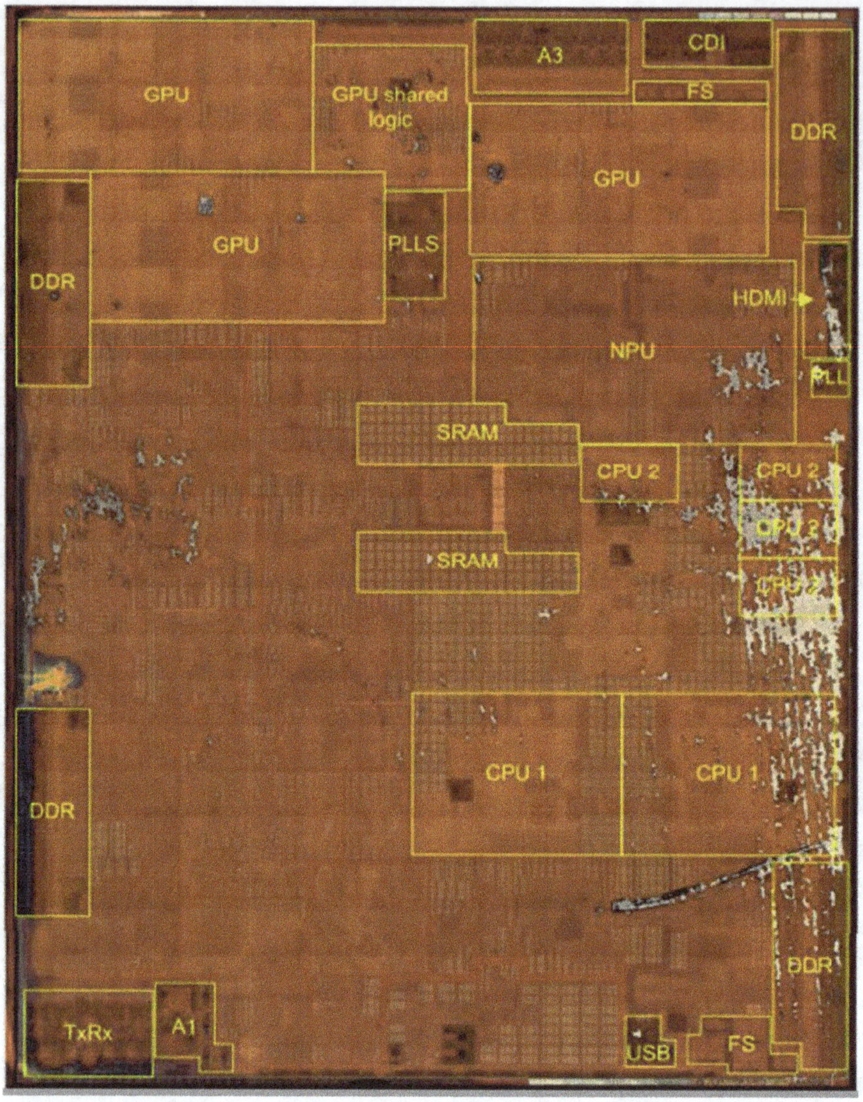

Fig. 10. Apple 11 floorplan with an NPU (Techinsights 2017)

7 Conclusions

To have sustainable computing, when the number of connected devices in the Internet of Things is fast increasing, it is fundamental the design of devices optimised regarding energy consumption. Most of the chips produced today use much more transistors than necessary to perform a function. So, there is a significant space for the optimisation of the number of components. In many devices related to critical applications, the application of techniques for fault tolerance is also fundamental, as nowadays circuits at ground level can have faults due to radiation effects. The reduction of power consumption must be treated at all design abstraction levels in a synthesis flow of integrated systems, from the specification of them in high-level languages to the physical synthesis. It was presented several works that were developed to reduce the power consumption and increase the reliability of integrated systems on a chip, and more details are shown in the mentioned references. The keyword in the age of the Internet of Things is **optimisation**.

Acknowledgements. We thank CNPq, FINEP, Fapergs, and CAPES for financial support for the development of our team's work, as well as the master's and doctoral students of PGMICRO and PPGC and students of Scientific Initiation who have contributed to the research works that served as the basis for this paper.

References

Aguiar, Y., Zimpeck, A., Meinhardt, C., Reis, R.: Permanent and single event transient faults reliability evaluation EDA Tool. In: Microelectronics Reliability, September 2016, vol. 64, pp. 63–67. Elsevier B.V., Amsterdam (2016). ISSN 0026-2714

AnandTech (2014). https://www.anandtech.com/show/8562/chipworks-a8

Conceição, C., Moura, G., Pisoni, F., Reis, R.: A cell clustering technique to reduce transistor count. In: 24th IEEE International Conference on Electronics, Circuits and Systems – ICECS 2017, Batumi, Georgia, 5–8 December 2017, pp. 186–189 (2017). https://doi.org/10.1109/icecs.2017.8291996

Gennaro, R., Rosa, F., Oliveira, A., Kastensmidt, F., Ost, L., Reis, R.: Analyzing the impact of fault tolerance methods in ARM processors under soft errors running Linux and parallelization APIs. IEEE Trans. Nucl. Sci **64**(8) (2017). https://doi.org/10.1109/tns.2017.2706519. ISSN 1558–1578

Geden, B.: Understand and avoid electromigration (EM) & IR-drop in custom IP blocks. Synopsys (2011)

Lazzari, C., Wirth, G., Kastensmidt, F., Anghel, L., Reis, R.: Asymmetric transistor sizing targeting radiation-hardened circuits. J. Electr. Eng. (2011A). https://doi.org/10.1007/s00202-011-0212-8. Accessed June 2011

Kastensmidt, F., Carro, L., Reis, R.: Fault-Tolerance Techniques for SRAM-Based FPGA, pp. 1–183. Springer, New York (2006). https://doi.org/10.1007/978-0-387-31069-5. ISBN 0-387-31068-1

Neuberger, G., Wirth, G., Reis, R.: Protecting Chips Against Hold Time Violations Due to Variability, pp. 1–107. Springer, New York (2014). https://doi.org/10.1007/978-94-007-2427-3. ISBN 978-94-007-2426-6

Nicolaidis, M.: Time redundancy based soft-error tolerance to rescue nanometer technologies. In: Proceedings of IEEE VLSI Test Symposium, vol. 17, pp. 86–94. IEEE Computer Society (1999)

Posser, G., Flach, G., Wilke, G., Reis, R.: Gate sizing minimizing delay and area. In: ISVLSI 2011, IEEE Computer Society Annual Symposium on VLSI, Chennai, India, 4–6 July 2011, pp. 315–316 (2011). https://doi.org/10.1109/isvlsi.2011.92. ISBN 978-0-7695-4447-2

Posser, G., Mishra, V., Jain, P., Reis, R., Sapatnekar, S.: Cell-internal electromigration: analysis and pin placement based optimization. IEEE Trans. Comput.-Aided Des. Integr. Circ. Syst. **35** (2), 220–231 (2016). https://doi.org/10.1109/TCAD.2015.2456427. ISSN: 0278-0070

Posser, G., Sapatnekar, S., Reis, R.: Electromigration Inside Logic Cells, 118 p. Springer (2017). https://doi.org/10.1007/978-3-319-48899-8. ISBN: 978-3-319-48898-1

Reimann, T., Sze, C., Reis, R.: Challenges of cell selection algorithms in industrial high performance microprocessor designs. In: Integration, vol. 52, pp. 347–354. Elsevier B.V., January 2016. https://doi.org/10.1016/j.vlsi.2015.09.001. ISSN 0167-9260

Reis, R.: Redução de Consumo pela Otimização de Componentes. In: SEMISH 2010, Anais do 37º Seminário Integrado de Software e Hardware, Belo Horizonte, 21 a 22 de julho de 2010, pp. 371–379 (2010). ISSN 2175-2761

Reis, R.: Design automation of transistor networks, a new challenge. In: IEEE International Symposium on Circuits and Systems, ISCAS 2011, Rio de Janeiro, Brasil, 15–19 May 2011, pp. 2485–2488. IEEE Press (2011A). https://doi.org/10.1109/iscas.2011.5938108. ISBN 978-1-4244-9472-9

Reis, R.: Power consumption & reliability in NanoCMOS. In: IEEE NANO, 11th International Conference on Nanotechnology, Portland, USA, 15–19 August 2011 (invited talk), pp. 711–714 (2011B). https://doi.org/10.1109/nano.2011.6144656. ISBN 978-1-4577-1515-0

The Connectivist (2014). http://ow.ly/i/5vph6/original

The Economist (2010). Accessed 6 Sept 2010

SIA: Semiconductor Industry Association, Rrebooting the IT Revolution (2015). http://www.semiconductors.org/clientuploads/Resources/RITR%20WEB%20version%20FINAL.pdf

IHS Markit: IoT Trend Watch 2018 (2018). https://ihsmarkit.com/forms/thankyou.html?efid=t+m2jEyFYkJQYyoP3YvuHA==&&gasc_id=862037098&&gasc_label=scrXCLnM7m0Q6siGmwM

Techinsights (2017). http://techinsights.com/about-techinsights/overview/blog/apple-iphone-8-teardown/

Vazquez, J., et al.: Delay sensing for long-term variations and defects monitoring in safety–critical applications. Analog Integr. Circ. Sig. Process. **70**(2), 249–263 (2012). https://doi.org/10.1007/s10470-011-9789-0. ISSN 0925-1030

Velazco, R., Fouillat, P., Reis, R.: Radiation Effects on Embedded Systems. Springer, New York (2007). ISBN 978-1-4020-5645-1

Shao, Y.S.: Design and modeling of specialized architectures. Ph.D. thesis, Harvard, May 2016. https://ysshao.github.io/papers/shao2016-dissertation.pdf

Ziesemer, A., Reis, R.: Physical design automation of transistors network. Microelectron. Eng. **148**, 122–128 (2015). https://doi.org/10.1016/j.mee.2015.10.018. ISSN 0167-9317

An Internet of Things (IoT) Model for Optimising Downtime Management: A Smart Lighting Case Study

Brenda Scholtz[1(✉)], Mando Kapeso[1], and Jean-Paul Van Belle[2]

[1] Nelson Mandela University, Port Elizabeth, South Africa
{brenda.scholtz,mando.kapeso}@mandela.ac.za
[2] University of Cape Town, Cape Town, South Africa
jean-paul.vanbelle@uct.ac.za

Abstract. In today's global, competitive economy, downtime has been identified as a key performance indicator for field service organisations. The emergence of an Internet of Things (IoT) has brought new enhancement possibilities to various industries such as the manufacturing and field service industry. This paper provides a vision and motivation for using IoT in Field Service Management (FSM) in order to address data quality and service delivery issues. The theory of information quality was used to undergird the research and a model for the optimisation of downtime management in the field service industry using the IoT is proposed. The model was used to drive the design of a "proof of concept" prototype, the KapCha prototype. The paper also includes a report on an empirical study of the application of the proposed IoT model in FSM. The experiment findings showed that the prototype reduced the round trip delay time for sending and receiving data and was scalable. As a result, access to quality information supporting advanced data analytics and artificial intelligence was provided. Therefore, service technicians can be alerted more quickly as soon as any potential technical problems occur. In turn improved diagnostics and more efficient decision making can be achieved. The model and the lessons learned provide valuable guidance to other researchers and fill the gap in research of empirical studies conducted on IoT implementations.

Keywords: IoT · Smart lightning · Design science research

1 Introduction

The lack of accurate, available and real-time information is a common challenge faced by field service organisations [1]. As a result downtime, which is an important performance measure in this domain, is negatively impacted. Downtime is defined as the time between a customer's request for service and the completion of the service by the field service team to rectify the problem [2]. Field service management (FSM) refers to the support provided by hardware and software in the management of field service operations and involves the management of the activities and processes that are associated with field services. There is a need for solutions that efficiently address the challenges of FSM and downtime management and that support the provision of

L. Strous and V. G. Cerf (Eds.): IFIPIoT 2018, IFIP AICT 548, pp. 89–104, 2019.
https://doi.org/10.1007/978-3-030-15651-0_9

quality information and ultimately improved decision making and service delivery levels [3].

One application of downtime management in the field service domain is that of the maintenance of smart lights. Smart lighting projects have been undertaken by municipalities as a result of a drive for improved energy management within cities [4]. In the context of cities, streetlights are one of the most important assets to maintain as they provide safe roads and enhanced security for homes, businesses and city centres. However, they are costly to operate and account for an estimated 40% of the amount of electricity spent in an urban city [5]. To address this issue, city managers are implementing smart lighting solutions. Smart lighting consists of heterogeneous and multidisciplinary areas of lighting management, with the possibilities of integrating a wide range of sensory and control technologies with ICTs. This integration can improve efficiencies in lighting products and lower the negative impact derived from the use of energy for illumination. Smart lighting provides intelligent features and interfaces for lighting solutions in the ambient, commercial and public domains [4, 6]. Smart lighting is linked to the concept of a smart city, which is an urban development that envisions the efficient management of a cities resources and services with the use of integrated ICT solutions [4]. Smart cities play an important role in the sustainable economic development of countries or states seeking to attain environmental sustainability. Smart cities are made possible through the abundance of smart devices, smart objects and the emergence and rapid growth of technologies such as the Internet of Things (IoT). The IoT is described as a decentralised system of “smart” objects with sensing, processing, and network capabilities [7].

Extensive research has been conducted related to the IoT [16, 18, 26]. In particular several studies have proposed various architectures for IoT, such as a general reference architecture [27] and others in certain domains such as smart metering [28]. However, limited studies can be found that report on empirical studies of IoT applications in practice and findings and lessons learnt from these applications. There is a need for research into how technologies in the IoT can be applied to various business domains [20].

This paper addresses this gap by investigating an IoT application in the domain of smart lighting. The purpose of this paper is to propose an IoT model that addresses the challenges of information quality leading to poor downtime management. The paper reports on the application of this model in the smart lighting domain. The model includes IoT compatible technologies and techniques (protocols and formats) to support successful downtime management. To address this purpose, a critical analysis of the literature related to FSM, downtime management and IoT was conducted (Sect. 2). The context was a smart lighting organisation in South Africa (Sect. 3). From the literature and consideration of the context, a theoretical model was derived (Sect. 4). The model was used to design the architecture of and to implement a prototype for the case study (Sect. 5). The experiments conducted revealed that the new architecture and protocols implemented resulted in a lower Round Trip Delay time and was scalable (Sect. 6). The quality of information was improved and provided a foundation for advanced data analytics and artificial intelligence (AI), since the system provided intelligent information to technicians and managers; thereby improving diagnostic decision making, downtime management and service delivery.

There are several contributions and implications for future research that are identified from this study (Sect. 7). The practical contribution is the model, which can provide guidance to practitioners working in the field service domain and for system designers. On a theoretical level the model and the implementation issues identified contribute to the body of knowledge regarding the application of IoT models, architectures and network protocols.

2 Literature Review

2.1 Challenges in Field Service Management (FSM) and Downtime Management

In a competitive global economy where every organisation is looking at ways to cut costs, increase efficiency and gain a competitive advantage, organisations have become more customer-centric. The effectiveness of field services provided by technicians affects everything from the retention of customers and the profitability of the organisation [1, 8]. With field-based services, customers receive either an on-site or a remote service [2]. FSM operations include tracking vehicles, scheduling and dispatching employees, and integration of these operations with a back-office system for inventory, logistics and marketing. FSM includes elements such as Enterprise Asset Management (EAM), maintenance support, sensor networks, Radio Frequency Identification (RFID) tags, technical support, contract management and product life-cycle management. The FSM market has seen a steady growth and evolution in the last 10 years [9], which can be attributed to new technology developments, as technology is a driver in improved after-sales service innovations.

Downtime management is an important measure of performance for field services for both the organisation providing the service and the customer [10]. From the customer's perspective, that is the organisation undergoing downtime, the downtime period has operational implications such as reduced productivity levels and delayed delivery of services to the organisation's clientele. It is therefore imperative that downtime is kept to a minimal period. Service providers have to adequately manage downtime in order to satisfy its customers and by doing so efficiently they may gain a competitive advantage. Agnihothri [2] classified downtime into two subcategories, response time and on-site time. Response time is the time between the customer's request and the service team's arrival on-site. On-site time is the duration of time taken between the service team's arrival at the customer's site and the rectification of the problem. Corrective maintenance occurs when the machinery breaks down and includes activities undertaken to diagnose and rectify a fault so that the failed machine, equipment or system can be restored to its normal operational state, thus reducing the extent of downtime.

A lack of information related to a technical breakdown can result in longer cycle times and possibly a second service visit, thus resulting in longer periods of downtime for customers [8]. A malfunctioning piece of industrial machinery on a manufacturing floor can translate into tens of thousands of dollars per minute. It is important to make critical information immediately available to field technicians and management with high levels of accuracy. Critical data related to the problem must be accurate, available anywhere, and dynamically changing along with the day-to-day operations of field service teams. Access to this information can assist with optimising the problem detection step in FSM and field service providers can determine strategies to ensure that downtime is minimised and managed with optimal efficiency. Within IS literature, information quality (IQ) can be used as a dimension of IS success [12]. Knowledge is functionally related to data and information, thus it follows a hierarchy (data → information → knowledge), termed as the knowledge hierarchy [11]. Our study classified the problems in FSM related to information that impact downtime management according to six of the attributes of IQ proposed by [12]. These are:

- Timeliness: lack of access to real-time information [1];
- Completeness: missing information [1, 3, 8];
- Accuracy: inaccurate information [1];
- Relevance: aggregated or de-aggregated information [14, 15];
- Consistency: lack of integration between enterprise and FSM systems [14].

This analysis also confirmed the findings of [13] showing a significant relationship between IQ and individual impact. Individual impact is measured in terms of decision-making performance, job effectiveness, and quality of work. Challenges faced by FSM organisations with regards to IQ resulted in negative impact on decision making and service delivery. Inaccurate or missing information and a lack of real-time availability of information to employees onsite in the field (for example dispatchers and service technicians) resulted in operational challenges [1, 3, 8]. Information related to the customer or the equipment under maintenance or repair is not always readily available to field service employees, resulting in the poor scheduling of field employees, the ineffective management of field service resources such as service parts [3] and ultimately in poor service delivery. In a study by Lehtonen [1], it was reported that service teams could not provide a service due to missing spare parts. The main reason for this was the inaccurate information on the spare parts that was taken to the client at the time of repair. Challenges in FSM within Enterprise Systems may also arise due to the lack of accessibility and integration of various systems [14]. For example, geographical data is found in Geographical Information Systems (GIS), whilst maintenance-related data and reports are often stored in an Enterprise Resource Planning (ERP) system, thus resulting in integration and consistency issues. Schneider [14] reported issues related to the use of aggregated data within an ERP system. For example, in an ERP system electricity usage data for a manufacturing plant is usually stored as an aggregated figure for all work centres within the plant. Aggregated data makes the operational performance monitoring of a single work centre or equipment within the plant difficult.

Access to real-time information aids organisations in optimising FSM since it can minimise the time for the service team to locate a client location by using GPS services and can reduce the on-site time spent servicing a clients' request [1, 2]. Real-time access to the clients' location eliminates the need for the service team to return to the service provider's facilities in order to get information about a new client's request, thereby optimising the scheduling element [3].

2.2 Applications of the IoT

The IoT has brought new functionality possibilities for many industries such as manufacturing and field services [16, 17]. It is expected that soon more than fifty billion devices ranging from smart phones, laptops, sensors and game consoles will be connected to the Internet through heterogeneous access network technologies [18]. However, the successful implementation of an IoT system introduces several other challenges. The abundance of data provided by sensors can introduce inefficiencies in data transfer and a need for aggregated data since sensor nodes are constrained by limited resources, for example computational power, memory, storage, communication, and battery energy [15]. These constraints provide an important challenge to design and develop approaches to information processing and aggregation that are efficient and make effective use of the data. For a given query, it may not be necessary or efficient to return all the raw data collected from every sensor – alternatively information should be processed and aggregated within the network and only processed and aggregated information returned. From a system level perspective, the IoT can be viewed as a dynamic, radically distributed, networked system, consisting of many smart objects that produce and consume information [19]. It can optimise business processes by leveraging on advanced analytics techniques applied to IoT data streams [19]. Thus, it provides good potential for addressing the downtime problem, if successfully implemented.

Although technology advances enable the possibility of the IoT, it is the application of the IoT which is driving its evolution [18]. The potential social, environmental and economic impact that the IoT has on the decisions we make and the actions we take is its main driving force. For example, having accurate information about the status, location and identity of things which are part of our environment opens the way for making smarter decisions. The application domains that the IoT includes can provide a competitive advantage beyond current solutions. In its inception the IoT was used in the context of supply chain management with RFID tags as the enabling technology [7]. However, in the past decade its applications have covered a wide range of industries, including transportation and utilities, to name just a few. Hwang et al. [20] classified the potential business contexts of IoT into three different factors: industry applications (for example government, education and finance); service domains (for example transportation, asset management) and value chain activities (for example sales and marketing, service or procurement). On the other hand, Borgia et al. [18], classified the IoT into three application areas: industrial (for example agriculture, logistics or other industrial applications), health/well-being and smart city. The smart city factor includes safety, mobility, buildings, road conditions, waste collection and public lighting.

3 Context of Research: Smart Lighting

The case study used in this research is a smart lighting system that is maintained at an engineering consulting and research organisation in South Africa. For purposes of anonymity, the organisation will be called LightCo. The smart lights that are used as outdoor luminous equipment for parking bays and security lights for building facilities and are grid independent; meaning they are not connected to a local or municipal electricity provider for the energy needed to light them. An interview was conducted with one of the senior engineers at LightCo in order to establish an overview of the environment as well as the challenges faced by the organisation in delivering maintenance services for the smart lighting environment.

Smart lighting consists of the integration of intelligent functionalities and interfaces at four complementary levels [4], namely: the embedded level; system level; grid level and communication and sensing level. The embedded level is the lighting engine or the light itself, whilst the system level is the luminaries and lighting systems. The grid level consists of the management and monitoring of the power sources, energy generation and plants and the distribution of utilities and appliances. The final level is the communication and sensing level, which provides complete lighting solutions with monitoring, control and management of the applications.

The smart light unit at LightCo consists of an on board 48-voltage battery pack that is used as an energy storage unit. The solar panel is used to harness solar energy and the wind turbine generates electricity by the turning of a generator. The architecture of the smart lighting system allows for remote monitoring. The smart light also contains sensors and actuators that enable it to measure environmental variables and to respond to specific conditions by means of the actuators. The sensors include ambient sensors on the solar panel and voltage and current sensors on the circuit board of the smart light. Furthermore, the smart light is uniquely identifiable and contains on-board microcontrollers that provide computational and communication capabilities. The microcontrollers receive voltage and current data readings from the solar panel and wind turbine and also record the voltage and current that is outputted to the LED light. The battery management system manages the flow of current to the battery. Once these readings have been recorded they are then sent to a remote server for processing.

Prior to starting this study, the smart lighting system at LightCo did not provide for efficient or effective downtime management. Technical problems with the lights were not being reported timeously and were not correctly diagnosed due to IQ issues reported in literature [1, 14]. These problems could be for example, an LED light or circuit board is damaged. The system that was in place for detecting technical problems with their lights used a Global System for Mobile Communications (GSM) SMS-based messaging/polling protocol to transfer data from a smart light to a server at a remote location. This protocol was reported as inefficient due to its high latency times and high data costs affiliated with the sending and receiving of SMS messages. Increasing the latency was not an option, since it would increase the data costs. Data transmission was not bi-directional and data was merely recorded in a CSV file, with no processing performed on it. An Arduino microcontroller was situated in each smart light with a GSM Shield, which allowed the Arduino board to send and receive an SMS as well as connect to the Internet using the GSM library. However, the system did not use the GPRS wireless component that would enable the Arduino to connect to the Internet. Technicians had to manually peruse the data to diagnose any issues or potential issues.

4 IoT Model for Downtime Management

The Three Phase Data Flow Process model proposed by Borgia et al. [18] (Fig. 1), the four layers of IoT [25], and IQ theory were used as the main guiding theories for the proposed IoT Model for Downtime Management (Fig. 2). The model describes the flow of data in the IoT over three phases [18], namely the Collection Phase; the Transmission Phase; and the Process Management and Utilisation phase and four layers [25] (the Sensing Layer; the Networking Layer; the Service layer; and the Interface layer). The Sensing Layer consists of hardware that senses and controls the physical world and acquires data. Examples are RFID, sensors and actuators. The Network Layer provides networking support and transfers data over either a wireless or a wired network. The Service Layer is responsible for the provision of services to satisfy the user needs and creates and manages services. The Interface Layer (or Application Layer) interacts with other applications and users.

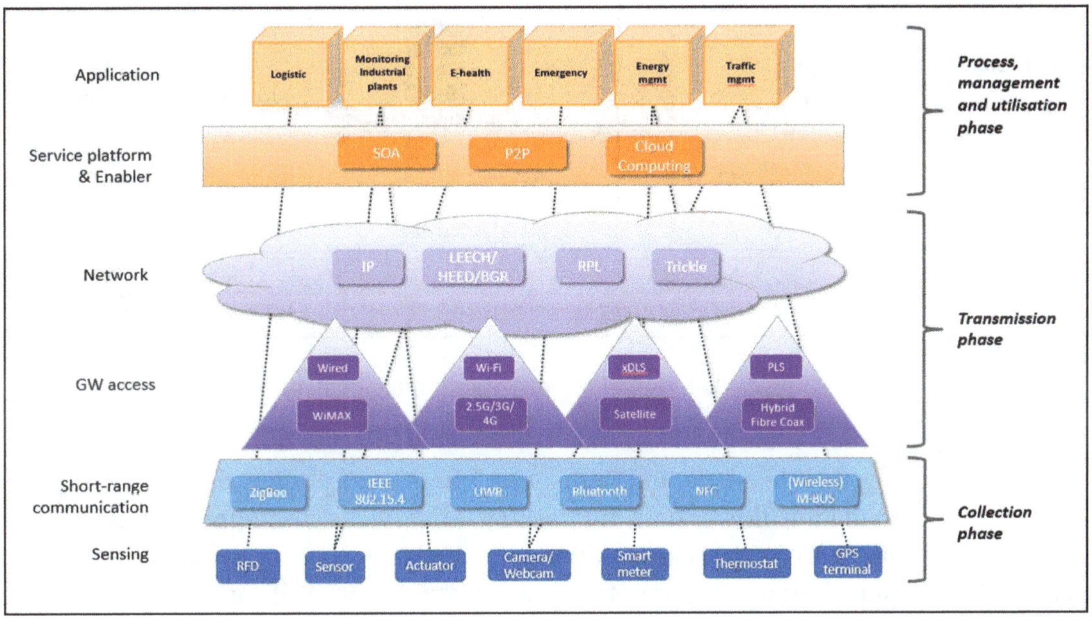

Fig. 1. The three phase data flow process [18]

The Collection Phase reports on the event driven processes during the collection and acquisition of the data from the environment [18]. Data acquisition technologies attached to sensors and cameras collect information about the physical environment (temperature, humidity and brightness), or about the objects (identify and state) in real-time; while data collection is accomplished by short range communications, which could be open source standard solutions or proprietary solutions. In the FSM context these would be integrated into the equipment or assets in the field, for example the smart light. The Transmission Phase involves mechanisms that deliver collected data to various applications and external servers [18]. Once data has been collected it must be transmitted across the network so that it can be consumed by applications. For wired technologies the standard is Ethernet IEEE802.3. The primary advantage that wired networks have for data transmission is that they are robust and less vulnerable to errors and interference. However, they are costly. Therefore Wireless LAN (WLANs) are often used to access the network. Due to the flexibility of WLANs, it is believed that they will be the main communication paradigm of the IoT. However, the restricted wireless spectrum available for cellular networks is a major limitation to their widespread use.

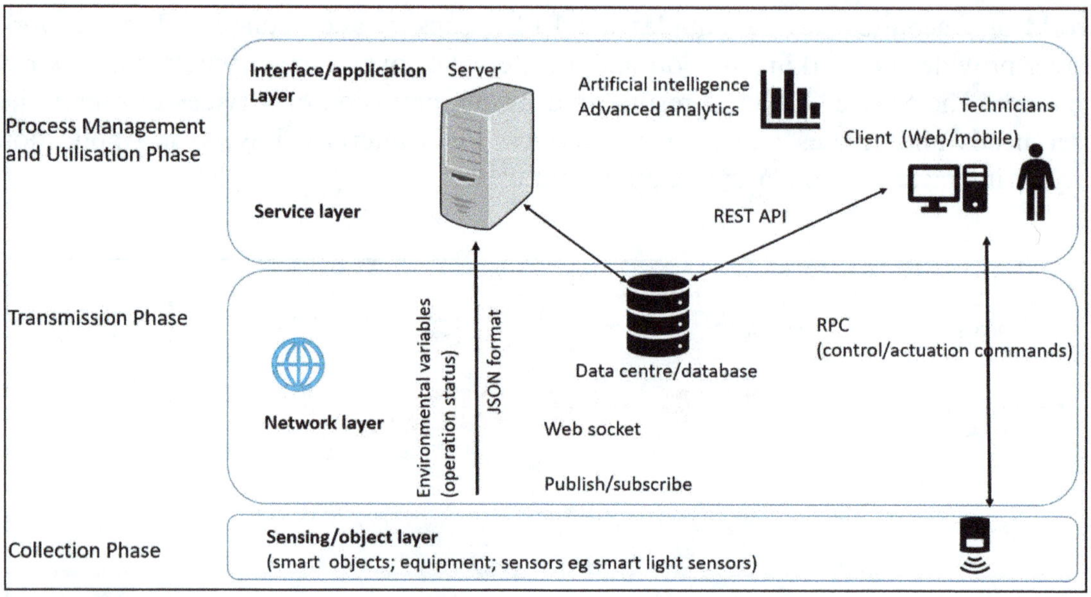

Fig. 2. IoT model for downtime management

The Processing, Management and Utilisation Phase incorporates the processing and analysing of information flows, data forwarding to services and applications and the provision of feedback to control applications [18]. It also involves device discovery and management, data filtering, aggregation and information utilisation. The Service Platform & Enabler sub-phase covers an important role for managing these functions and is necessary in order to hide the heterogeneity of hardware, software, data formats, technologies and communication protocols that are a key feature of the IoT. Its responsibility is to abstract all the features of objects, networks and services, and to provide a loose coupling of components.

5 Methodology and Development of the Prototypes

5.1 Methodology

The Design Science Research (DSR) methodology [21] was adopted in this study to create and evaluate the artefacts (model and prototype). The model was derived from a systematic literature review as well as from the case study of smart lighting maintenance, which was used for implementing and evaluating the model. The Technical and Risk efficacy evaluation strategy from the Framework for Evaluation of Design Science (FEDS) is used in the DSR methodology for evaluations conducted in the design cycle of DSR and was used in this study to evaluate both the model and the KapCha prototype [22]. An artificial-summative evaluation was used to evaluate the design of the model, but due to space limitations these results are not reported on in this paper but are available on request. Iterative formative evaluations were conducted during the development of the prototype; after which a summative-naturalistic evaluation was conducted in order to determine the performance of the prototype under real-world conditions.

5.2 The Prototypes and Their Mapping to Requirements

The KapCha prototype was developed using an incremental prototyping process comprising of three prototype components (Table 1). **ProWebSoc** is the web socket protocol; **ProObjWeb** is the web socket client; and **ProDT** is the interface layer and web socket server. The IoT Model for Downtime Management (Fig. 2) was used to design the architecture of the prototypes.

Table 1. Prototype components

Collection and transmission phases		Process management and utilisation phase
ProWebSoc web socket protocol	ProObjWeb web socket client	ProDT (interface layer) web socket server
Data transmission protocols; security and standardisation	Transmission of data from the smart light and integration of CPS principles	Intelligent algorithms, advanced analytics and interfacing with applications and mobile technologies

Collection and Transmission Phases (ProWebSoc and ProObjWeb)
As an alternative to the SOAP/XML data transmission protocols used by LightCo prior to this intervention, a protocol based on JavaScript Object Notation (JSON) was implemented. JSON, is a text-based open standard format that is designed for human-readable data interchange and used for the serialisation of structured data making it easy for machines to parse and generate it. JSON is ideal for low processing computational capabilities (such as the smart light) and can result in less data that needs to be generated as compared to SOAP/XML.

ProObjWeb, through the web-socket client, enabled the smart light in the case study, as an OEM, to interface with a remote web-server using the KapCha web-socket protocol and to transmit data over a web socket protocol (**ProWebSoc**). Web sockets enable bi-directional communication (upstream and downstream) through the introduction of an interface and the definition of a full-duplex single communication channel that operates through a single socket [23]. They provide a reduction in network traffic and latency as compared to polling and long-polling solutions that are used to simulate a full-duplex connection by maintaining two connections. They also reduce the amount of port openings on the server side, as compared to the traditional means of retrieving resources such as polling. This reduction also reduces maintenance of connection channels from the server side, therefore decreasing the overhead network traffic. The web socket protocol also has the ability to traverse firewalls and proxies, which is a problem for other protocols. The protocols provide real-time communication (RTC) between a smart object and a central system or other smart objects and supports ad hoc and continuous data transfer as well as operational status communication and Remote Procedure Calls (RPCs).

A GPRS wireless component was used to enable the Arduino to make use of web socket technology. The web socket client was developed on the Arduino board using the Arduino open source software and several web socket methods. During connection, the web socket detects the presence of a proxy server and automatically establishes a tunnel to pass through the proxy. The tunnel is established through the opening of a TCP/IP connection. The connection is established by the client issuing an HTTP connect statement to the proxy server for a specific host and port. Upon the tunnel being set up communication flows uninterrupted through the proxy.

The web socket protocol (**ProWebSoc**) was designed to work with existing web infrastructure, therefore the protocol specification defines that the web socket connection starts as an HTTP connection [24]. This guarantees full backwards compatibility with HTTP based communication protocols. The upgrade from an HTTP to web socket is referred to as a handshake. In this process the client sends a request to the server indicating that it wants to switch protocols from HTTP to Web sockets, by means of an upgrade header. During the handshake process the server accepts the request and responds with an upgrade switch header. The server acknowledges receipt of the client's request by taking the |Sec-Web socket-Key| value and concatenating it with a Globally Unique Identifier (GUID) in string form. An SHA-1 hash (160 bits) base64-encoded of this concatenation is then returned in the server's response. This prevents an attacker from tricking a web socket server by sending it carefully crafted packets using XMLHttpRequest or a form submission.

Web sockets are ideal due to the ability to use customised protocol calling depending on the service being offered [23]. In ProObjWeb, when the client receives a response with no errors the connection is upgraded to a web socket over the same TCP/IP connection. Once the connection is established data frames between clients and servers can be transferred. Once the web socket client application connects to the webserver, the webserver initiates an upgrade sequence to upgrade the connection from an HTTP connection to a web socket server. ProObjWeb was functionally tested using the web socket.org echo server, which allows developers of web socket applications to test the ability of their applications to successfully upgrade the connection from HTTP to a web socket protocol. The test results showed that ProObjWeb successfully managed to connect to the web.org server and upgrade from HTTP to web sockets.

Management and Utilisation Phase

The third prototype (**ProDT**) focused on the development of the web-socket server application, a decision tree algorithm implementation and a REST (Representational

State Transfer) API web interface. REST APIs with web socket Requests/Responses were used to form an intermediate layer between a client and the database, translate the raw data from the database to a format that the client requests and transmit the data. Most databases provide real-time notifications for added or updated data. However, real-time notification passage between the database and the client was required, therefore an Interface Layer was created in ProDT using a web socket server. The web-socket server also handled communication with the database, which is the core of the application architecture. These techniques (including the protocols) provided real-time notification between the database and the client, eliminating the need for the Ajax techniques of polling. The database contained information about each smart light such as the date of manufacture and installation, its GPS location, object data sent by the Smart Light, the fault issue result after data analysis and job card data.

In order to generate an issue, data analysis using a decision tree learning algorithm was implemented. A decision tree is a tree structure consisting of nodes that each represent a test of an attribute with each branch representing a result of the test [29]. The tree splits observations into mutually exclusive subgroups until observations can no longer be split. The ID4.5 is a popular splitting algorithm that builds a decision tree by employing a top-down, greedy search through the given sets of training data to test each attribute at every node. Decision trees require little effort for data preparation unlike some statistical techniques and they are easy to interpret. The data collected was categorised data and therefore is ideal for decision tree. Furthermore, as there was no historical information on the diagnosis of faults or issues the decision tree was the ideal AI technique to be used as the classifier would be developed from the expert's opinion of plausible issues. The diagnosis of a set of problems based on these opinions was determined as a classification problem.

The improvements in the quality of information provided by these techniques thus allowed for advanced data analytics and intelligent algorithms (such as decision trees) to be conducted on the IoT data streams. The ability to interface with mobile technologies was also provided.

6 Experiment Procedure and Findings

The aim of the experiments was to evaluate the Round-Trip Delay time (RTD) of messages, latency, accuracy of the decision tree analysis and scalability. Due to space constraints this paper only provides details of the RTD and accuracy experiments.

Round-Trip Delay time (RTD). The RTD experiment measures the time taken for a client to send a signal to a server and the time it takes for the server to acknowledge the signal and send a response [22]. In this context the client was the smart light and the server was the remote web socket server application. For the RTD experiment a connection had to be established between the smart light and the web socket server application. The experiment procedure involved running the applications in three cycles; the first cycle involved sending a data packet 10 times, then the second cycle 100 times and the third cycle 1000 times. The data packet was an array data object that was instantiated and sent to the server.

Two phases of experiments were performed: the first phase (local testing) consisted of running the server applications on a local host machine; and the second phase (remote testing) of the experiment involved running the server applications on a remote server. The performance metrics for the RTD evaluation were delay time and messages per second.

From the results of all three cycles it is evident that the KapCha web socket had a lower RTD time as compared to the Ajax protocol (Table 2). The results can be attributed to the fact that there are fewer HTTP overheads when using web sockets as compared to Ajax requests. Upon the connection being established all messages are sent over the single socket connection rather than the creation of new connections for new HTTP request and response calls created every time a message is sent over the Ajax protocol.

Furthermore, the web socket protocol had more messages sent per second as compared to that of the Ajax protocol. The messages per second for web sockets are higher because the web sockets establish the connection once over a single socket, unlike Ajax techniques that require multiple connections to be opened and closed during request/response calls. Therefore, web sockets do not have messages delayed during the connection process and can send more messages per second. The messages sent per second over the web socket protocol increased exponentially with the number of iterations completed.

Table 2. Experiment results – RDT and messages per second

First phase: local host					
Cycle	Num packets	Time (sec)		Messages	
		Ajax	Kapcha	Ajax	Kapcha
1	10	0.130	0.082	80.135	150.235
2	100	0.435	0.082	301.720	1502.235
3	1000	3.104	0.558	340.832	2215.621
Second phase: remote testing					
Cycle	Num packets	Time (sec)		Messages	
		Ajax	Kapcha	Ajax	Kapcha
1	10	1.241	3.705	3.212	1.752
2	100	22.016	17.213	2.907	3.352
3	1000	153.352	147.25	3.191	3.714

The results from the remote testing set of experiments revealed that the web socket protocol had a lower RTD time as compared to the Ajax protocol when the number of packets was lower than a certain level. This result could be due to the upgrade sequence overhead during the web socket handshake process. The additional overhead connection, however, is not significant as the number of iterations increase due to the maintenance of the single socket connection. The RDT results highlighted the advantages of applications that use web sockets have over HTTP polling mechanisms.

The advantages are lower latency and the provision of a single socket connection that enables the web server to push data to the client at will, creating a fully duplex bi-directional data exchange web-protocol.

Accuracy of decision tree: Prior to the development of the prototype there wasn't any data stored regarding the cause of a fault or the documentation of the diagnosis of a fault at LightCo. Therefore, the accuracy of the training dataset created was based on the expert's verification. The C4.5 decision tree algorithm was used to analyse the data and deduce the cause of the faults that occurred. For the experiment, the algorithm was deployed/executed to analyse three sample data set sizes of 50, 100 and 175. The number of correct predictions after each execution was recorded and verified by an expert at LightCo. This process was undertaken to establish the accuracy of the algorithm in diagnosing faults. The execution time of the algorithm was also recorded to determine the turnaround time of the fault diagnosis. The formula used for determining the accuracy percentage was:

$$\text{Accuracy} = \frac{\text{Number of correct predictions}}{\text{Total number of predictions}} = \frac{f_{11} + f_{100}}{f_{11} + f_{10} + f_{01} + f_{00}}. \quad (1)$$

The accuracy results are summarised in Table 3. The sample size of fifty (n = 50) resulted in a percentage accuracy of 82.2% meaning that 41 out of the 50 predictions were correct. The sample size of 100 had 79 correctly predicted faults with a percentage accuracy of 79%. The final sample size had an accuracy percentage of 77% that is 96 faults were correctly predicted. Whilst the accuracy results were all above 70% additional testing is required to determine accuracy of larger datasets. However, this could not be done since previous records were non-existent and the training set was small. This is a limitation of this study. Future studies should perform the accuracy tests on the larger data set, which will increase rapidly with time. However, in spite of this limitation useful results and lessons learned were obtained regarding the IoT techniques used in the model.

Table 3. Accuracy results

Size of dataset	Accuracy (%)
50	82
100	79
125	77
Mean	**79**

7 Conclusions

In this paper a theoretical prescriptive model for optimising downtime management is proposed that was derived from a systematic literature review of FSM, IoT and IQ theory. The use of intelligent algorithms and data accessibility are features of the model that can aid in the reduction of downtime. The model also supports geographically dispersed devices and clients. From a practical viewpoint, an organisation in the smart lighting industry was used to test the model as a proof of concept. In the case of the smart lighting scenario, prior to the intervention of our study, an SMS/Ajax polling system was used that was slow and expensive due to the data costs. As a results insufficient data was provided to assist with detecting and diagnosing problems. The solution lacked real-time information and field service technicians had to rely on human 'diagnostics' and sometimes travelling to the smart lights in order to physically detect problems. The proposed IoT model for downtime management was used to design an architecture and to develop and implement a system prototype for optimising downtime management in the smart lighting environment.

The evaluations of the prototype revealed that web-sockets are more efficient and cost-effective than other web-based data transfer protocols such as Ajax. The implementation of a web-socket based protocol provided a low-cost data communication protocol with real-time bi-directional capabilities and fully duplex communication between a smart light and a remote server. The use of IoT-enabled communication protocols reduced the latency time and data exchange costs. Furthermore, the web-socket server implements an expert system mechanism using intelligent algorithms for data analysis. The intelligent algorithm, a C4.5 decision tree, automates fault detection and provides an issue report. The intelligent algorithms can assist service technicians to identify and diagnose problems. The practical contributions of this research are therefore the model, which can be used by FSM organisations in the implementation of IoT. The results of the evaluations revealed that the implementation of the various techniques and features of the model optimised downtime within the smart lighting environment. A problem encountered during the study related to restrictions on GSM protocols by the mobile service providers, some of which do not support the use of web-socket connections. Another challenge was inventor patents on the smart lights in the case study that restricted testing of the prototype in its natural environment. As a result only historical data was used for testing. A further limitation was that not all elements of the model could be tested due to time and resource constraints. However, the findings of this study can still be used by other researchers as a valuable source of reference when conducting similar research. The lessons learnt can be useful to other researchers and practitioners working in FSM and similar industries that can benefit from IoT.

The combination of advanced big data analytics, cloud-computing and IoT enables users to not only gather vast amounts of data but also enable them to process it without having to acquire high infrastructural costs. This leads to several opportunities for researchers in these fields. Future research directions could extend the study to include functionality such as predictive maintenance. AI mechanisms can be implemented in the model to support the prediction of faults before they occur. Additional intelligence can be achieved by interacting with other systems in the same environment that have a direct impact on the equipment's performance. The addition of predictive mechanisms as well as enabling object interaction with other systems will transform regular equipment into a self-aware and self-learning machines, and consequently improves overall performance and maintenance management. The model serves as a reference model for standards and protocols in an IoT-based implementation in the field of downtime management within the after-sales industry. Although the study was limited to evaluating the prototype in only one environment it provided valuable lessons that could be used by other practitioners and researchers to guide the implementation of IoT in FSM.

Acknowledgements. The financial assistance of the National Research Foundation (NRF) towards this research is hereby acknowledged. Opinions expressed and conclusions arrived at are those of the author and are not necessarily to be attributed to the NRF.

References

1. Lehtonen, O.: Taking advantage of after-sales product information in a multi-company environment. Masters thesis, Helsinki University of Technology, Department of Industrial Engineering and Management, Finland (2005)
2. Agnihothri, S., Sivasubramaniam, N., Simmons, D.: Leveraging technology to improve field service. Int. J. Serv. Ind. Manag. **13**(1), 47–68 (2002). https://doi.org/10.1108/09564230210421155
3. Petrakis, I., Hass, C., Bichler, M.: On the impact of real-time information on field service scheduling. Decis. Support Syst. **53**(2), 282–293 (2012). https://doi.org/10.1016/j.dss.2012.01.013
4. Castro, M., Jara, A.J., Skarmeta, A.F.G.: Smart lighting solutions for smart cities. In: Proceedings - 27th International Conference on Advanced Information Networking and Applications Workshops, WAINA, pp. 1374–1379 (2013)
5. Basu, C., et al.: Sensor-based predictive modeling for smart lighting in grid-integrated buildings. IEEE Sens. J. **14**(12), 4216–4229 (2014). https://doi.org/10.1109/JSEN.2014.2352331
6. Koh, L.H., Tan, Y.K., Wang, Z.Z., Tseng, K.J.: An energy-efficient low voltage DC grid powered smart LED lighting system. In: IECON Proceedings (Industrial Electronics Conference), pp. 2883–2888 (2011)
7. Kortuem, G., Kawsar, F., Fitton, D., Sundramoorthy, V.: Smart objects as building blocks for the Internet of things. IEEE Internet Comput. **14**(1), 44 51 (2010). https://doi.org/10.1109/MIC.2009.143
8. Jose, G.J., Kumanan, S., Venkatesan, S.P.: Optimize field service management through analytics. In: Proceedings of the International Conference on Advances in Production and Industrial Engineering 2015, pp. 529–534 (2015)
9. Gartner. Magic Quadrant for Field Service Management (2017). https://www.gartner.com/doc/3808464/magic-quadrant-field-service-management
10. Knotts, R.M.H.: Civil aircraft maintenance and support. J. Qual. Maint. Eng. **5**(4), 335–348 (1999). https://doi.org/10.1108/13552519910298091
11. Nonaka, I.: A dynamic theory of organizational knowledge creation. Organ. Sci. **5**, 14–37 (1994)
12. Delone, W.H., Mclean, E.R.: The DeLone and McLean model of information systems success: a ten year update. J. Manage. Inf. Syst. **19**, 9–30 (2003)
13. DeLone, W.H., McLean, E.R.: Information systems success: the quest for the dependent variable. Inf. Syst. Res. **3**(1), 60–95 (1992)
14. Schneider, J., et al.: Asset management techniques. Int. J. Electr. Power Energy Syst. **28**(9 SPEC. ISS), 643–654 (2006). https://doi.org/10.1016/j.ijepes.2006.03.007
15. Przydatek, B., Song, D., Perrig, A.: SIA: secure information aggregation in sensor networks. In ACM SenSys, pp. 255–265 (2003)

16. Bi, Z., Da Xu, L., Wang, C.: Internet of things for enterprise systems of modern manufacturing. IEEE Trans. Industr. Inf. **10**(2), 1537–1546 (2014)
17. Coetzee, L., Eksteen, J.: The Internet of Things – Promise for the Future ? An Introduction. In: IST-Africa 2011 Conference Proceedings, pp. 1–9 (2011)
18. Borgia, E.: The internet of things vision: key features, applications and open issues. Comput. Commun. **54**, 1–31 (2014)
19. Miorandi, D., Sicari, S., De Pellegrini, F., Chlamtac, I.: Internet of things: vision, applications and research challenges. Ad Hoc Netw. **10**(7), 1497–1516 (2012)
20. Hwang, Y.M., Kim, M.G., Rho, J.J.: Understanding internet of things (IoT) diffusion: focusing on value configuration of RFID and sensors in business cases (2008–2012). Inf. Dev. **32**(4), 969–985 (2016)
21. Hevner, A.R., Gregor, S.: Positioning and presenting design science research for maximum impact. MIS Q. **37**(2), 337–355 (2013)
22. Venable, J., Pries-Heje, J., Baskerville, R.: FEDS: a framework for evaluation in design science research. Eur. J. Inf. Syst. **25**, 77 (2016). https://doi.org/10.1057/ejis.2014.36
23. Fette, I.: The WebSocket protocol. Internet Eng. Task Force, Request for Comments **53**(9), 1–79 (2011). https://doi.org/10.1017/CBO9781107415324.004
24. Lubbers, P., Greco, F.: HTML5 web sockets: A quantum leap in scalability for the web. SOA World Magazine, Article (2010)
25. Da Xu, L., He, W., Li, S.: Internet of things in industries: a survey. IEEE Trans. Industr. Inf. **10**(4), 2233–2243 (2014)
26. Datta, P., Bhisham, S.A.: Survey on IoT architectures, protocols, security and smart city based applications. In: 8th International Conference on Computing, Communication and Networking Technologies (ICCCNT), pp. 1–5. IEEE (2017)
27. Yaqoob, I., et al.: Internet of things architecture: recent advances, taxonomy, requirements and open challenges. IEEE Wirel. Commun. **24**(3), 10–16 (2017). https://doi.org/10.1109/MWC.2017.1600421
28. Lloret, J., Tomas, J., Canovas, A., Parra, L.: An integrated IoT architecture for smart metering. IEEE Commun. Mag. **54**(12), 50–57 (2016)
29. Kohavi, R., Quinlan, J.R.: Data mining tasks and methods: Classification: decision-tree discovery. Handbook of data mining and knowledge discovery. 267–276. Oxford University Press, Inc. New York, NY. USA (2002)

IoT Enabled Process Innovation: Exploring Sensor-Based Digital Service Design Through an Information Requirements Framework

Niclas Carlén, August Forsman, Jesper Svensson(✉), and Johan Sandberg

Department of Informatics, Umeå University, 901 87 Umeå, Sweden
{niclas.carlen, august.forsman, jesper.svensson, johan.sandberg}@umu.se

Abstract. Through digitisation of physical artefacts and environments, the Internet of Things carries vast potential for process innovation. However, navigation of the quickly evolving technological landscape and identification of emerging opportunities for value creation remains challenging. To this end, we combine existing frameworks on information requirements, IT capability, and business value of IT. We evaluate the usability of these frameworks for IoT enabled innovation in our analysis of two sensor-based process innovation projects. We investigate the fit between process characteristics and technological functionality, and the implications of this alignment. Our analysis demonstrates that the framework provides a practically useful and theoretically coherent conceptual device for analyzing process characteristics and digital options to innovate processes. Furthermore, we find that IoT sensors are well suited to address connectivity and uncertainty requirements. However, in order to leverage them to address high equivocality requirements designers need deep contextual understanding to align IoT capability with information requirements.

Keywords: Process innovation · Internet of Things · Information requirements

1 Introduction

The ongoing pervasive digitisation of physical artefacts and environments, often collectively referred to as the Internet of Things (IoT), signifies a new paradigm in data processing and communication. It is not a new technology per se, Wortmann and Flüchter (2015) describes IoT as "a global infrastructure for the Information Society, enabling advanced services by interconnecting (physical and virtual) things based on, existing and evolving, interoperable information and communication technologies". IoT has evolved into an ecosystem of possible objects or things to connect to the internet where basically anything that has an on and off switch can be connected e.g. sensors. Combined with an expected battery life of several decades for many sensors allows for data collection around the clock. Sensors like this are making headway around the world with the emergence of smart cities, i.e. cities that are connected and efficient collecting data to manage its resources and serve its citizens in the best way

L. Strous and V. G. Cerf (Eds.): IFIPIoT 2018, IFIP AICT 548, pp. 105–120, 2019.
https://doi.org/10.1007/978-3-030-15651-0_10

possible (Sundmaeker et al. 2010). The global market for IoT is growing tremendously, resulting in significant market opportunities and an expected turnover at around 8.9 trillion dollars combined with an estimated 26–100 billion connected devices by the year 2020 (Statista 2017). Currently, there are significant uncertainties when companies engage in IoT; lack of standards, low understanding of technology and security issues are all sizeable problems hindering development (Forbes Insight 2017). Most companies feel uncertain which IoT-solution will collect the data they need, this results in a discrepancy in what companies need and what they get with regards to data and information (Forbes Insight 2017). In this paper, we argue that this uncertainty can be mitigated by synthesising two theoretical frameworks combining both analysis of information requirements and corresponding digital options with effects on processes by different IoT implementations.

We have been involved extensively in two IoT-projects and have seen issues regarding information requirements and process analysis arise throughout both. Both cases illustrate the need to understand the working environment and the technology at hand. While most studies thus far have focused either on the technical or business side of IoT (Forbes Insight 2017), we argue that there is a need to understand both aspects to generate successful outcomes. Since in most cases there is going to be humans interacting with the technology in their daily work life, we also argue that it is of great importance to understand the duality of technology and social activity. We have, therefore, focused on a micro-level perspective by investigating how IoT-systems affect work practices. This paper seeks to examine the effects of implementing sensor-based systems in organisations, i.e. how the implementation effects the process and value chain. This study will be limited to two separate case studies where sensor-based systems have been both designed and implemented in the organisations. Specifically, we explore the following research question:

How can IoT sensors be used for digital service design to innovate processes?

2 Internet of Things in Business Processes

With the emergence of ICT in the 20th century a lot of IT projects have had lacklustre results, one reason is the assumption that technological functionality solves organisational issues (Alter 2006). The argument against this is that an IT system should be viewed as a resource for the solution and not the solution itself (Alter 2006; Meyer et al. 2013). IoT is also argued to have a decentralising effect on the value chain in business as parts of it become connected. As the value chain becomes decentralised the decision-making rights are moved to the individual components in the chain, and the different parts become more independent, arguably creating a more efficient and streamlined process chain throughout (Haller et al. 2008). We would add to the current research by enacting these principles in real-world implementations. Doing so with the intention of showing real-world scenarios with the technology in place, we argue that the current body of research will benefit by the holistic perspective applied in this study.

2.1 A Framework for Analysing Process Effects with IoT and IoT Capability

In this paper, we synthesise two different theoretical frameworks. The first is a framework developed to identify what digital options are available to organisations and what information requirements different processes have (Sandberg et al. 2014). The second framework is intended to measure the effects of the chosen solution on the process (Mooney 1995). By synthesising we refer to using the frameworks in tandem, iteratively, throughout the process analysis, implementation and evaluation of the systems. This in turn contributes to the body of research with a practical framework encompassing the entire process of implementing IoT in an organisation with intent to innovate business processes.

Information Requirements

Information requirements are used to identify what digital options there are for a specific business process. Digital options should here be understood as opportunities for leveraging IT in process innovation. The conceptualisation is grounded in earlier research, but Sandberg et al. (2014) further develop the concept of a specific tasks requirements about uncertainty and equivocality by adding connectivity to modernise the theory. We extend existing applications of the framework by using the information requirements in an IoT context. Establishing information requirements for each case is the first step of the innovative work process to map if and how IoT can support or transform a business process. This analysis, enables generation of the digital options available to organisations. To identify information requirements there are three aspects to consider and analyse: connectivity, uncertainty and equivocality.

Connectivity relates to the informational dependencies between processes and systems within an organisation, i.e. the need for information sharing across boundaries in an organisation (Malhotra et al. 2005). If the connectivity need is regarded as high, the focus for managers should be to counteract technical or social barriers by increasing information *reach*, characterised as "the number information sources that can be accessed during task execution" (Sandberg et al. 2014, p. 428). If information can be accessed across organisational and geographical boundaries, process information requirements have low connectivity requirements. When the connectivity need is low, it can be relevant to increase *richness* which refers to "the number of data points available regarding a given object during task execution" (Sandberg et al. 2014, p. 428).

Uncertainty refers to the availability and accuracy of information needed for actors to execute their task within an organisation. Uncertainty requirements can be addressed by continually balancing information production and information consumption (Ramaprasad and Rai 1996). Information *production* occurs when actors generate new information based on stimuli in the process and its environment. Information *consumption* turns the existing and available information into business process actions. If the information requirements are high in uncertainty, i.e. the current information is inaccurate, unreliable or insufficient, organisations should aim to increase production of information as they should not want to consume unreliable information. When uncertainty requirements are low, organisations can instead focus on consumption of information. If the information is reliable, available options for consumption emerge which can drive an organisation to make better data-driven decisions.

Equivocality refer to confusion and lack of mutual understanding when executing a task, or the level of complexity and ambiguity in the tasks information processing (Sandberg et al. 2014) (Mathiassen and Sørensen 2008). When a task is to be executed, there may be a need for mutual understanding between actors or processes, as they may have to rely on contextual knowledge. Conversely, there can be situations where actors or processes can rely on their codified knowledge and routines. If information requirements are high in equivocality, then the situation or task context is unknown for the involved parties. A *relationship* enables success in these situations; there needs to be a high level of understanding and trust within the system and in the systems supporting situational knowledge and contexts. If the requirements are low, however, then the characteristics are based on *encounters* where standardised protocols and workflows are utilised.

Table 1. Information requirements and digital options characteristic (Adapted from Sandberg et al. 2014)

Information requirement	Corresponding digital option characteristic		Example of IoT capability investment
Connectivity	High	**Reach**: the number of information sources that can be accessed through IoT during task execution	Open data sharing of sensor data between organisational departments, generating easy access to new information
	Low	**Richness**: the number of data points available through IoT about a given object during task execution	Flow sensors generating exact measurements of waste flow in a waste management facility
Uncertainty	High	**Production**: the extent to which IoT supports the creation of information from stimuli	Multiple sensor measuring soil and crop health in modern agriculture
	Low	**Consumption**: the extent to which IoT support translation of information into action taken	Heatmaps showing movement patterns of visitors in a public building
Equivocality	High	**Relationship**: extent to which IoT supports contextual consideration and development of trust by adaptation and sharing of information across subsequent episodes	Correct analysis of contextual environment with the implementation of sensors that measure the exact values needed for the task
	Low	**Encounter**: IoT based on a standardised approach without variation across customers; limited regarding time and flexibility but efficient due to uniformity	Photoelectric sensors measuring visitors entering and leaving a facility from a permanently fixed position

IoT Capabilities in Organisations
Sandberg et al. (2014) refer to the organisation's IT capabilities as a firm's previous investments in IT resources, such as technology or IT competence. We use the concept and expand upon it to fit the field of IoT and thereby refer to them as IoT capabilities. Table 1 shows both information requirements, their corresponding digital options and examples of IoT capabilities that reflect the requirement characteristic.

2.2 Measuring Effects of IoT on Processes

We draw on Mooney's (1995) framework for assessing the business value of IT. Business performance is best measured from the performance of its processes (Ray et al. 2004; Mooney 1995). Sensors collect a limited range of data in an environment which in turn supports business processes. Therefore, we conclude that examining sensor implementation impact is most efficiently done in the context of the processes which they intend to support. In this study, we analyse the automational, transformational and informational effects of the IT-systems designed for each case, which are classifications derived from Mooney's process-oriented framework and have been used in similar studies (Stenmark and Jadaan 2010; Visich et al. 2009).

The automational dimension relates to how sensors data collection can substitute manual labour. Different kind of sensors can continuously collect data which are to support or initiate processes. Automational effects on business value are gained through aspects such as improved customer service, increased productivity and a more efficient labour distribution (Stenmark and Jadaan 2010; Visich et al. 2009).

Informational effects are those that are caused by IT-enabled collection, storage, processing and spread of information acquired from the sensors. Case studies of RFID implementations have shown that business value can arise from improved resource management and reduced manual labour (Stenmark and Jadaan 2010; Visich et al. 2009).

The transformational dimension affects and supports process innovation and transformation. Sensor data may support and improve existing processes but may also be utilised for business innovation. Data acquired to support a specific process chain can be used in combination with other aspects of the organisations' knowledge base to innovate the business (Stenmark and Jadaan 2010).

3 Methodology

For this paper we conducted a multiple case study consisting of two cases where sensor-based IoT-systems, through collection and visualisation of data, were designed and implemented to support different process chains. Case studies are a preferred strategy when research questions related to "how" and "why" are posed (Yin 2003), and multiple case-studies when the logic of the study is to "produce contrasting results but for predictable reasons" (Yin 2003, p. 47). We argue that this makes a case-study approach viable with regards to the framing and research question stated earlier. By evaluating this innovation process through multiple cases, we intend to generate general findings and propose practices which could be built upon in further research.

We chose the cases based on an analysis of two different research sites. The classification for inclusion was that the case should present one or several concrete problems in a process chain where sensor-based technology could be a solution. These problems could either be a lack of ability in performing activities which could be enabled by the technology or addressing problems currently present in an organisation.

A process is "a structured, measured set of activities designed to produce a specified output for a particular customer or market" (Davenport 1993, p. 5) and can be classified into two different categories; operational processes and management processes (Mooney 1995). Operational processes are the set of activities an organisation performs to produce something that generates value and is referred to as an organisation's primary activities. Management processes are related to streamlining and improving the efficiency of an organisation's primary set of activities such as coordinating and handling different information. Process innovation in this context refers to the practice of analysing an organisation's processes and redesigning them using innovative technology to improve performance and support the processes (Davenport 1993). In this case, that innovative technology is LoRa-sensors, which enables remote monitoring and control of different aspects of a process, and the IT-artefacts of the software designed to visualise or manipulate the data generated by the sensors. Each case process chain was broken down into sub-processes depending on what type of activities and the complexity of the tasks performed. We then mounted sensors at each research site to collect data and designed IT-artefacts with the purpose of solving specific problems related to the sub-process. The effectiveness of these systems was analysed in the context of what type of value and effects the data generated when innovating operational and management processes.

3.1 Research Sites and Sensor Technology

The sensors used in the project are based on LoRa technology, and a specific type of gateway delivers connectivity to the sensors. Because of lacking infrastructure in the northern municipality, we were tasked to mount two base-stations; this implementation took place in September 2017. One of these base-stations was installed on the highest point in the town, which is a water tower, the other one on the roof of the local secondary school. We also installed a base-station in the city where the cleaning company project took place to further the existing coverage. The base-stations have guaranteed coverage of a 3 km radius, however, depending on disruption and quality of air it may be greater than that (LoRa-alliance 2015).

LoRa stands for Long Range and is the physical layer utilised to create long-range communication links. LoRa is based on chirp spread spectrum modulation, using its entire spectrum of bandwidth and is therefore very resistant to channel noise. LoRaWAN is based on Low Power, Wide-Area Networks i.e. LPWAN, and defines the communication protocol and system architecture for the network. LoRaWAN has a great influence on battery times for nodes, network capacity and security. LoRaWAN is explicitly designed for sensors and applications that need to send small amounts of data over long distances at different time intervals, making it ideal for IoT sensors applications. As IoT is still a new phenomenon and standards are currently lacking, other technologies are competing to become the business standard. In likeness with LoRa, several LPWAN networks are emerging as competitors; examples are Sigfox and Narrowband IoT that operate similarly (LoRa-alliance 2015).

In this study, we have used two different types of LoRa-sensors that measure different values while having some similar readings; temperature inside the casing, humidity at the sensor and battery-level (Table 2).

Table 2. LoRa Sensors utilised in projects with corresponding properties

Sensor name	Properties
ERS	Passive infrared (PIR) sensor registering movement in its field of view
ELT-1	Analogue input sensor capable of coupling with external analogue measurement tools, e.g. thermometer, voltmeter, ultrasonic level indicator

3.2 Data Collection and Analysis

The data collection process consisted of an analytical phase where we in conjunction with each organisation collected data regarding the problem background of their process chains. An implementation phase studying the physical environment of the research site, collected data relevant to the practical implementation of the system, and an evaluation phase where the data related to the results of the system was collected. All interviews conducted are semi-structured and were conducted throughout all three phases to capture viewpoints from the participants on both current problematic aspects, initial impressions of the implemented system, and impressions regarding its effects. Observations refer to activities where we have studied staff members performing the process chains, as well as documenting areas of interest. This was performed mainly during the analytical phase in order discover details relevant to mapping the process chains and capture insights possibly missed using the other methods. Workshops are meetings where we collected data related to our subsequent design choices and was mainly conducted in the analytical phase with participants in each innovation project. Informal encounters are the interactions with the organisation where we have performed different tasks or exchanged minor pieces of information related to the projects, a method which was applied throughout all three phases.

A total of 9 interviews, 11 observations, 7 workshops and 46 informal encounters were conducted, spanning all three cases in the study during a time frame spanning from 20th September 2017 to the 29th of Mars 2018 (Table 3).

Table 3. Data collection overview

Case	Interviews	Observations	Workshops	Informal encounters
Swimming pool	4	5	2	7
Cleaning company	5	6	5	39

The data analysis was performed in iterations together with the organisation throughout the time-frame of the data collection, where the input in the analytical phase formed the basis for our description of the information requirements and IT-capabilities in each case. The results of the evaluation period (testing the systems in practice) formed the input for the process effects each system had on the corresponding process chain it supported.

4 Results

This section consists of the results of our research, each case will be presented with a description of the research site, problem background and information requirements of the process chains, with a subsequent description of practical implementation and effects from each case.

4.1 Swimming Pool

Research Site

The research site of the public swimming pool-case is in a municipality in the north of Sweden and is run by a small organisation of six people who maintain the pool, a gym and a gymnasium in the same building. The public pool is a facility open during weekdays and Saturdays on regular weeks.

Process Chains and Problem Backgrounds

The organisation lacks data on the number of visitors and which hours and days during the week generate most activity. The main areas of activity which the organisation found interesting were the entrance to estimate the overall number of customers, the cafeteria to investigate the air quality during peak hours, and the locker rooms to investigate differences in attendance between the genders. This data is interesting for the organisation when optimising staffing and air quality, and to create an overview of when and how much the facilities are used during the week. To achieve these informational effects, the sensor implementation sought to address the high uncertainty and low connectivity information requirements through continuous collection of visitor data. Further, the information regarding the number of visitors is non-equivocal as the collected data is readily interpreted in the context.

The second process chain in the case is optimising heating of the swimming pool. According to the person responsible for this routine, the pools are heated to 32 °C every week during Tuesday nights, and then the temperature falls successively to around 27 °C during the weekly cycle. This practice leads to uncertainty amongst the customers on the current temperature and generates phone calls to the organisation increasing the workload. Further, the facilities have shown signs of increased wear in forms of mould and moisture damage due to the increased evaporation generated by higher temperatures. The organisation seeks informational effects on the managerial level through an increased amount of temperature data points and implementing sensors to address the connectivity and uncertainty requirements. The equivocal requirements were low as temperature data is readily understood in the context.

The third process chosen for this case is the documentation of pool water quality, which is a process chain performed by the staff daily to discover anomalies and potential health risks related to the pool water. Water samples are collected, analysed and documented as the first task of every day: water temperature, pH-value and chlorine-levels. To collect this data, the staff places a thermometer in the pool water where it is submerged for 15 min. During this time, they gather two water samples which are analysed using a pool water quality kit establishing its pH-value and amount of chlorine. This data is then documented manually in a binder and stored in the staff office of the facilities. Due to the repetitive manner of the data collection and documentation, the organisation seeks to explore to what extent it could be automated using IoT sensors. To achieve these effects, automatic production of information regarding temperature, pH-value and chlorine levels is required, which characterises an information requirement high in uncertainty. We found the connectivity and equivocality requirements to be low as the information is to be utilised within task entity boundaries and well understood in the context.

Implementation

To support the first process chain, we mounted four sensors at areas for which the organisation had expressed interest. The main units of observation these sensors were to measure were motion activity and temperature in each respective area. The sensors were placed at the entrance of each respective area at the height of around 150 cm's ensuring measurements of every individual passing.

This motion activity and temperature-data is uploaded every 30 min to a database, imported into tables and transformed into graphs, both real-time and historical. The information was made accessible to the organisation through a web application where it could be studied and form part of the basis for process innovation. The implemented system has the characteristics referring to the production of information to address uncertainty requirements. As this process aims to collect information about motion and temperature in the facility we argued that the four sensors would address the uncertainty requirements.

To support the second chain, we mounted one temperature sensor in the bottom of the swimming pool, hidden behind a ladder. This sensor uploaded water temperature every 30 min to a database and was imported into tables and graphs made available to the organisation. The historical data generated by the sensor can be utilised to measure how much time it takes to heat the pool to the preferred temperature and get a more detailed overview of its heating cycle. This data could serve as a basis for innovating the heating process chain and minimise the problems of their current practices. The third process chain utilised the same temperature sensor as the second as the only relevant unit in the process chain collected and documented is the temperature data. This data was then uploaded every 30 min and presented in the form of tables and graphs. For this process, we addressed the information requirements with the intent to increase richness by collecting data with the sensor as well as produce more information to lower uncertainty.

Effects

The first process chain showed primarily informational effects. The data collected from the motion sensors generated an estimate of which areas has the most activity, and during which hours can be established by studying the graphs in the web application. The organisation had ideas of using the data to optimise the air conditioning. However, the functional capabilities of adjusting the air conditioner cycles to reflect usage or be automated by the data seemed to be limited which was uncovered later in the project when this issue was discussed with a janitor responsible for the air conditioning. A side-effect of studying the comprehensive dataset was the discovery that the temperature in the cafeteria rises around 2–3 °C during the nights when the facility is closed. This occurrence was unknown to the organisation when they were informed of it, and according to one of the staff members, may be related to the underfloor heating being active during the night time when the ventilation is inactive.

The effects on the second process chain had informational effects. The historical data generates a clear and consistent timeframe over how long it takes for the swimming pool to reach its intended temperature and shows some anomalies. An example is the re-warming of the pool, which usually happens around 4 h after it has reached its maximum temperature. Why this happens is unknown to us right now but will be of interest in further evaluation of the system. The third process chain has potential to be completely automated, generating both automational and transformational effects, but since the sensors automate only 1/3 of the data collection, the staff must still perform a majority of the process chain in the same manner as before. A future update of the system will be to implement sensors collecting data of the chlorine level and pH-value. With a complete system in place, the whole process will be performed continuously and automatically document the data in the same way as current practice. The permanent character enables transformational possibilities in the sense that with a system documenting the water quality continuously, anomalies in the water can be discovered faster.

4.2 Cleaning Company

Research Site

The research site for the case of the cleaning company is located in a university building. The organisation is responsible for cleaning all facilities and have a staff of six managing and executing this task at the research site.

Process Chains and Problem Backgrounds

The staff have expressed a problem of prioritising which order that classrooms are cleaned after the weekend in an effort to work more condition-based. The current situation is such that the activity in the classrooms during the weekends is unknown to the staff when they begin cleaning on Mondays, and they clean each room in a set routine. The consequence of cleaning in a routine-based manner could result in rooms with less cleaning needs getting cleaned, and rooms with higher cleaning need left unattended. The cleaning process of each room constitutes four sub-processes: cleaning the floor, cleaning the tables, wiping the whiteboard and emptying the waste bin, and the cleaning need of each sub-process in combination is what constitute the cleaning need of the classroom. The organisation seeks informational effects through collection of information regarding classroom cleaning need. This information requirement has the characteristics of high equivocality, as assessing cleaning need is non-algorithmic and is based on situated knowledge about the specific context. The process chain has high connectivity and both high and low uncertainty requirements as cleaning need information must be collected and accessed remotely. Since the organisation currently lacks data on the activity in the classrooms during the weekends, it cannot innovate its processes in such a way that it aligns with the ambition of working more condition-based.

The second process chain presented as problematic by the organisation is assessing if a room is vacant. In the current situation, the staff do not clean rooms which are occupied and wait until the rooms are vacant to clean them. This problem means in practice that they sometimes spend time visiting rooms only to discover that they cannot be cleaned, and delay that process until later, having wasted time moving to the classroom. The organisation seeks informational effects on the operational level through remote access to information with regards to classroom vacancy. To achieve these effects, vacancy information need to be produced and remotely accessible to cleaning staff, which characterises the information requirements as high in connectivity and uncertainty. Lastly, information regarding classroom vacancy is non-equivocal as the room is either vacant or not.

The third process chain is the comparison between the presumed usage based on the booking schedule and actual usage of the specific classrooms. According to the organisation, it is not uncommon for a room to be booked during the week, but its actual usage is unclear. The staff can plan the cleaning of classrooms only to discover that they have not been used and, therefore, not in need of cleaning. This could also be used as a basis when negotiating terms with its currently largest customer which is the university itself. Part of how many hours the company can bill the university is based on the number of hours booked in the electronic booking schedule. The organisation seeks informational effects on the managerial level through remote information collection of classroom usage. High connectivity, high uncertainty, and low equivocality characterises its information requirement. The multiple data collection points increase reach and production of this non-equivocal information.

Implementation

To support the process chains described in the case we mounted sensors in classrooms collecting motion data. The sensors were placed at the entrance around 170 cms from the floor, registering every motion near the entrance door. This data was uploaded every 10 min to a database. We then designed a web-application containing various artefacts which utilise this data to address the information requirements in the process chain. Due to the high connectivity requirements the purpose was to increase reach through multiple data collection points. For the uncertainty requirements, there was a need for both production and consumption to address the requirements relating to uncertainty. The sensors installed addressed the information production aspect, and the web application was developed to increase consumption of information. As the equivocality requirements were high, the need for a relationship characteristic was of high priority. Due to the organisation wanting to measure cleaning need in the rooms, which is a highly equivocal measurement, the sensors and web application needed to be utilised in conjunction with the cleaning staffs' knowledge and routines.

The artefacts contained in the application display three sets of data; accumulated motion in each room, a two colour-button signalling if motion has been detected the last 10 min and historical data available for export in the form of graphs. The application was made accessible for the cleaning staff in their day-to-day work by a tablet placed on their cleaning cart.

The system was tested for three weeks, during which the staff had access and utilised it when performing their tasks. Furthermore, they graded the experienced cleaning need which was defined on a three-grade scale where one was clean, two was normal and three related to a high cleaning need. Interviews with the staff were conducted before, during and after the test period. During this period, we also tested the hypothesis that an increased motion value from a classroom during the weekend represents a higher cleaning need. This hypothesis was tested by photographing every aspect related to the sub-processes of the cleaning process chain after the weekends, comparing the empirical findings with motion data captured by the sensors.

Effects

The implemented system had various effects on the organisation depending on which process chain it supported, but how well it improves the general organisational performance remains inconclusive and needs to be evaluated further. Although the system generated the motion data we presumed when designing and implementing the system, the usability of this data in the context of the first process chain, determining the cleaning need of a specific classroom, is still unclear. The system was designed to have mainly informational effects on the first process chain, by presenting information to the staff which could be used to determine which classrooms that had a more significant cleaning need. The empirical findings, however, related to the hypothesis that higher motion value represents a higher cleaning need are vague. We believe that further evaluation of the system is necessary to establish its effects.

The effects on the second process chain, which was to inform the staff if a classroom is vacant and possible to clean, has mainly been of informational and automational character, with the intended ability successfully generated. According to the staff, the system correctly identifies if a classroom is vacant or if there are students present, which informs them in a way that improves their performance. Since they do not have to spend time collecting this information manually, it has automated the process chain. The long-term effects of having this ability, its possible flaws (no motion input if students are very still) and how great of a value it brings to the organisation, due to it solving a relatively minor problem, will have to be further evaluated.

The system has generated the desired ability to analyse and compare between the booked hours in the electronic booking schedule and the actual amount of activity in the classrooms, which would classify it as having a transformational effect on the organisation's ability to innovate. This ability may contribute to having informational effects which improve performance, depending on how generated data is utilised. The organisation has expressed an ambition to integrate the graphs, and sensor data with the current electronic booking schedule to easier compare the data, but this feature has yet to be implemented.

5 Discussion

To provide actionable guidance for the use of IoT sensors to innovate processes through digital service design, we have illustrated the applicability of a synthesised framework facilitating opportunity recognition, design and analysis of effects. The analysis provides insight both to the general applicability of the framework across the innovation process, and the bearing of specific components of the framework for IoT sensors.

Although developed for different tasks, our application of the framework suggests that it is beneficial to apply the whole chain of analysis in the different subparts of the innovation process. While the business value of IT provides support for retrospective analysis of effects (Stenmark and Jadaan 2010; Visich et al. 2009), the desired outcomes in terms of informational, automational and transformational effects should guide the design of the digital service system. Thus, in accordance with Alters (2006) arguments regarding a holistic view in systems design, such ambitions need to be considered in the initial analysis phase. By establishing information requirements for a process chain or specific sub-processes during this phase, potential complexities related to generating the desired effects can be discovered, e.g. processes with a high level of equivocality. With a desirable effect-outcome and the information requirements necessary for generating this outcome established, we argue that this provides a more well-grounded basis for process innovation with sensors.

For sensor-based process innovation, the process information requirements in part determine the degree of automational effect that can be achieved. A process with the purpose of simply collecting or communicating one type of data may be automated in its entirety through implementing a sensor-based system. Automational effects of this kind are shown in the swimming pool case where the process chain of documenting pool water quality has the potential of being automated completely by the utilisation of sensor-based systems. This high degree of automational effects arises from alignment between information needed to complete the task and sensor capacity to produce data output. This outcome differs from a process with high equivocal information requirements, such as the process of evaluating the cleaning need where there are four sub-processes to complete the process chain. Each sub-process requires information with regards to its specific cleaning need, and the sum of the informational output from these sub-processes are then what constitutes the cleaning need of the classroom. The sensor used to support this process chain provides information of movement around the entrance to the classroom. This information of movement does not map precisely to any of the sub-process outputs of assessing a cleaning need. For example, to assess if a whiteboard needs cleaning there is a requirement of visual examination of the whiteboard and from this draw a conclusion regarding its need for cleaning. Information of movement is only a proxy variable that does not directly respond to use of the whiteboard. Similarly, to assess if the floor needs mopping, information is required on the amount of dust and dirt that is currently present on its surface. Again, the type of information provided by the sensor used does not immediately support an assessment of mopping need.

The sensor-produced data may be used to make assumptions of cleaning need based on the information of activity around the sensor, without showing a one to one relationship between the amount of movement and the equivocal cleaning need. For instance, while movement information does not show how dusty or dirty the floor is, it shows the cause of this effect: people have walked on the floor. Any value of activity data means that the floor has been walked upon. If the floor has been walked upon, it is reasonable to assume that some amount of dirt and dust have been transferred from the shoes to the surface of the floor. Thus, a value of activity data increases the need of mopping the floor.

This reasoning may be used on the other sub-processes of the cleaning case as well, though with a weaker conclusion. We have argued that movement information show a relationship with the degree of dirt on the floors. However, movement information is not directly correlated with the use of whiteboards. Recorded activity data means that there has been a person around the entrance of the classroom. It does, however, not capture the type of activity the person has engaged in, e.g. if they used the whiteboards. Similarly, the data does not show if the person(s) moving close to the classroom entrance also throw waste into the waste bin. The IoT sensor capabilities do not address these equivocal information requirements directly. Thus, conclusions regarding the cleaning need of these processes cannot be drawn solely from the information provided by the sensor. Movement information may, however, be used in conjunction with visual evaluation of the state of classrooms over time to show statistical probabilities of whiteboard cleaning need, waste bin level and table dirt. Cleaning staff collected this data during the testing phase of the cleaning case by grading the classrooms total cleaning need in conjunction with them cleaning it. This method of evaluation could be improved by splitting it into an evaluation of each sub-process, thus increasing its accuracy. There are degrees to this relationship between process information requirements and sensor data output. This relationship spans from misaligned, exemplified by assessing cleaning need of whiteboards with movement sensors, to aligned, as shown by addressing temperature requirements with a temperature sensor. Thus, we argue that IoT sensors could be implemented to processes with various degrees of success depending on the process equivocality information requirements (Table 4).

Table 4. General descriptions of IoT capabilities addressing information requirements.

High connectivity *Reach*	IoT-sensors by nature increases reach due to many individual data collection points that are accessible over organisational borders
High uncertainty *Production*	IoT-sensors can continuously produce data outside human intervention, day as night
High equivocality *Relation*	IoT-sensors can supply relations, however, important to match sensor capabilities with the process information requirements
Low connectivity *Richness*	IoT-sensors add richness and granularity due to continuous, focused data collection
Low uncertainty *Consumption*	IoT-sensors do not directly address consumption, but through data-analysis and visualisation of sensor-data consumption can be addressed
Low equivocality *Encounter*	IoT-sensors can fortify encounters through stabile data collection that supports codified knowledge and routine-based tasks

6 Conclusion

In this paper, we provide a synthesised framework for IoT sensor-based process innovation. The framework draws on extant theory on (1) the role of information requirements analysis in identification of IT-based process innovation opportunities and (2) effects on business value. The synthetisation of these theoretical devices enables a holistic analysis, from opportunity recognition to evaluation of achieved effects. We have explored the practical usability of the framework through an analysis of two different implementations of IoT systems and associated organisational effects. We found areas where the sensors have shown potential for process innovation and demonstrated the applicability of an information requirements perspective in an IoT context. Through this we have been able to identify areas where complexity becomes an issue for implementation of IoT systems. In particular, the results point to IoT sensors general capacity for responding to high connectivity and uncertainty requirements, and the need for aligning functionality with organisational needs to respond to high equivocality requirements. Thus, the functionality provided by IoT sensors does not reduce the importance of organisational ability for process analysis and identification of values to measure. We also identify the effects and relate them to levels of alignment between information requirements in the process and sensor capacity. Lastly, we have argued for a need to understand IoT through a micro-level perspective in organisational processes and proposed a set of practices for overcoming challenges encountered in the cases. As the field continues to grow we believe it is essential for organisations to further understand how to utilise IoT-technology when innovating their work processes.

References

Alter, S.: The Work System Method, 1st edn. Work System Press, Larkspur (2006)

Davenport, T.H.: Process Innovation - Reengineering Work Through Information Technology, 1st edn. Harvard Business School Press, Boston (1993)

Insight, F.: Internet of Things - From Theory to Reality. Forbes Insight, Jersey City (2017)

Haller, S., Karnouskos, S., Schroth, C.: The Internet of Things in an Enterprise Context. Springer, Vienna (2008). https://doi.org/10.1007/978-3-642-00985-3_2

LoRa-alliance: LoRaWAN - What is it? A technical overview of LoRa and LoRaWAN, San Ramon, CA: LoRa® Alliance Technical Marketing Workgroup (2015)

Malhotra, A., Gosain, S., Sawy, O.: Absorptive capacity configurations in supply chains: gearing for partner-enabled market knowledge creation. MIS Q. **29**, 145–187 (2005). https://doi.org/10.2307/25148671

Mathiassen, L., Sørensen, C.: Towards a theory of organizational information services. J. Inf. Technol. **23**, 313–329 (2008). https://doi.org/10.1057/jit.2008.10

Meyer, S., Ruppen, A., Magerkurth, C.: Internet of Things-Aware Process Modeling: Integrating IoT Devices as Business Process Resources. Springer, Valencia (2013). https://doi.org/10.1007/978-3-642-38709-8_6

Mooney, J.G.: A Process Oriented Framework for Assessing the Business Value of Information Technology. Center for Research in Information Technology and Organizations, University of California, Irvine (1995)

Ramaprasad, A., Rai, A.: Envisioning management of information. Omega. **24**, 179–193 (1996). https://doi.org/10.1016/0305-0483(95)00061-5

Ray, G., Barney, J., Muhanna, W.: Capabilities, business processes, and competitive advantage: choosing the dependent variable in empirical tests of the resource-based view. Strateg. Manag. J. **25**, 23–37 (2004). https://doi.org/10.1002/smj.366

Sandberg, J., Mathiassen, L., Napier, N.: Digital options theory for IT capability investement. J. Assoc. Inf. Syst. **15**(7), 422–453 (2014)

Statista: Statista - The statistics portal (2017) https://www.statista.com/statistics/512673/worldwide-internet-of-things-market/. Använd 13 March 2018

Stenmark, D., Jadaan, T.: Enabling process innovation through sensor technology: a multiple case study of RFID deployment. In: ECIS 2010 Proceedings, Gothenburg (2010)

Sundmaeker, H., Guillemin, P., Friess, P., Woellflé, S.: Vision and Challenges for Realising the Internet of Things. Publications Office of the European Union, Luxemburg (2010)

Visich, J.K., Li, S., Khumawala, B.M., Reyes, P.M.: Empirical evidence of RFID impacts on supply chain performance. Int. J. Oper. Prod. Manag. **29**(12), 1290–1315 (2009)

Wortmann, F., Flüchter, K.: Internet of things - technology and value added. Bus. Inf. Syst. Eng. **57**(3), 221–224 (2015)

Yin, R.: Case Study Research, 3rd edn. SAGE Publications, Thousand Oaks (2003)

An Internet of Things Based Platform for Real-Time Management of Energy Consumption in Water Resource Recovery Facilities

Mário Nunes[1], Rita Alves[2], Augusto Casaca[1](✉), Pedro Póvoa[2], and José Botelho[2]

[1] INOV/INESC-ID, R. Alves Redol, 1000-029 Lisbon, Portugal
mario.nunes@inov.pt, augusto.casaca@inesc-id.pt
[2] Águas do Tejo Atlântico, Fábrica de Água de Alcântara, Av. de Ceuta, 1300-254 Lisbon, Portugal
{rita.alves,p.povoa,j.botelho}@adp.pt

Abstract. The article describes the design of an Internet of Things based platform having as main objective the real-time management of energy consumption in water resource recovery facilities and their integration in a future demand side management environment. The monitoring of several electrical parameters, including energy consumption, is done via a dedicated energy meter, whose design is detailed in the article. The high level data communication from the energy meters to a central platform of the wastewater utility is done via the MQTT protocol. Within the water resource recovery facility, the access network is based either on Wi-Fi or LoRa, which are two enabling technologies for the Internet of Things. The meters are deployed in pilot demonstrators located in two water resource recovery facilities in Lisbon, Portugal.

Keywords: Wastewater management · Internet of Things · Smart cities · Energy meters

1 Introduction

The Internet of Things (IoT) is the support for a large number of applications. Many of these applications are fundamental for implementing the concept of smart cities, namely in domains like e-health, smart buildings, transportation systems, energy grids and wastewater management. In this paper we focus into a smart wastewater management application, supported in an IoT infrastructure, having in view the real-time control of energy consumption in Water Resource Recovery Facilities (WRRF) of a Portuguese Wastewater Utility.

Energy is often the second-highest operating cost at WRRF after the labor cost; it can be above 50% of an utility′s total operating costs [1]. The reason for this is that

L. Strous and V. G. Cerf (Eds.): IFIPIoT 2018, IFIP AICT 548, pp. 121–132, 2019.
https://doi.org/10.1007/978-3-030-15651-0_11

most of the processes that occur in WRRF require energy for their operation and are intensive energy consumers. Also, when the drainage system is not gravitational, energy is required for operating pumping stations. In Portugal, the Águas de Portugal (AdP) Group, which is the utility in charge of water distribution and wastewater treatment plants in Portugal, represents about 1.4% of the total electrical consumption of the country and the energy cost represents 60% of the operating costs of AdP.

On the other hand, nowadays, new challenges appear due to the limited water and nutrient resources, to the existence of the circular economy framework and to climate changes concerns associated with the fossil fuel consumption; additionally there is an increasing cost of energy for the utility. In this context, a new paradigm for the use of the domestic wastewater was created. Domestic wastewater is being looked more as a resource than a waste and the wastewater treatment plants now are known as WRRF, where it is possible to recover nutrients and water to achieve a more sustainable use of the wastewater energy potential, and become a driver for the circular economy [2].

Águas do Tejo Atlântico (AdTA), which is one of the companies of the AdP group, is in charge of the wastewater treatment in the Lisbon region and in the west region of Portugal. AdTA is a consortium member of the running European Union H2020 research project "Intelligent Grid Technologies for Renewables Integration and Interactive Consumer Participation Enabling Interoperable Market Solutions and Interconnected Stakeholders", which has the acronym INTEGRID. The main objectives of INTEGRID are to test the flexibility of electrical energy consumption for domestic and industrial consumers, to test energy storage systems and make forecasts of renewable energy production and consumption. The main role of AdTA in this project is to manage the flexibility of its internal processes in order to minimize the energy costs according to the market and to the requirements of the grid operators, leading to an optimization of the AdTA internal processes.

The AdTA focus on the flexibility of energy consumption and in the new challenges of turning a wastewater treatment plant into a WRRF is an important path towards its objective of achieving operational optimization and flexibility of processes. To optimize and make processes more flexible it is essential to know the performance of the processes. Thus, one of the variables to monitor is the energy consumption of the process or equipment. This paper is related with the specific work done for real-time monitoring of the electrical energy consumption in WRRF. It is being developed by AdTA, within the INTEGRID project, in collaboration with INOV, a Portuguese research institute.

The objective of this collaboration is to design and implement a low cost smart energy meter capable of being integrated in an Internet of Things (IoT) environment. The meter will periodically measure electrical energy consumption and several other electrical parameters, and will communicate those measurements to a central system and a database. The meter has a bi-directional communication with the central system, being allowed a remote control of the meter, namely for altering the configuration parameters. The meter is equipped with a state of the art communication technology compatible with the IoT communication protocols. Low cost for the meter is a must, as a large number of meters will be required for the complete universe of WRRF. Pilot demonstrators are being deployed in two WRRF in Lisbon, Portugal. The demonstrators have a total of 30 energy meters, and two different IoT communication technologies were chosen to be tested in the two pilots. Each of the pilots also follows an IoT deployment framework with respect, not only to the communication protocols, but also to the used platforms.

The article is organized as follows. In Sect. 2 related work is reviewed, and in Sect. 3 the communication architecture is presented. Section 4 deals with the meter structure. The pilot deployment is treated in Sect. 5 and the last section concludes the paper.

2 Related Work

In the context of the ability to collect, transmit and process data, with a view to make the most of the collected information by transforming it into knowledge, there was a need at AdTA to implement systematic and integrated approaches, i.e., the implementation of decision support tools. Thus, the AQUASAFE platform was developed at AdTA [3], integrating data already existing in the company, in order to produce answers to the specific needs of the operation and management. The AQUASAFE platform is a structure that allows managing all the information flows necessary to obtain an adequate response in the context of the management problems (overflows, energy management, emergency response, etc.). The measured data, mainly from water flows, is imported in real-time and the models run periodically in the forecast mode in simulation scenarios chosen by the user. The AQUASAFE platform is in full use in AdTA nowadays.

With regard to energy use, energy systems are sensitive to energy consumption spikes and, therefore, measurements have to be taken, either to optimize energy generation and distribution or better to reduce or shift peak power demands. While there is plenty of experience in optimizing energy generation and distribution, it is the demand side management that is receiving increasing attention by research and industry [4]. Thus far, there still exists a gap between energy consumption and costs since there is no generalized cost model describing current energy tariff structures to evaluate operating costs at WRRF [5]. In most energy studies, the energy consumption is multiplied by an average energy price. However, operating costs significantly depend on the energy tariff structure applied. Different time-of-use and/or peak penalty charges may change the cost efficiency of a control solution completely [6].

For the first time, an application of a real energy pricing structure was applied to a calibrated model for evaluating operational strategies in two large WRRF, in the context of the Portuguese "SmartWater4Energy" project [7]. The importance and need of mathematical modelling for energy optimization of specific energy costs at real WRRF processes was assessed. Time periods with potential for further optimization were identified, supporting a smart grid basis in terms of water and energy markets that respond to the demands [6]. This work was developed in the AQUASAFE platform, where the different models and the data from different sensors (flow, energy consumption, dissolved oxygen concentration, NO3 concentration, etc.) were included for calibrating and evaluating the models. However, in the AQUASAFE platform, the energy consumption measurements are done in an indirect way, through the SCADA system.

There is, however, a need to have accurate measurements on the energy consumption and other electrical parameters in real-time for all the WRRFs. Also, those measurements need to be communicated to a central platform with analytical capability, which allows extracting information from the data being measured. Based on the analytical studies performed at the platform it will be possible to devise a strategy for shifting peak loads and reducing energy consumption on the whole. These are the main reasons that originated the current developments described in this paper.

On what concerns the development of dedicated energy meters to measure several electrical parameters like current, voltage and power in real-time, and adapted for wireless sensor network communications, there is previous work already done for the smart grid environment [8, 9]. In the present case, the energy meters will be different from those ones as they must have the following distinctive characteristics: (i) to be adapted to the constraints of a WRRF deployment; (ii) to measure the parameters required in WRRF; (iii) to comply with the IoT communications paradigm and platform architecture, which is the state of the art for smart cities deployment; (iv) to be low cost.

3 Communication Architecture

The basic design idea for the communication architecture is to consider each meter, and the respective equipment to which it is connected, as a "thing" in an IoT context and collect the information from all the "things" in a central platform of AdTA, where the data can be stored in a database and data analytics be performed. Secure communication is a must and for that purpose we have available the AdTA private communication network that provides a security guarantee for the wide area communication.

The first decision to be taken was concerned with the IoT communication protocol (s) to use. From the universe of IoT communication protocols [10], we have considered that Wi-Fi and LoRa are two appropriate standard communication technologies for use in this solution and, therefore, in the pilot demonstrators. Wi-Fi is a well - known technology, having low cost communication modules for the meters, a low cost Access Point (AP), and high data rates (Mbps). As low cost is a key objective, the choice of Wi-Fi as one of the candidate technologies looked promising.

LoRa was the second candidate technology selected for the tests. LoRa is the physical layer containing the wireless modulation utilized to create a long range communication link. The complete stack of protocols used over LoRa is known as LoRaWAN. Compared to Wi-Fi, LoRa is a higher cost technology, namely for the LoRaWAN gateway, and has lower data rates (Kbps). However, it enables a longer communication distance than Wi-Fi, which is very useful for the communication between some remote equipment in the WRRF and the LoRaWAN gateway. The decision for the pilot demonstrations was to test both technologies, Wi-Fi in one WRRF (Chelas WRRF) and LoRa in the second one (Beirolas WRRF).

As it is required to transmit the data from the meters to the Control Centre, we had to establish a communication architecture that allows a seamless and secure transmission. The chosen architecture is shown in Fig. 1 for the Wi-Fi access case.

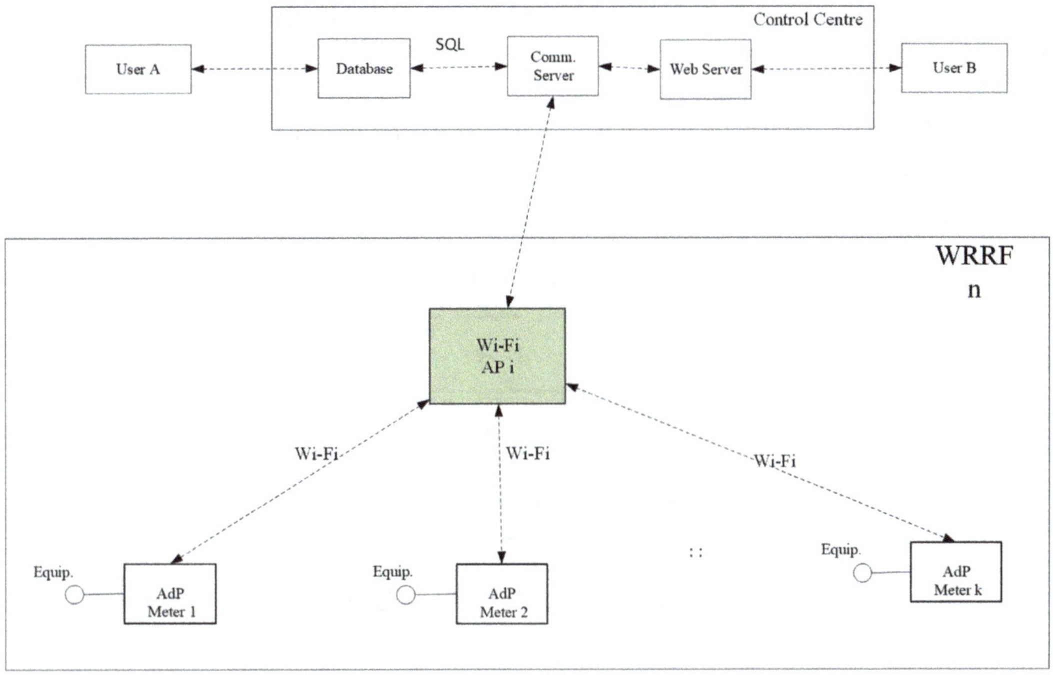

Fig. 1. System communication architecture based on Wi-Fi access

There might be several Wi-Fi APs installed in a WRRF. The WRRF energy meters, from now on called AdP meters, are deployed at the different WRRF equipments, e.g., recirculating pumps, equalization pumps, ventilators, etc. The meters communicate to the nearest Wi-Fi AP, sending a message containing the meter identification, followed by the electrical measurements. The data is forwarded from the Wi-Fi AP to the Communication Server (CS) located at the Control Centre via the AdTA private communication network. The CS will upload the data into the database, by means of the SQL protocol. The users can access the data either via a direct connection to the database or indirectly through a Web server.

Figure 2 shows a simplified protocol stack of the Wi-Fi based access network. A conventional TCP/IP stack of protocols is used over the Wi-Fi Medium Access Control (MAC) and Physical (PHY) layers. The Network server is implemented as one of the components of the CS in the Control Centre. The Wi-Fi AP converts Wi-Fi into Ethernet and communicates with the CS via the AdTA private wide area network.

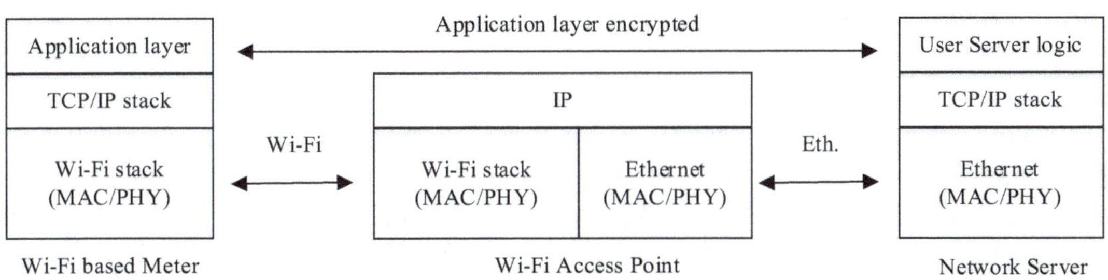

Fig. 2. Protocol stack of the Wi-Fi based access network

For LoRa, the system communication architecture is similar to the one shown in Fig. 1, having as main difference the use of a LoRaWAN Gateway instead of the Wi-Fi AP.

Figure 3 shows the protocol stack of LoRaWAN, which comprises 4 layers: RF layer, Physical layer, MAC layer and Application layer.

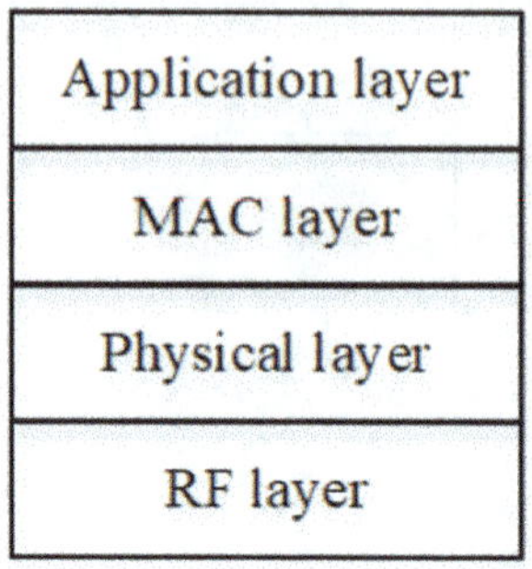

Fig. 3. LoRaWAN protocol layers

The RF layer defines the radio frequency bands that could be used in LoRa, namely for Europe and USA. We adopted the 868 MHz band available for Industry, Scientific and Medical (ISM) applications in Europe.

The LoRa physical layer implements a derivative of the Chirp Spread Spectrum (CSS) scheme. CSS was first developed in 1951 at Bell Telephone Laboratories for the military radars. It aimed to offer the same efficiency in range, resolution and speed of acquisition, but without the high peak power of the traditional short pulse mechanism. The MAC layer defines 3 classes of end nodes, respectively Class A, B and C. In this project we use only Class A, since it is the most energy efficient and the only one that is mandatory. To achieve this high energy efficiency, the nodes in this class are 99% of the time not active (neither transmitting nor receiving) and are only ready to receive immediately after transmitting a message. The Application layer is related with the user application layer.

As LoRa is a communication technology dealing with many connected nodes, it needs a robust end-to-end security. LoRa achieves this by implementing security at two different levels: the first one at the network level and a second one at the application level. Network security ensures authenticity of the node in the network and application security ensures that the operator has not access to the end user's application data.

The basic components of the LoRaWAN architecture are the following: nodes, gateways and network server. The nodes are the elements of the LoRa network where the sensing or control is undertaken. The gateway receives the data from the LoRa nodes and then transfers them into the backhaul system. The gateways are connected to the network server using standard IP connections. On this way the data communication uses a standard protocol, but any other communication network, either public or private, can be used. The LoRa network server manages the network, acting to eliminate duplicate packets, scheduling acknowledgements, and adapting data rates. The network server is also included in the CS, as it happened in the Wi-Fi solution. Figure 4 shows a simplified protocol stack of the three components interconnected.

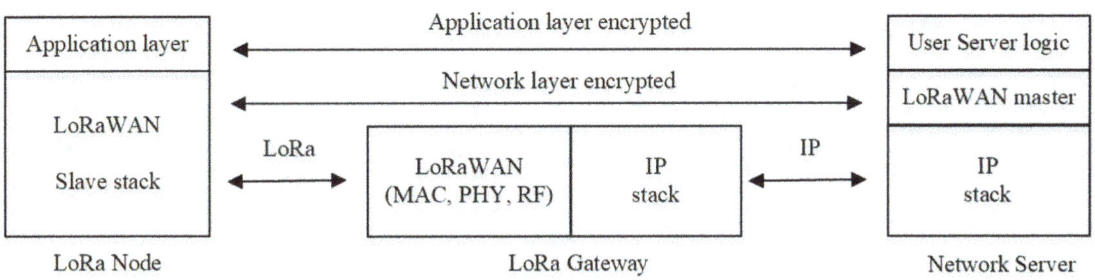

Fig. 4. Protocol stack of the LoRa based access network

The high level communication between the AdP meter and the CS (see Fig. 1) uses the Message Queuing Telemetry Transport (MQTT) protocol. MQTT is an IoT connectivity protocol. It was designed as a lightweight broker-based publish/subscribe messaging protocol, which is open, simple, lightweight and easy to implement. These characteristics make it ideal for use in constrained environments, for example, where the network has low bandwidth or is unreliable, as is the case of wireless sensor communications, or when run on an embedded device with limited processor or memory resources, as is the case of the AdP meters.

The AdP meter contains a MQTT client and the CS a MQTT Server or Broker. Periodically, e.g., every 5 min, the meter sends a MQTT Publish message to the MQTT Broker, located in the CS, with the following structure: Meter ID, Voltage, Current, Power, Power Factor, Energy, Service Time, Timestamp. For configuration of the different parameters in the AdP Meter the MQTT Server uses Subscribe messages with different topics, namely: Change of the measurement period, Change of the communication parameters (specific of Wi-Fi or LoRA), Set date/time, Set the initial value of the energy counter, Set current transformer ratio, Set Power Threshold (defines the power threshold to consider the equipment is in service), Set Meter mode (tri-phasic or 3 x mono-phasic).

In the MQTT architecture the elements that generate information are called Publishers and the elements that receive information are called Subscribers. The Publishers and Subscribers are interconnected through the MQTT Broker, as shown in Fig. 5.

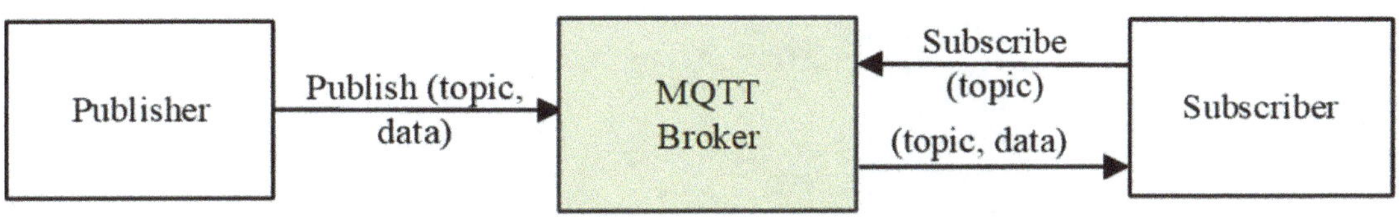

Fig. 5. MQTT communication architecture

The CS transmits the received information to the database by using the Structured Query Language (SQL). In the CS a software module converts the received messages coming from the Wi-Fi or LoRa based meter to a SQL message and transmits it to the database.

4 The AdP Meter

The AdP meter was designed to allow the monitoring, not only from energy consumption, but also of other electrical parameters like current, voltage, power and power factor. The AdP meter has the electrical interfaces shown in Fig. 6, and can be connected to a tri-phase electrical system.

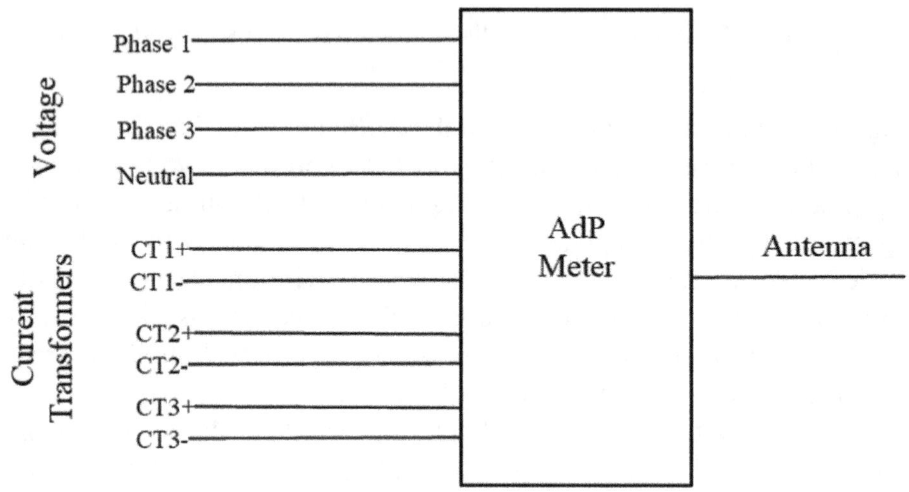

Fig. 6. AdP meter interfaces

There are 4 inputs for the three voltage phases and neutral connection on the top left. On the bottom left, there are 6 inputs for the connection of 3 current transformers, one for each phase. In Fig. 7, we can see the physical layout of the AdP meter, with the Voltage connectors and the antenna connector on the top and the current connectors on the bottom.

Fig. 7. AdP meter prototype

The AdP meter block diagram is shown in Fig. 8 and comprises four main modules: Measurement module, Processing and Communication module, Galvanic Isolation module and AC/DC dual power supply module.

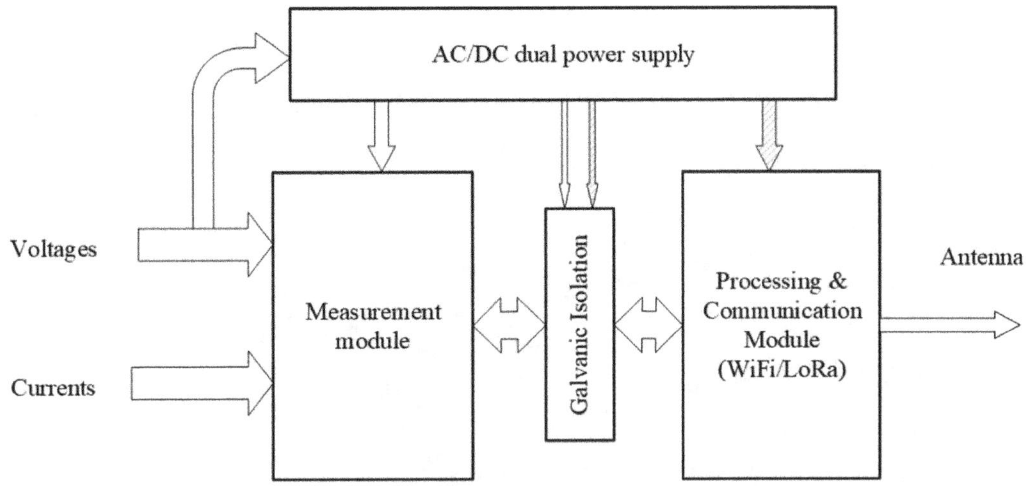

Fig. 8. AdP meter block diagram

The Measurement module and the Processing and Communication module are galvanic isolated for user protection, namely for the antenna connector and antenna cable handling. This requires a dual power supply with one of them connected to the Measurement module and the other to the Processing and Communication module. The Galvanic Isolation module requires to be connected to both.

The power, power factor, energy consumption and service time are calculated internally in the AdP meter from the voltage and current readings. They are transmitted to the CS, via MQTT protocol messages, using the following units for the different parameters: Voltage: 0.1 V, Current: 0.1 A, Power: Watt, Power Factor: 0–100 (100 correspond to PF = 1), Energy: 0.1 kWh (accumulated value), Service Time: minutes (accumulated value), Time Stamp: seconds.

5 Deployment

The meters are being tested in two large WRRF in the Lisbon area, named Chelas and Beirolas. Meters with the Wi-Fi module are installed in Chelas, while meters with the LoRa module are installed in Beirolas. The first objective is to test both communication technologies in order to make an evaluation of their strong and weak aspects, from the technical and economic points of view. The second objective is that AdTA is able to perform demand side management operations. By having the knowledge on the real-time energy consumption and on the values of other electrical parameters, in a demand management situation, AdTA will be able to shift loads in a controlled way so that the impact is minimized in the WRRF.

The Chelas WRRF covers an area of around 37,500 m2 (250 m × 150 m) in a central area of Lisbon. Figure 9 shows the plant of the Chelas WRRF where Pi signals the points where the meters equipped with Wi-Fi are located. There are two meters in each Pi. The meters are connected to different WRRF equipment, such as pumps and ventilators. The total number of Wi-Fi APs to be deployed depends on the result of the on-going communication tests.

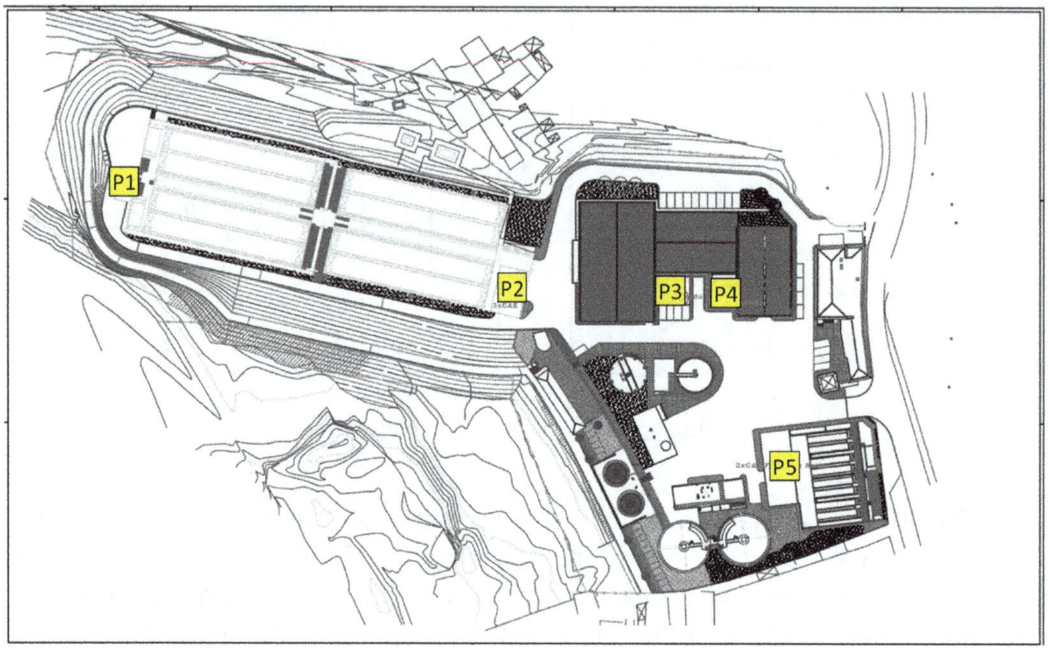

Fig. 9. Chelas WRRF

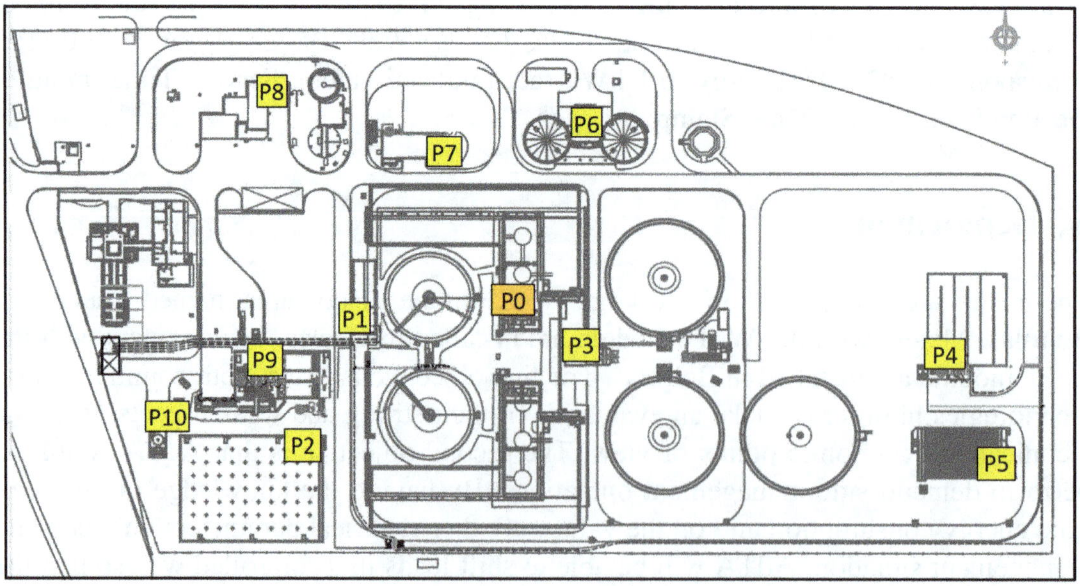

Fig. 10. Beirolas WRRF

The Beirolas WRRF covers a larger area of around 100,000 m2 (400 m × 250 m) in Lisbon. Figure 10 shows the plant of the Beirolas WRRF where Pi are the points where the LoRA meters are located. There are also two meters located in each Pi. P0 is the location of the LoRa gateway and antenna. The communication tests have already been performed and have validated this configuration with a single LoRa gateway.

6 Conclusion

An IoT based platform for real-time management of energy consumption in WRRF was presented. The developed work included the design and implementation of the adequate meters for measuring different electrical parameters (including energy consumption), the deployment of those meters in two WRRFs in the Lisbon area, the economical and performance analysis of two IoT communication protocols (Wi-Fi and LoRa) for access networks in the WRRF and the transmission of the data from either Wi-Fi APs or LoRa gateway to a central platform and database, where data analytics will be performed.

The objective of the pilots is, in first place, to decide on the communication technology to be used, when a more extended deployment of the system is done for other WRRF. The second objective is to be able to do demand side management operations, having in view the shifting of loads from peak load situations so that a better balance of the energy consumption can be achieved.

This work has to do with the so-called smart wastewater management, which is an important component of the smart city concept. It is worthwhile noticing too, that the project uses IoT technologies and architecture, which makes it up to date with the status of communications and platforms in smart cities. The future work includes the running of the platforms, extraction of the meter data and performance of data analytics on those data, so that guidelines can be designed for the extension of the platform to other WRRF.

Acknowledgment. The research leading to this work is being carried out as a part of the InteGrid project (Demonstration of INTElligent grid technologies for renewables INTEgration and INTEractive consumer participation enabling INTEroperable market solutions and INTErconnected stakeholders), which received funding from the European Union's Horizon 2020 Framework Programme for Research and Innovation under grant agreement No. 731218. The sole responsibility for the content of this publication lies with the authors.

References

1. United States Environmental Protection Agency, Energy efficiency for water and wastewater utilities (2015). https://www.epa.gov/sustainable-water-infrastructure/water-and-energy-efficiency-utilities-and-home
2. International Water Association, Water Utility Pathways in a Circular Economy (2016). http://www.iwa-network.org/wp-content/uploads/2016/07/IWA_Circular_Economy_screen.pdf

3. AQUASAFE: an R&D complement to Bonn Network tools to support water safety plans implementation, exploitation and training, IWA Newsletter, vol. 1, no. 3 (2009)
4. Palensky, P., Dietrich, D.: Demand side management: demand response, intelligent energy systems, and smart loads. IEEE Trans. Ind. Inform. **7**(3), 381–388 (2011)
5. Aymerich, I., Rieger, L., Sobhani, D., Rosso, D., Corominas, L.: The difference between energy consumption and energy cost: modelling energy tariff structures for water resource recovery facilities. Water Res. **81**, 113–123 (2015). https://www.sciencedirect.com/science/article/pii/S0043135415002705
6. Póvoa, P., Oehmen, A., Inocêncio, P., Matos, J.S., Frazão, A.: Modelling energy costs for different operational strategies of a large water resource recovery facility. Water Sci. Technol. (2017). https://doi.org/10.2166/wst.2017.089
7. SmartWater4Energy project (2015). http://smartwater4energy.hidromod.pt/
8. Grilo, A., Casaca, A., Nunes, M., Bernardo, A., Rodrigues, P., Almeida, J.: A management system for low voltage grids. In: Proceedings of the 12th IEEE PES PowerTech Conference, (PowerTech 2017), Manchester, United Kingdom, June 2017
9. Silva, N., et al.: Fault detection and location in low voltage grids based on distributed monitoring. In: Proceedings of the IEEE International Energy Conference (ENERGYCON 2016) Conference, Leuven, Belgium, April 2016
10. Keysight Technologies, The Internet of Things: Enabling technologies and solutions for design and test (2017). https://literature.cdn.keysight.com/litweb/pdf/5992-1175EN.pdf?id=2666018

A New Reconfigurable Architecture with Applications to IoT and Mobile Computing

Amir Masoud Gharehbaghi(✉), Tomohiro Maruoka, and Masahiro Fujita

The University of Tokyo, Tokyo, Japan
{amir,maruoka}@cad.t.u-tokyo.ac.jp, fujita@ee.t.u-tokyo.ac.jp

Abstract. Traditional reconfigurable devices known as FPGAs utilize a complicated programmable routing network to provide flexibility in connecting different logic elements across the FPGA chip. As such, the routing procedure may become very complicated, especially in the presence of tight timing constraints. Moreover, the routing network itself occupies a large portion of chip area as well as consumes a lot of power. Therefore, limiting their usage in mobile applications or IoT devices with higher performance and lower energy demands. In this paper, we introduce a new reconfigurable architecture which only allows communication between neighboring logic elements. This way, the routing structure and the routing resources become much simpler than traditional FPGAs. Moreover, we present two different method for scheduling and routing in our new proposed architecture. The first method deals with general circuits or irregular computations and is based on integer linear programming. The second method is for regular computations such as convolutional neural networks or matrix operations. We have shown the mapping results on ISCAS benchmark circuits as general irregular computations as well as heuristics to improve the efficiency of mapping for larger benchmarks. Moreover, we have shown results on regular computations including matrix multiplication and convolution operations of neural networks.

Keywords: Reconfigurable architecture · Placement and routing · FPGA · Mobile computing · IoT · Convolutional neural network

1 Introduction

Recently, with the advances in internet of things (IoT) technology as well as the increase in the computing power of mobile devices, there is a growing interest in performing different computational tasks on IoT or mobile platforms, especially for edge computing solutions.

In the edge computing paradigm, it is essential to reduce the amount of data that is transferred between IoT nodes and the servers. Therefore, the IoT nodes or mobile devices require to perform more computation tasks. This way, the

L. Strous and V. G. Cerf (Eds.): IFIPIoT 2018, IFIP AICT 548, pp. 133–146, 2019.
https://doi.org/10.1007/978-3-030-15651-0_12

communication bottleneck due to data transfer bandwidth or communication latency is avoided.

Programmable hardware devices, such as Field Programmable Gate Arrays (FPGAs), have shown to be superior in term of performance as well as energy efficiency for different computation tasks compared to using CPUs or GPUs [1–5]. Consequently, very promising to be used in IoT or mobile platforms. Another category of programmable devices is Coarse Grain Reconfigurable Architecture (CGRA). CGRAs usually provide a less complicated and more regular communication among the processing elements or the processor cores compared to FPGAs to enable acceleration of applications [6–9].

In this work, we have proposed a new reconfigurable hardware architecture suitable for IoT or mobile platforms with the following characteristics.

1. Traditional FPGA devices have a complicated routing architecture to provide flexibility in connecting internal logic blocks together. Consequently, mapping an application to an FPGA device may become very difficult when the utilization of internal blocks is high, or the timing constraints are very tight and hard to achieve. Therefore, we have proposed an architecture which provides connectivity only to neighbors employing a mesh topology, similar to CGRAs; consequently, simplifying the routing architecture as well as the routing method greatly.
2. In the traditional FPGA devices, the routing network, because of its complexity, occupies a large portion of the chip area; consequently, increasing the power consumption. However, in our proposed architecture, because of connectivity to only neighbors, the routing network is greatly simplified, reducing its size as well as the power consumption.
3. Traditional FPGA devices are very fine grained, meaning that the basic functional blocks can only implement basic logic functions. However, in our architecture, the basic functional blocks may be more complicated, for example ALUs or more complicated processing elements. However, unlike CGRAs the functional blocks are not very coarse grained.

In addition to the new proposed architecture, we have provided a scheduling and routing algorithm using integer linear programming (ILP). Starting from a data-flow graph model of the application, ILP formulation results in efficient mapping of the application to our proposed architecture, as well as the optimum latency for executing the application. Moreover, we have introduced heuristics to improve the efficiency of the routing method for larger circuits.

The proposed mapping method is general and may be used for random logic or irregular computations as well as regular computations such as operations on a matrix or convolution operations in neural networks. However, for regular computations there is a more efficient way that is scalable to even very large problems that employs the inherent regularity of the operations. Our proposed mapping method for large regular computations is based on automatic mapping for the small instances of the problem, and induction-based generalization for larger problem.

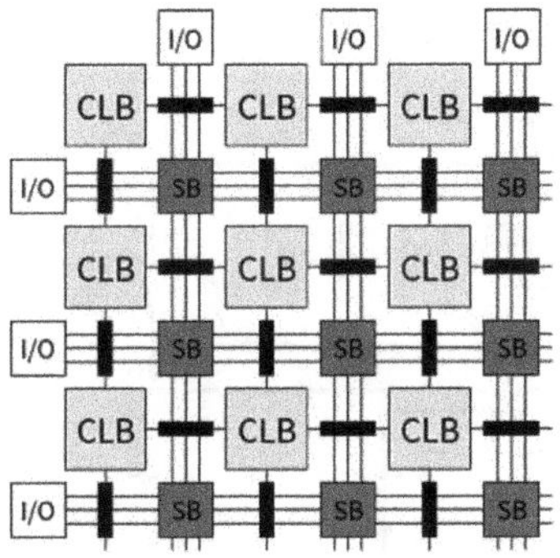

Fig. 1. Traditional FPGA architecture

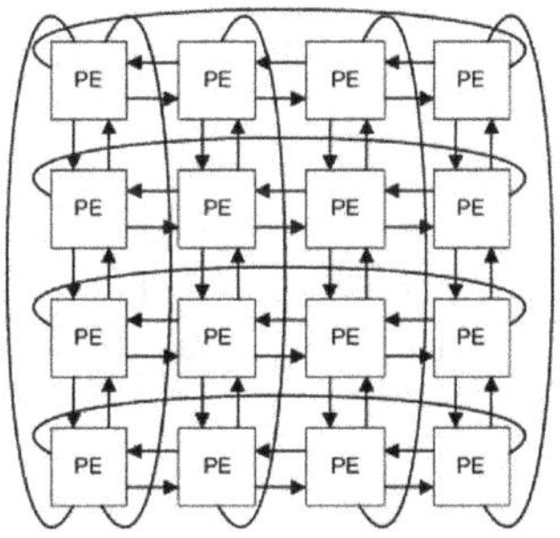

Fig. 2. Traditional CGRA architecture

Please note that because of our simpler and more regular routing architecture compared to traditional FPGA devices, it is possible to achieve very deep pipelining with higher clock frequency, consequently improving the performance of the computation on our proposed architecture.

The rest of the paper is organized as follows. Section 2 gives a background on reconfigurable devices and ILP. Section 3 presents our proposed hardware architecture. Section 4 presents our scheduling and routing (mapping) method for general circuits or irregular computations. Section 5 presents our method for regular computations. Section 6 shows the experimental results. Section 7 concludes the paper and gives some future directions.

2 Background

2.1 Reconfigurable Hardware

Field-programmable gate array (FPGA) is a semiconductor device with a matrix of programmable logic blocks and a programmable routing network. Figure 1 shows a simple architecture of a FPGA. Configurable logic blocks (CLBs) contain 1 or more lookup-tables (LUT) to implement small logic functions. LUTs may have 4 or more inputs and can implement any logic function of 4 or more inputs. Each CLB may contain 1 or more LUTs. The routing network consists of programmable switch blocks (SB) and a number of links connecting SBs together. By programming SBs, CLBs can be connected together to implement larger logic functions. Moreover, some SBs are connected to input/output (I/O) pins to be able to transfer data between FPGA and the outside world.

Coarse grain reconfigurable architecture (CGRA) is another kind of reconfigurable device, shown in Fig. 2. One main difference between CGRA and FPGA is the communication network. CGRAs usually use 2-D mesh or torus network. Moreover, the processing elements of CGRA are processor cores or some complicated processing units, providing coarse grained parallelization of operations or tasks.

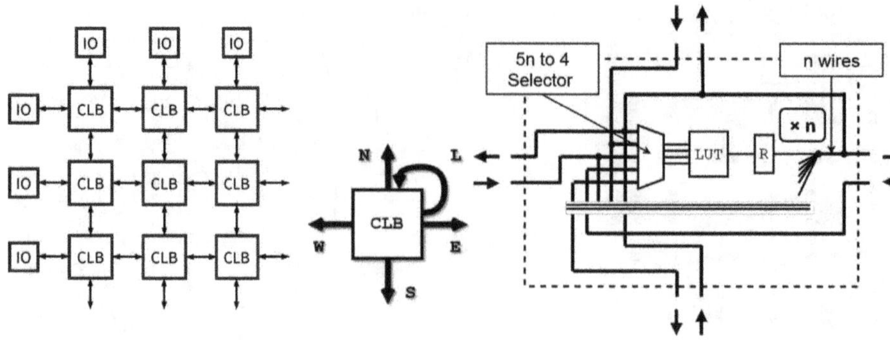

Fig. 3. Proposed architecture

2.2 ILP

Integer linear programming (ILP) is an optimization method that tries to find the values for a set of integer variables given a set of linear constraints, such that a linear function becomes minimized or maximized.

For example: minimize $x + 6 * y$ subject to:

$$2 * x + y \leq 7,\ 3 * x + 5 * y \leq 15,\ x, y \geq 0$$

There are numerous problems in the field of electronic design automation (EDA) that can be mapped to an ILP problem, including scheduling and routing, which is the target of this paper.

3 Hardware Architecture

In this section, we present our proposed hardware architecture and comparison to the traditional FPGA architecture.

The general architecture is shown in Fig. 3 (left). The basic building blocks are configurable logic block (CLB), that are connected in a 2-D mesh architecture. Each CLB is connected to its four neighboring CLBs (North, South, East, West), as shown in Fig. 3 (center). Moreover, each CLB's data can be used in the next cycle with the Local link. CLBs at the edges are connected to I/O pins to transfer data to/from the device.

Inside each CLB is shown in Fig. 3 (right). Each CLB contains a number of 4-input lookup tables (LUTs). LUTs can be used to implement any 4-input logic function. The 4 inputs of the LUT are selected from the 5 inputs (N, S, E, W, L). Output of each LUT is latched and is send to all the four neighbors.

Each CLB may have a number of LUTs (n). Therefore, n different logic functions may be implemented in a CLB. Also, because of the connectivity to all neighbors, n data line exists between every two neighboring CLBs.

Although in the architecture shown in Fig. 3, LUTs are used inside CLBs, LUTs may be replaced with more complex processing elements such as ALUs. This way, higher-level applications, instead of logic functions, can be mapped to the hardware easily.

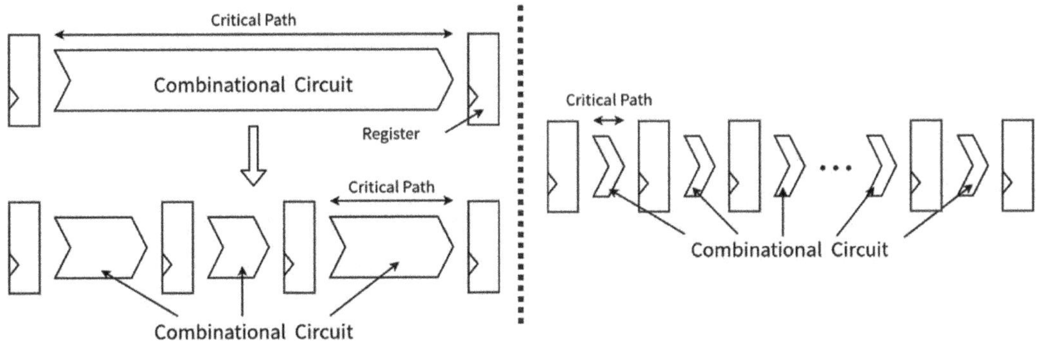

Fig. 4. Comparison of pipelining in a FGPA (left) and the proposed architecture (right)

Following are the main differences between the proposed architecture and a traditional FPGA.

In the proposed architecture, data can be transferred only from a CLB to a neighboring CLB. Therefore, to transfer data from a CLB to other non-neighboring CLBs, some CLBs in between should be used as transfer points. However, in a FGPA data may be transferred from any CLB to any other CLB as long as there is an available routing resource. Consequently, data transfers in FPGA may take a long time, increasing the critical path delay, and reducing the clock frequency. However, in our proposed architecture, all data transfers are between two neighboring CLBs, and take exactly one clock cycle. Moreover, the critical path delay is fixed, and so the clock frequency.

This means that a given application, when mapped to our architecture, may result in very deep pipeline. In general, having a very deep pipeline helps to improve the performance, although the latency may be increased. Another important feature of our proposed architecture is that the critical path delays are fixed; hence, the timing closure problem may not happen. Figure 4 illustrates the differences in the pipelining of a FPGA and our proposed architecture.

4 General Mapping Method

In this section, we present our mapping method for the proposed hardware architecture. The input of the mapping method is the data-flow graph (DFG) of the application, and the general information about the hardware such as the architecture mesh size, and the number of LUTs in a CLB. The output of the method specifies that each node of the DFG is executed on which LUT of which CLB, and at which cycle. For example, the simple DFG shown in Fig. 5 (left) will be mapped to the proposed architecture as shown in Fig. 5 (right).

4.1 ILP Variables

We have formulated the problem of mapping as an integer linear programming (ILP) problem that can be solved with any ILP solver, as follows. We have defined the binary variable D to represent the data transfers.

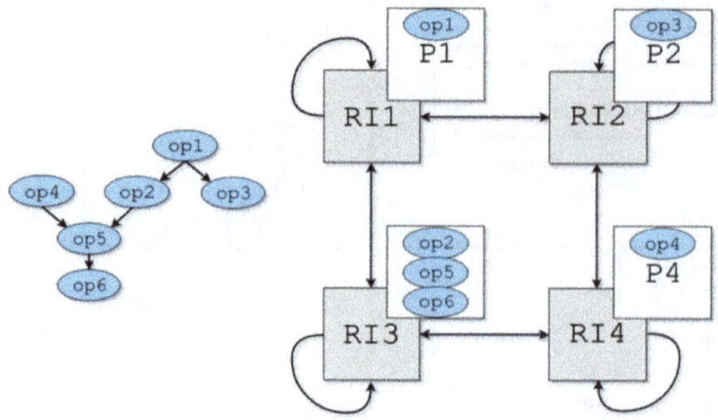

Fig. 5. Example of mapping a DFG in to the proposed architecture

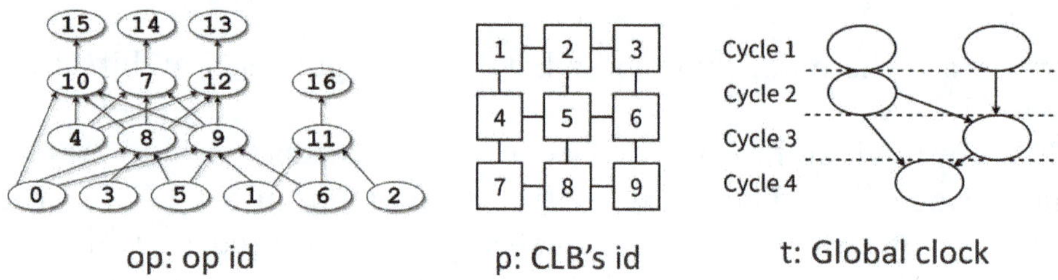

Fig. 6. Parameters in mapping DFG nodes

$D(op, t, p)$: *op* data is mapped to be used at cycle t on CLB number p
op, t and p parameters are shown in Fig. 6.

An example of binding is shown in Fig. 7. Assuming, each gate in the figure is going to be executed on one LUT, one possible way is as follows. Gate1 is executed in CLB5 at time 2, and data is transferred at time 3: D(1, 3, 5) = 1. Gate2 is assigned to CLB8, which is a neighbor of CLB5, and executes at time 3, and its output is transferred at time 4: D(2, 4, 8) = 1.

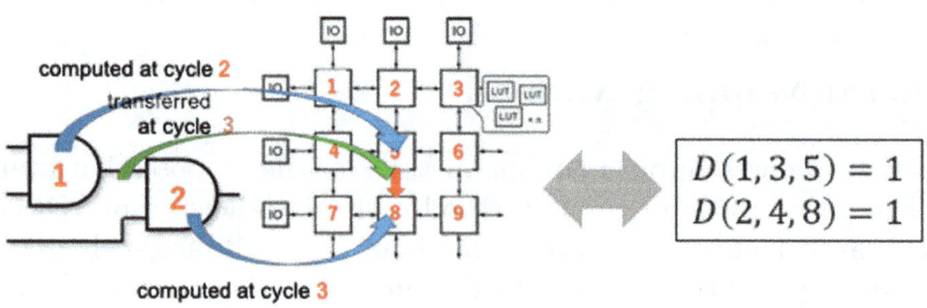

Fig. 7. Mapping example

4.2 ILP Constraints

There is a constraint that all the nodes' data should appear at least once, meaning that all the operations are performed, as follows:

$$\forall op, \sum_t \sum_p D(op, t, p) \geq 1$$

Note that in the definition of variables, we have assumed that any op can be mapped to any CLB, meaning that all CLBs are capable of executing any DFG node function. However, in general, we may have different DFG node types and different CLB types, and each type of DFG node may be mapped to different CLB types. In that case, we need additional constraints to define not allowed resource bindings, by adding constraints that which data transfers are not feasible. It means that some $D(op, t, p)$ variables are always 0.

Data transfer constraints make sure that all the edges of DFG are assigned at least once. Moreover, because of the proposed architecture, data transfer constraints make sure that correct sequence of data transfer is performed, meaning that data is only transferred to the neighboring nodes in one cycle. The constraints are as follows:

$$\begin{aligned}
&\forall op, t, p, op_{par},\\
&-D(op,t,p) + \sum\nolimits_{p' \in p_s} D(op, t-1, p') + \sum\nolimits_{p' \in p_s} D(op_{par}, t-1, p') \geq 0\\
&\forall op, t, p,\\
&-D(op,t,p) + \sum\nolimits_{p' \in p_s} D(op, t+1, p') + \sum\nolimits_{op_{chi}} \sum\nolimits_{p' \in p_s} D(op_{chi}, t+1, p') \geq 0
\end{aligned}$$

The other constraint is regarding the number of registers in a block. Assuming the number of registers is n, maximum n operations may be performed in a block:

$$\forall p, \sum\nolimits_{op} \sum\nolimits_{t} D(op, t, p) \leq n$$

4.3 Objective Function

In our problem, the goal is to map in such a way that the latency is minimum, meaning that the last cycle that any DFG node is executed (T) be minimum. The constraint for the objective function is as follows:

$$\forall op, t, p, (t * D(op, t, p) \leq T)$$

However, practically we can avoid adding the above constraint, as the additional constraints slow down the ILP solver. In our solution, when we are generating the problem for the ILP solver, we only add $D(op, t, p)$ variables for $t \leq T$. This way, if the problem has a solution with time limit of T, it can be solved. Otherwise, the problem has no solution, meaning that the execution of the given DFG in the given architecture cannot be finished in less than T cycles.

5 Regular Computations Mapping Method

The general mapping method presented in the previous section works for any kind of circuit. However, it is required to employ heuristics to become scalable to larger circuits, and, heuristics may largely affect the quality of results. Therefore, we are proposing another mapping method that is both scalable and optimal

$$\begin{pmatrix} I_{stim}1 \\ I_{stim}2 \\ I_{stim}3 \\ I_{stim}4 \end{pmatrix} = \begin{pmatrix} w11 & w12 & w13 & w14 \\ w21 & w22 & w23 & w24 \\ w31 & w32 & w33 & w34 \\ w41 & w42 & w43 & w44 \end{pmatrix} \cdot \begin{pmatrix} I_s1 \\ I_s2 \\ I_s3 \\ I_s4 \end{pmatrix}$$

Fig. 8. Matrix-vector multiplication

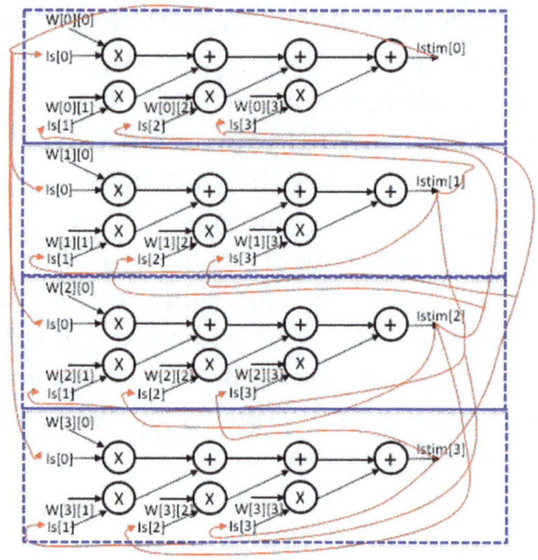

Fig. 9. Multiplication solution with global communication

for large regular computations. One of the important characteristics of regular computations, like matrix operations or convolutions on neural networks, is that the general flow of the operations is very similar or the same for different sizes of the problem. Therefore, if the optimal solution for the small size problem is known, its generalization to larger size problems is possible.

The general flow of the proposed mapping method for regular computations is as follows:

1. Map the smaller size problem optimally by an automatic method, like the proposed method in the previous section.
2. Use induction methods to generalize the solution of small problem for large one, semi automatically by human guidance.
3. Map the large problem optimally, automatically, utilizing the induction.

The generalization phase results in a set of constraints that basically limits the search space of the solver; consequently, larger problems can be solved very efficiently by an automated method. Following, the method is shown on two different examples.

5.1 Matrix-Vector Multiplication

Matrix-vector multiplication is one of the basic operations on matrices that have many applications in different domains including neural networks. Figure 8 shows the multiplication of a 4×4 matrix, and Fig. 9 shows its corresponding data flow graph that is mapped to 4 blocks. The flow of data among the blocks is like a ring connection, and the mapping is followed by the "natural" order of operations by a human. As shown in the figure, the mapping in this case is not optimal as it requires a lot of global data transfers among the blocks.

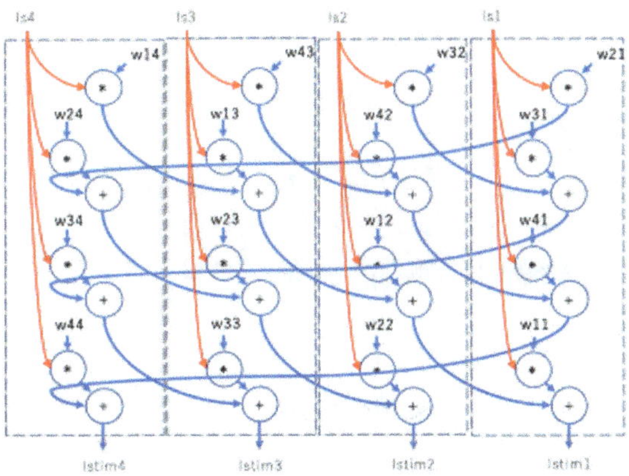

Fig. 10. Multiplication solution 1: local transfer of partial products

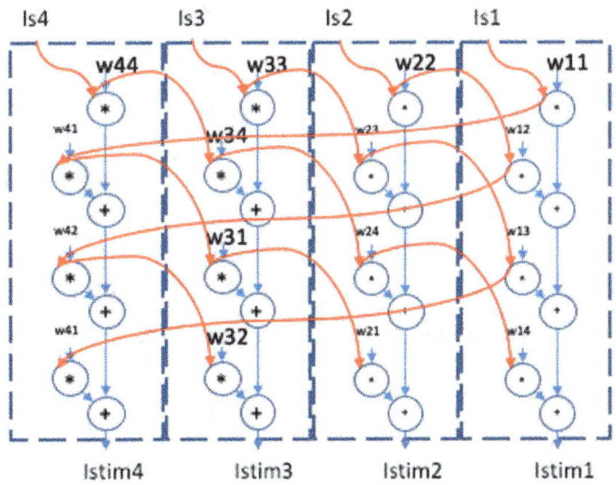

Fig. 11. Multiplication solution 2: local transfer of input vector

Following the proposed method, we have tried to find the optimal solution for this matrix-vector multiplication. Two different optimal results are obtained that are shown in Figs. 10 and 11. In the first solution, the partial products are propagated from one block to its neighbor block, while in the second solution, the input vectors are propagated.

The above observations regarding the flow of data in the solutions can be done by a human, and that knowledge can be used in a program to automatically generate and verify the solution for larger size matrices, as shown in the experimental results section.

5.2 Convolutional Neural Networks

Nowadays, convolutional neural networks (CNNs) are used in many applications; hence, acceleration of the convolution operations are very important. In this section, we present an optimal mapping of convolution operations in one convolution layer of CNN for image classification as an example.

Figure 12 shows a typical neural network for image classification. At first, a moving window of different sizes performs feature extraction on the input image, using convolution operations. At the end a fully connected neural networks performs image classification based on the extracted features from the image.

The convolution operation on a moving window usually requires a lot of processing power; hence, a target of acceleration. We have proposed a sequence of operations for a window, following ring connection-like order of operations as well as moving the window on the input image to maximize the utilization of processing element in each block as well as making data transfers locally. Figure 13 shows the order of operations for 4×4 window, though it can be extended to other window sizes. Figure 14 shows the data flow graphs for image of 4×4 and window size of 2×2. Similarly, it can be extended to any image size and any window size.

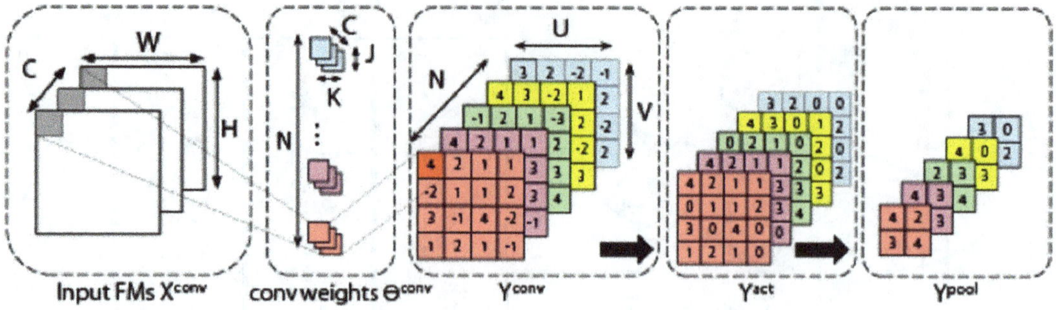

Fig. 12. An example CNN for image classification

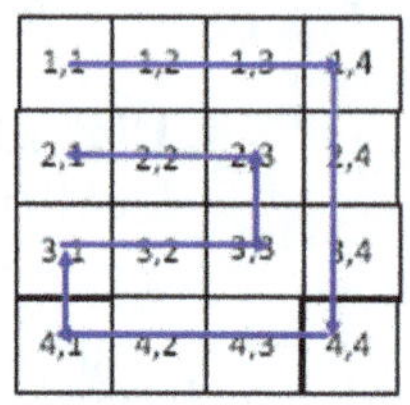

Fig. 13. Order of convolution operations: ring connection in mesh architecture

6 Experimental Results

In this section, we present our experimental results on mapping different DFGs into our proposed architecture. In our experiments, we have used DFGs obtained from ISCAS benchmark circuits and mapped them to our proposed hardware assuming LUTs in our blocks. Similarly, the DFGs may be obtained from other applications, and the block contents may be ALUs or other more complex processing elements, without affecting the mapping process or the mapping results. The process of obtaining DFGs is as follows:

1. The original circuit is synthesized and mapped into to netlist of LUTs with ABC tool [11]
2. The netlist of LUTs is converted to DFG as follows: each LUT in the netlist becomes a node in DFG, and for each connection in the netlist we have the corresponding edge in the DFG.

We convert DFGs to ILP formulas with our mapping program written in Python. For the experiments, we have used Gurobi optimizer [12]. All the experiments are performed on a server with Xeon E5 2.2 GHz processor and 512 GB memory running Linux kernel 4.16.

In the first experiment, we generated DFG for the combinational ISCAS benchmark circuits, as explained above. The DFG are then mapped to our hardware structure, as shown in Table 1. Columns 1 and 2 show the circuit name, and its number of inputs/outputs, respectively. Columns 3, 4, and 5 show the number of nodes, edges, and levels in the DFG, respectively. Columns 6 shows the size of the mesh structure. Columns 7 and 8 show the size of the ILP problem in terms of number of variables and number of constraints of ILP formula.

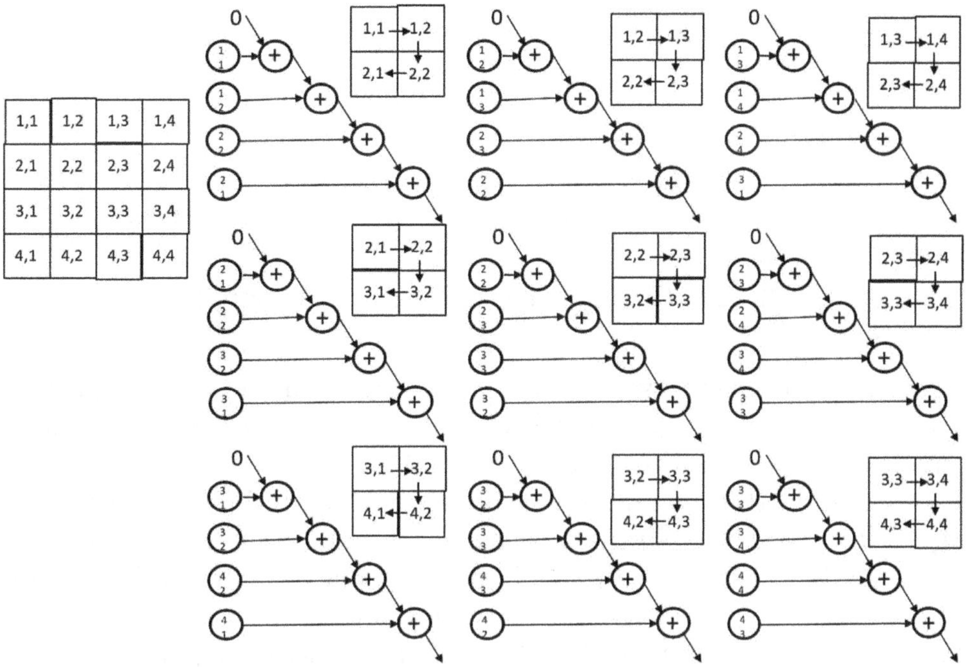

Fig. 14. Data flow graphs for 4×4 image and window size of 2×2

Table 1. Experiment 1: mapping of DFGs from ISCAS benchmark circuits

Circuit	DFG				Mesh size	ILP		Latency	Mapping time
	I/O	Nodes	Edges	Level		Var.	Const.		
s298	17/20	42	148	6	6×6	4,528	12,693	6	7.0 s
s344	24/26	44	147	6	6×6	5,484	13,615	6	17.4 s
s382	24/27	56	201	6	6×6	5,368	15,214	6	19.5 s
s400	24/27	55	203	6	6×6	5,336	15,409	6	19.0 s
s420	34/17	59	216	7	8×8	9,364	27,019	N/A	>1 day
s444	24/27	55	216	6	6×6	5,284	15,085	6	17.6 s
s510	25/13	98	353	7	8×8	11,692	41,840	7	32,664 s
s526	24/27	83	299	6	8×8	9,773	30,406	6	836.5 s
s641	35/24	79	234	9	8×8	31,356	75,939	N/A	>1 day

Column 9 shows the latency of the mapped circuit that is the number of clock cycles to finish executing the DFG on the target hardware. Column 10 shows the execution timr of the ILP solver to find the optimum solution.

As shown in the results, the complexity of finding optimum solution increases by increasing the number of DFG nodes as well as the number of I/O of the circuit. Therefore, for some circuits the optimum results could not be found even in 1 day.

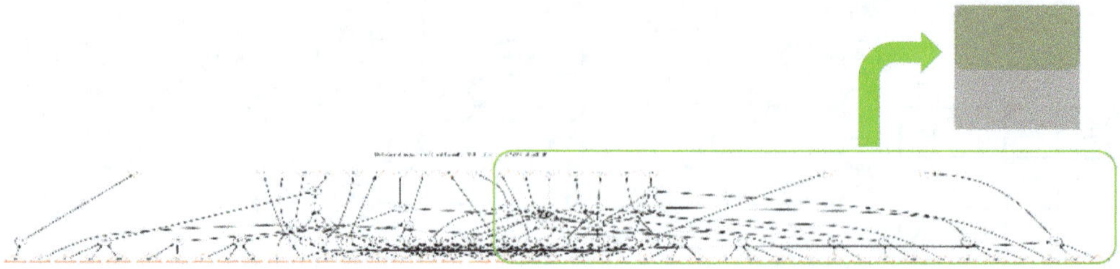

Fig. 15. Partitioning of the architecture into 2

In the next experiment, we tried to improve ILP solving time by partitioning the DFG into 2 sections, such that each section will be implemented in one of the 2 partitions of the hardware as shown in Fig. 15.

We have used hMETIS graph partitioning tool [13]. hMETIS tries to partition the graph into 2 subgraphs in a way that each subgraph has almost the same number of nodes, and the number of edges crossing a subgraph into another subgraph is minimum. In other words, the number of data transfers among the subgraphs is minimum, while almost uniformly distributing the DFG nodes. The results are shown in Table 2 for the four hardest cases. Comparing the results without graph partitioning and with graph partitioning, the latency is not increased while the execution time of ILP solver is reduced by an average more than one order of magnitude. Note that hMETIS is very fast and for all the DFGs finishes in less than 100ms. Moreover, for one of the cases that could not be solved because of timeout, the optimum solution is obtained. However, for one of the circuits we still cannot find optimum solution, and we need other heuristics to reduce the runtime further, and it is part of our future work.

In the next experiment, we used the proposed mapping method for matrix-vector multiplication. First, we tried the mapping for 4×4 matrix, as explained before, as the guidance for generalization to larger matrix operations. Then, we added constraints to the mapping program to limit the flow of operations for arbitrary size matrices similar to the case of 4×4. The results of mapping larger matrices are shown in Table 3. Without the generalization of the solution for 4×4 matrices, the problem for matrices larger than 8×8 could not be finished in one day. However, with the proposed generalization methods, matrix size of 32×32 can be mapped into 4 cores in less than 25 min.

Table 2. Experiment 2: mapping after partitioning original DFG to 2

Circuit	Mesh size	Sub-ILP		Whole-ILP		Latency	Mapping time (no partition)	Mapping time (w/partition)
		Var.	Const.	Var.	Const.			
s420	8 × 8	4,374	13,745	5,224	14,625	8	>1 day	18,936 s
s510	8 × 8	2,602	8,413	4,241	15,231	7	32,664s	1,415 s
s526	8 × 8	2,284	7,532	3,795	10,411	6	836.5s	40.0 s
s641	8 × 8	7,030	17,934	N/A	N/A	N/A	>1 day	>1 day

Table 3. Experiment 3: mapping of matrix-vector multiplication

Matrix dimension (N)	# cores (M)	Mapping time (s)
15	3	14
16	4	15
8	2	1.2
12	4	1.6
32	4	1437

7 Conclusions

In this work, we have presented a new reconfigurable architecture for IoT and mobile platforms. Our hardware consists of several logic blocks connected through a mesh network. The proposed hardware architecture provides a general platform for both fine- and coarse-grained computation. Compared to traditional FPGA devices, our proposed hardware can achieve easily very deep pipelining; hence, providing high performance computation.

In addition, we have proposed the general mapping method based on ILP formulation and heuristics to improve its efficiency. Our mapping method starts from the data-flow graph (DFG) of an application and results in optimal latency. The general mapping method works for any kind of computation. However, for regular computations such as matrix operations or convolutions on CNN, we have proposed a method scalable to large designs. The method is based on solving the problem automatically for small problem, generalize it by human, and solve the problem for larger problems automatically.

Our future work is improving the efficiency of the general mapping as well as experimenting with mapping high-level applications to coarse-grained blocks. Moreover, we are working on automation of the generalization process.

References

1. Rafique, A., Kapre, N., Constantinides, G.A.: Enhancing performance of tall-skinny QR factorization using FPGAs. In: International Conference on Field Programmable Logic and Applications (FPL), pp. 443–450 (2012)
2. Aluru, S., Jammula, N.: A review of hardware acceleration for computational genomics. IEEE Des. Test **31**(1), 19–30 (2014)
3. Morcel, R., et al.: Minimalist design for accelerating convolutional neural networks for low-end FPGA platforms. In: International Symposium on Field-Programmable Custom Computing Machines (FCCM), p. 196 (2017)
4. Zhang, X., et al.: Machine learning on FPGAs to face the IoT revolution. In: International Conference on Computer-Aided Design (ICCAD), pp. 894–901 (2017)
5. Song, M., et al.: In-situ AI: towards autonomous and incremental deep learning for IoT systems. In: International Symposium on High Performance Computer Architecture (HPCA), pp. 92–103 (2018)

6. Farmahini-Farahani, A., Ho Ahn, J., Morrow, K., Sung Kim, N.: DRAMA: an architecture for accelerated processing near memory. IEEE Comput. Arch. Lett. **14**(1), 26–29 (2015)
7. Liang, S., Yin, S., Liu, L., Guo, Y., Wei, S.: A coarse-grained reconfigurable architecture for compute-intensive MapReduce acceleration. IEEE Comput. Arch. Lett. **15**(2), 69–72 (2016)
8. Tanomoto, M., Takamaeda-Yamazaki, S., Yao, J., Nakashima, Y.: A CGRA-based approach for accelerating convolutional neural networks. In: International Symposium on Embedded Multicore/Many-Core Systems-on-Chip (MCSoC), pp. 73–80 (2015)
9. Bae, I., Harris, B., Min, H., Egger, B.: Auto-tuning CNNs for coarse-grained reconfigurable array-based accelerators. IEEE Trans. Comput.-Aided Des. Integr. Circuits Syst. **37**(11), 2301–2310 (2018)
10. ISCAS'89 benchmarks. http://www.pld.ttu.ee/~maksim/benchmarks/iscas89/
11. Berkeley Logic Synthesis and Verification Group, ABC: A System for Sequential Synthesis and Verification. http://www.eecs.berkeley.edu/~alanmi/abc/
12. Gurobi optimization. www.gurobi.com
13. hMETIS - Hypergraph & Circuit Partitioning. http://glaros.dtc.umn.edu/gkhome/metis/hmetis/overview

Unexpected Inferences from Sensor Data: A Hidden Privacy Threat in the Internet of Things

Jacob Kröger(✉)

Technische Universität Berlin, Straße des 17. Juni 135, 10623 Berlin, Germany
kroeger@tu-berlin.de

Abstract. A growing number of sensors, embedded in wearables, smart electric meters and other connected devices, is surrounding us and reaching ever deeper into our private lives. While some sensors are commonly regarded as privacy-sensitive and always require user permission to be activated, others are less protected and less worried about. However, experimental research findings indicate that many seemingly innocuous sensors can be exploited to infer highly sensitive information about people in their vicinity. This paper reviews existing evidence from the literature and discusses potential implications for consumer privacy. Specifically, the analysis reveals that certain insufficiently protected sensors in smart devices allow inferences about users' locations, activities and real identities, as well as about their keyboard and touchscreen inputs. The presented findings call into question the adequacy of current sensor access policies. It is argued that most data captured by smart consumer devices should be classified as highly sensitive by default. An introductory overview of sensors commonly found in these devices is also provided, along with a proposed classification scheme.

Keywords: Privacy · Sensors · Internet of Things · Inference attacks · Information leaks

1 Introduction

At the latest since the advent of smartphones, a variety of embedded sensors is constantly surrounding us – whether we are at work, in transit, or even within our own four walls. The emerging Internet of Things (IoT) is predicted to further increase the number of sensors in our everyday environment by many orders of magnitude [17].

New services and business models are enabled through the increasing pervasiveness and interconnection of sensors which promise to bring transformational improvements in many areas including health, safety, security, convenience, productivity and sustainability. At the same time, with sensing technologies reaching ever deeper into people's lives, there is growing concern about potential privacy violations. These concerns need to be addressed before IoT technologies are widely deployed – not only to protect the fundamental right to informational self-determination, but also to foster trust and acceptance among users.

L. Strous and V. G. Cerf (Eds.): IFIPIoT 2018, IFIP AICT 548, pp. 147–159, 2019.
https://doi.org/10.1007/978-3-030-15651-0_13

While cameras, microphones and navigation systems like GPS are commonly perceived as privacy-sensitive [26, 32] and require explicit user permission in current mobile operating systems [6], many inconspicuous sensors such as accelerometers, gyroscopes and barometers are less well-understood in terms of their privacy implications, and also less protected [57]. Countless embedded sensors in consumer electronics, such as smartphones, smartwatches, and smart home appliances, can be freely accessed by various possibly untrusted parties ranging from device manufacturers [48] and service providers [59] to third-party apps installed on mobile devices [6] and even website operators [8].

Numerous studies have shown that highly personal information can be inferred from seemingly innocuous sensor data. Accordingly, an international group of data protection and privacy commissioners argued in the *Mauritius Declaration on the Internet of Things* that all IoT sensor data should be treated as personal data [33]. This paper substantiates this view with empirical evidence from the existing literature and illustrates potential implications for consumer privacy.

2 Sensors in IoT Devices

2.1 Classification

A wide variety of sensors can be found in consumer IoT devices. Depending on the type of device and its field of application (e.g. home automation, fitness monitoring, gaming), sensor measurements fulfil many different purposes. In the context of IoT consumer privacy, sensors can be meaningfully classified according to the following properties:

Measured Variable. Sensors can be classified based on the specific physical or chemical property they measure (e.g. air pressure, temperature, acceleration), or – in the case of fusion sensors which combine the results of multiple underlying sensors – the computed result they provide (e.g. absolute orientation of a device).

In the privacy context, this seems more accurate and meaningful than the widespread classification of sensors based on their intended purpose. In Android, for instance, accelerometers are exclusively classified as motion sensors because their declared purpose is to monitor a device's motion [1]. More relevant for assessing their potential privacy impact, however, is the fact that accelerometers can also be used to infer much more sensitive information, including a user's location [24, 27], activities [55], and login credentials [49]. Therefore, a classification of sensors based solely on their most common purpose can be misleading.

Internal or External Focus. It can be differentiated between sensors which measure internal properties of their encapsulating device (e.g. internal temperature) and sensors which measure environmental properties (e.g. ambient illumination).

Possible Deployments. Depending on their size, functionality and intended purpose, sensors can vary in mobility. While some sensors are usually stationary (e.g. carbon dioxide sensors) or even wall-mounted (e.g. passive infrared motion detectors), others can be carried around or even be embedded into mobile devices (e.g. microphones, gyroscopes, accelerometers).

Reporting Mode. Sensors can be classified based on how frequently they generate events. Android, for instance, differentiates between continuous reporting (events are generated at a constant rate), on-change reporting (only if the measured values have changed), one-shot reporting (upon detection of a specific event) and special reporting (according to specific sensor requirements) [2].

Level of Protection. Depending on the assumed sensitivity of their data and other factors, sensors in IoT devices enjoy different levels of legal and technical protection. Specific protection mechanisms and access policies can vary significantly between devices of different manufacturers [6]. Further insights into the sensitivity and protection of different types of sensor data are provided in Sect. 2.2.

Accuracy. The measurement accuracy of sensors can greatly differ and often depends on their technological complexity and production quality. Sometimes, the granularity of sensor data is intentionally reduced to enhance privacy [16].

Visibility. Sensors can also be classified based on their degree of visibility. While some sensors can be completely hidden within a device (e.g. accelerometer) or even sense through walls (e.g. radio tomography), other sensors require visual contact to function (e.g. infrared). Also, the size and appearance of a sensor should be considered when assessing its degree of visibility.

2.2 Sensitivity and Protection of Sensor Data

There are considerable differences in the perceived privacy intrusiveness of different sensor types. Cameras, for instance, are commonly regarded as highly privacy-sensitive [34] and therefore often rejected in private rooms [44]. Similarly, microphones [13], biometrical sensors [44], and GPS data [32] are widely believed to intrude user privacy. By contrast, sensors that do not directly record or locate the user are often considered harmless. Examples include inertial sensors such as accelerometers [32] and sensors capturing environmental data such as room temperature [44].

This sentiment is reflected in the permission policies of current mobile operating systems. All mainstream platforms, including iOS, Android and Windows Phone, allow third-party apps to access various built-in sensors without requiring security permission [6]. An overview of common smartphone sensors and their permission requirements on Android is provided in Table 1. While Google's mobile operating system leaves numerous sensors unprotected, access to GPS, camera and microphone is restricted [38].

It can be expected that the policies of technology and market leaders like Apple, Google and Microsoft will substantially inspire and shape data protection mechanisms in the future IoT. Apart from mobile devices, other IoT devices such as smart meters [16, 23, 59], motion detectors [25, 59] and smoke alarm systems [48] have also been shown to share potentially sensitive data with service providers and device manufacturers without privacy-related restrictions. It is therefore important to investigate whether the widely assumed innocuousness of certain sensors matches reality.

Table 1. Overview of common smartphone sensors

Sensor type	Output	Restricted in Android [6, 38]
Accelerometer	Acceleration of device	No
Ambient temperature	Room/air temperature	No
Camera	Recorded image or video	Yes
GPS	Geographical location	Yes
Gravity	Force of gravity	No
Gyroscope	Device's rate of rotation	No
Light	Level of ambient illumination	No
Magnetometer	Ambient geomagnetic field	No
Microphone	Recorded audio	Yes
Orientation	Device's degrees of rotation	No
Pressure	Ambient air pressure	No
Proximity	Proximity of an object to the device's screen	No
Relative humidity	Relative ambient air humidity	No
Temperature	Temperature of the device	No

3 Localization

3.1 Indoor Localization and Occupancy Monitoring

Various unobtrusive sensors can be used for the purpose of monitoring room occupancy and locating people indoors. A technology commonly found in home security systems are passive infrared (PIR) sensors which detect moving objects based on changes in ambient temperature. Besides from binary room occupancy, PIR sensors have been used to infer the number of occupants and even to identify people [59].

Since humans naturally exhale carbon dioxide (CO_2), the air composition in a room or building can also be an indicator of occupancy. CO_2 sensors have already been exploited to estimate the number of room occupants with high accuracy [3]. Similarly, human presence can be detected through measuring other environmental parameters, such as ambient humidity, illumination, and sound rate [4].

Even the on/off state of household appliances and their level of power consumption over time allow inferences about binary [16] and ranged [59] room occupancy. The energy usage patterns required for such inferences can be derived from residential smart meter readings [18] which are commonly shared with electric utilities for the official purpose of demand-response management and billing [59].

Radio Tomographic Imaging is another technique that has been exploited for human presence detection. This approach is based on the fact that the human body absorbs and thereby weakens a radio signal between sender and receiver, which can be measured in terms of the received signal strength (RSS). Within wireless sensor networks, which are considered an enabling technology for IoT [52], radio tomographic imaging can be used for indoor localization [10] and even multi-target tracking [45] without requiring any additional hardware.

Radar sensors have also been proposed for the purpose of indoor localization. Aside from just detecting human presence and motion, existing approaches can sense through walls [21] and investigate the physical characteristics of targets [31]. Other technologies that are being explored for unobtrusive indoor positioning and room-level tracking include ultrasonic sensors [26], door-operated switches [30], and pressure-sensing floors [51]. In contrast to some of the data sources mentioned earlier, sensors like radar and ultrasound are unlikely to be underestimated in terms of their sensitivity. However, these technologies may be completely invisible to the tracked person which could be utilized for covert intrusions of privacy.

Indoor location information can be highly privacy-sensitive. Among many other possible inferences, indoor location traces have been used to obtain personal properties of targets, such as age, work role, coffee consumption and smoking habits [41].

3.2 Geographical Localization

Studies have shown that sensors in mobile devices can be exploited for geographical user localization, even when GPS is disabled. For instance, accelerometers in smartphones can reveal the device's location while the user is driving a car [24] or using a metropolitan train system [27]. These approaches are either based on supervised learning with labeled training data or on mapping the phone's motion trajectory to the shape of existing routes on a map through computing a similarity score.

Smartphone owners can also be located while they are walking or travelling on a train or plane by exploiting a combination of easily accessible mobile sensor data and publicly available auxiliary data [43]. For this approach, neither training data nor prior knowledge about the user is required. Researchers have even shown that a smartphone's location can be learned from tracking its battery level over time [42]. This method builds on the fact that the level of power consumption is affected by the distance and any obstacles between a phone and its current cellular base station.

Highly sensitive information can be inferred from location traces. Through spatial clustering and the identification of temporal mobility patterns, it is possible to obtain the true identity as well as the home address and points of interest of a person from his or her location history [19]. Spatio temporal information can also be used to infer a person's mode of transportation and to predict where a driver will drive [35]. It is important to understand that certain visited locations alone (e.g. betting office, mosque, vegetarian restaurant) can reveal sensitive personal properties such as habits, preferences or religious affiliation. In combination with various unprotected smartphone sensors, location data has even been used to draw inferences about a user's emotional state [37].

4 Activity Recognition

Data from various inconspicuous sensors in IoT devices can be used to infer information about basic physical activities (e.g. walking, running, climbing) and activities of daily living (e.g. grooming, cooking, washing dishes) of individuals in their vicinities.

Recent studies in the field of sensor-based human activity recognition have mostly focused on accelerometer data from wearable devices such as smartphones, smartwatches, or wrist-worn fitness trackers [11]. In [55], 3-axis accelerometry collected with an off-the-shelf smartwatch was successfully used to recognize eating moments of users in free-living conditions. Data from wrist-worn inertial sensors has also been used to recognize various other actions including drinking and cigarette smoking [50, 54]. Whole-body motions, such as descending and ascending stairs, walking, jumping, and jogging, can be recognized with high accuracy from smartphone inertial sensor data [11]. Motion sensors in smartphones have even been used for the assessment of driving behavior [29].

Another unobtrusive but revealing data source for activity recognition in an IoT environment are smart electric meters. Various behaviors of residents including bathroom activities, cooking, housework, sleep cycles, and meal times can be inferred from seemingly non-sensitive smart meter readings [16]. It has been shown that even the current TV channel and specific audiovisual content displayed on a television can be identified based on the corresponding household's electricity usage profile [23].

Data from infrared motion detectors, which is normally used for monitoring room occupancy and often shared with security companies [59], has also been exploited for activity recognition. In [25], passive infrared sensors were used to detect the operation mode of kitchen appliances, such as water cooker and toaster, as well as human actions, such as opening a refrigerator and taking a shower. While many current techniques for automated activity recognition require pre-processing of collected data, approaches have already been presented for extracting activity-related information from infrared sensor data in real-time [34].

In a smart home environment, data from multiple sources can be combined for improved recognition accuracy. Nef et al. [47] used a set of sensors measuring several parameters including luminescence, temperature and ambient motion to recognize eight different activities of daily living such as grooming, cooking, eating, and watching TV.

5 User Input Inference

Among the most sensitive information in the context of consumer electronics is the input that users provide through touchscreens and keyboards, which includes personal notes, text messages, transaction details, and login credentials.

Multiple so-called *keystroke inference attacks* have been developed for inferring such user inputs from seemingly innocuous sensor data. Most of these attacks are based on the observation that the keys typed into a device correlate with micro-motions of the user's hand, and – in the case of mobile devices – with micro-motions of the device itself. Owusu et al. [49] show that data from accelerometers in smartphones can be used to obtain entire sequences of text entered through the touchscreen, including passwords. The same kind of data can also be exploited to infer graphical password patterns [5]. As demonstrated by Spreitzer [53], even ambient-light sensors in mobile devices may leak sensitive user inputs such as the personal identification number (PIN).

Not only can embedded sensors reveal user inputs to their encapsulating device, they can also allow inferences about what users type into other devices. Motion sensors in modern smartwatches, for instance, have been exploited to recover text typed on laptop and desktop keyboards [40, 56].

The possibility to infer user inputs from sensor data could enable malicious parties to gain insight into sensitive communications and transactions. Beltramelli [7] even suggests that a user's entire technological ecosystem could be compromised when passwords are leaked through embedded sensors in consumer IoT devices. Although current keystroke inference attacks are mostly based on accelerometer and gyroscope data, it has been proposed that other potential side channels such as magnetic field sensors should also be investigated [56].

6 Identification

6.1 De-anonymization of Sensor Data

Sensor data collected through consumer IoT devices is particularly sensitive when it can be linked to the real identity of the user. In scenarios where data is accessed by untrusted service providers or device manufacturers, identifying information such as name, address and bank account is often already available to them from the respective service or purchase agreement.

Even if this is not the case, the sensor data itself and inferred location information can often reveal a user's identity to the data controller. As detailed above, work and home addresses of individuals can be derived from their geographical location traces [19]. Such information – even at coarse resolution – can be used in conjunction with employment directories, white pages, tax records, and other public or private datasets to uniquely identify a tracked person [22]. Social networks have also been proven to be excellent sources of auxiliary data for the de-anonymization of smartphone sensor data [36]. Some researchers even argue that no method exists to reliably prevent the de-anonymization of location data [46].

The linkage of data sources has been recognized as one of the major privacy threats in IoT [60]. The term *quasi-identifier*, coined by Dalenius [14], is generally used to describe pieces of information that are not personally identifiable when considered in isolation but can quickly become unique identifiers when combined with other data sources. When it comes to IoT sensor data, an adversary's auxiliary information does not even need to be drawn from external sources (e.g. information brokers, public datasets) but can also be collected from within a user's own ecosystem of connected devices. As shown in [36], mobile sensor data can become personally identifiable through linkage with less protected data streams of the same user. Seemingly innocuous sensors could thus be used as gateways to de-anonymize sensitive streams of user activity.

6.2 Tracking and Profiling of Anonymous Users

Even in cases where an adversary is not capable of obtaining a target's real identity from collected IoT sensor data, substantial privacy issues may arise. For some of the most common intentions behind data misuse, such as price discrimination and targeted advertising, it can be fully sufficient to distinguish between anonymous individuals without ever learning their real names.

In the context of consumer IoT devices, unidentified users can be told apart based on their physical characteristics and movement patterns, which are often reflected in sensor data from mobile devices. According to Jain et al. [28], body movements can serve as biological fingerprints if they are universal, repeatable, collectible, and distinctive. It has been shown that head movements, as captured through the sensors of head-worn IoT devices, fulfill these requirements [39]. Similarly, users of sensing devices can be uniquely distinguished based on their typing motion behavior [20] and other natural gestures such as lowering/raising an arm [58]. The required motion data can be drawn from sensors in smartphones [9] and wrist-worn devices [58] without requiring any permission or conscious participation from the user. Where accessible through IoT sensors, physical characteristics such as body weight may also be used to distinguish observation targets from one another [26].

Following another approach called *device fingerprinting*, users can be told apart based on imperfections and specific features of their personal devices. Even calibration errors in sensors commonly regarded as non-sensitive, such as gyroscopes and accelerometers, have been exploited to uniquely identify IoT devices [8, 15].

The ability to recognize and track individuals through sensor data is a potential basis for behavioral profiling [60] and can thus result in people being treated differently, even without names attached to the data.

7 Discussion and Implications

As shown in the previous sections, sensitive information regarding a user's location, activities and device inputs can be obtained from seemingly benign IoT sensor data. Through cross-linking different sources of sensor data with auxiliary information, an adversary can potentially identify the victim and draw further undesired inferences about his or her habits and preferences. Thus, even if an IoT device is not designed or expected to capture sensitive information, its data streams can indirectly enable serious invasions of user privacy.

It can be assumed that this threat will continue to grow with further improvements of sensor technologies in terms of size, cost and accuracy, further advances in machine learning methods, and – most importantly – the predicted rapid proliferation of consumer IoT devices [17]. Therefore, the privacy-intrusion potential of seemingly innocuous sensors needs to be addressed and dealt with urgently in order to effectively protect consumers' fundamental right to privacy.

The level of legal and technical protection of sensor data should always be chosen in consideration of all reasonably conceivable inferences that can be derived from the data, and not based on the sensor's official purpose. No distinct line can be drawn, for instance, between GPS data and currently less protected sensors such as accelerometers and gyroscopes when it comes to their potential of revealing sensitive information [24, 27]. Further research into the privacy impact of specific sensors is needed, taking into account state-of-the-art data mining and machine learning techniques. As it is extremely difficult, however, to meaningfully determine the limits of continuously advancing inference attacks, most types of IoT sensor data should be classified as highly sensitive by default.

Consumers need to be warned about the invisible privacy threats of IoT. Although surveys have shown that many individuals do not want IoT devices to record all of their inhome behaviors [12] and worry about inferences from otherwise anonymous data [44], people are not particularly concerned about unobtrusive sensors such as the ones discussed in this paper [32, 44]. It seems apparent that the possibilities and implications of data linkage and pattern recognition are not well-understood by the average consumer. Thus, truly informed consent to data processing, as required by the EU's General Data Protection Regulation and other data protection laws, can often not be obtained. Improved education of consumers and their voiced objection against the insufficient protection of sensitive sensor data could also exert pressure on policy makers and device manufacturers to incorporate effective privacy preserving mechanisms in IoT systems and the corresponding regulation.

In order to enable consumers to remain in control of their personal data and understand the complex privacy implications of IoT sensor technology, information on data collection and processing must be presented in an intuitive and easily understandable manner. For this purpose, new tools and approaches need to be developed.

8 Conclusion

The emerging Internet of Things promises to improve our quality of life in many ways. However, the large variety of sensors embedded into connected devices also poses a rising threat to consumer privacy. The overview provided in this paper illustrates that even sensors that are generally thought to be harmless can be used to infer highly sensitive personal information, such as a user's location, activities and real identity, as well as keyboard and touchscreen inputs. Since the access to seemingly innocuous sensors is often unrestricted, various parties can regularly capture and use their potentially revealing data, including device manufacturers, service providers, and third-party apps installed on mobile devices.

Many sensors discussed in this paper are usually hidden inside their encapsulating device and thus completely invisible to the user. Where no access permission is required, these sensors might enable fully covert surveillance of device owners and other people in their vicinity. Considering the extensive protection of sensors which are commonly believed to be privacy-sensitive, such as cameras, microphones and GPS, it is important to prevent malicious parties from using less-protected sensors as substitutional data sources.

Judging from the research findings presented in this paper, many disregarded types of sensor data in the IoT should be classified as sensitive by default and protected accordingly. Furthermore, improved consumer education and more intuitive ways of presenting privacy-related information are necessary to achieve true informational self-determination in an increasingly complex and diverse environment of sensing devices. This paper, however, provides only an initial exploration of the topic. Further empirical and conceptual research into the privacy implications of sensors in IoT devices is strongly encouraged.

References

1. Android Developers: Motion Sensors. https://developer.android.com/guide/topics/sensors/sensors_motion.html
2. Android Open Source Project: Reporting modes. https://source.android.com/devices/sensors/report-modes
3. Ang, I.B.A., et al.: CD-HOC: Indoor Human Occupancy Counting using Carbon Dioxide Sensor Data. arXiv170605286 CsHC (2017)
4. Ang, I.B.A., et al.: Human occupancy recognition with multivariate ambient sensors. In: Pervasive Computing and Communication Workshops (PerCom Workshops), pp. 1–6 (2016)
5. Aviv, A.J., et al.: Practicality of accelerometer side channels on smartphones. In: Proceedings of the 28th Annual Computer Security Applications Conference, pp. 41–50 ACM (2012)
6. Bai, X., et al.: Sensor guardian: prevent privacy inference on Android sensors. EURASIP J. Inf. Secur. **2017**, 1 (2017)
7. Beltramelli, T., Risi, S.: Deep-Spying: Spying using Smartwatch and Deep Learning. arXiv151205616 Cs (2015)
8. Bojinov, H., et al.: Mobile device identification via sensor fingerprinting. arXiv:1408.1416. (2014)
9. Buriro, A., et al.: Please hold on: Unobtrusive user authentication using smartphone's built-in sensors. In: Identity, Security and Behavior Analysis (ISBA), pp. 1–8. IEEE (2017)
10. Cao, X., et al.: A lightweight robust indoor radio tomographic imaging method in wireless sensor networks. Prog. Electromagn. Res. **60**, 19–31 (2017)
11. Chen, Y., Shen, C.: Performance analysis of smartphone-sensor behavior for human activity recognition. IEEE Access **5**, 3095–3110 (2017)
12. Choe, E.K., et al.: Living in a glass house: a survey of private moments in the home. In: Proceedings of the 13th International Conference on Ubiquitous Computing, p. 41. ACM Press (2011)
13. Cook, D.J., Krishnan, N.: Mining the home environment. J. Intell. Inf. Syst. **43**(3), 503–519 (2014)
14. Dalenius, T.: Finding a needle in a haystack or identifying anonymous census records. J. Off. Stat. **2**(3), 329–336 (1986)
15. Das, A., et al.: Tracking mobile web users through motion sensors: attacks and defenses. In: Network and Distributed System Security Symposium (NDSS). Internet Society (2016)
16. Eibl, G., Engel, D.: Influence of data granularity on smart meter privacy. IEEE Trans. Smart Grid **6**(2), 930–939 (2015)
17. Evans, D.: The internet of things - how the next evolution of the internet is changing everything. https://www.cisco.com/c/dam/en_us/about/ac79/docs/innov/IoT_IBSG_0411FINAL.pdf
18. Fan, J., et al.: Privacy disclosure through smart meters: reactive power based attack and defense. In: Dependable Systems and Networks (DSN), pp. 13–24. IEEE (2017)

19. Freudiger, J., Shokri, R., Hubaux, J.-P.: Evaluating the privacy risk of location-based services. In: Danezis, G. (ed.) FC 2011. LNCS, vol. 7035, pp. 31–46. Springer, Heidelberg (2012). https://doi.org/10.1007/978-3-642-27576-0_3
20. Gascon, H., et al.: Continuous authentication on mobile devices by analysis of typing motion behavior. In: Proceedings of GI Conference "Sicherheit", pp. 1–12 (2014)
21. Gennarelli, G., et al.: Real-Time through-wall situation awareness using a microwave doppler radar sensor. Remote Sens. **8**(8), 621 (2016)
22. Golle, P., Partridge, K.: On the anonymity of home/work location pairs. In: Tokuda, H., Beigl, M., Friday, A., Brush, A.J.B., Tobe, Y. (eds.) Pervasive 2009. LNCS, vol. 5538, pp. 390–397. Springer, Heidelberg (2009). https://doi.org/10.1007/978-3-642-01516-8_26
23. Greveler, U., et al.: Multimedia content identification through smart meter power usage profiles. In: Proceedings of the International Conference on Information and Knowledge Engineering (IKE), p. 1. WorldComp (2012)
24. Han, J., et al.: Accomplice: Location inference using accelerometers on smartphones. In: Communication Systems and Networks (COMSNETS), pp. 1–9. IEEE (2012)
25. Hevesi, P., et al.: Monitoring household activities and user location with a cheap, unobtrusive thermal sensor array. In: Proceedings of the 2014 ACM International Joint Conference on Pervasive and Ubiquitous Computing, pp. 141–145. ACM, New York (2014)
26. Hnat, T.W., et al.: Doorjamb: unobtrusive room-level tracking of people in homes using doorway sensors. In: Proceedings of the 10th ACM Conference on Embedded Network Sensor Systems, pp. 309–322. ACM (2012)
27. Hua, J., et al.: We can track you if you take the metro: tracking metro riders using accelerometers on smartphones. IEEE Trans. Inf. Forensics Secur. **12**(2), 286–297 (2017)
28. Jain, A.K., et al.: An introduction to biometric recognition. IEEE Trans. Circuits Syst. Video Technol. **14**(1), 4–20 (2004)
29. Júnior, J.F., et al.: Driver behavior profiling: an investigation with different smartphone sensors and machine learning. PLOS ONE. **12**(4), e0174959 (2017)
30. Kim, S.H., et al.: Improved occupancy detection accuracy using PIR and door sensors for a smart thermostat. In: Proceedings of the 15th IBPSA Conference, San Francisco, CA, USA, pp. 2753–2758 (2017)
31. Kim, Y., et al.: Human detection using doppler radar based on physical characteristics of targets. IEEE Geosci. Remote Sens. Lett. **12**(2), 289–293 (2015)
32. Klasnja, P., Consolvo, S., Choudhury, T., Beckwith, R., Hightower, J.: Exploring privacy concerns about personal sensing. In: Tokuda, H., Beigl, M., Friday, A., Brush, A.J.B., Tobe, Y. (eds.) Pervasive 2009. LNCS, vol. 5538, pp. 176–183. Springer, Heidelberg (2009). https://doi.org/10.1007/978-3-642-01516-8_13
33. Kohnstamm, J., Madhub, D.: Mauritius declaration on the internet of things. https://edps.europa.eu/sites/edp/files/publication/14-10-14_mauritius_declaration_en.pdf
34. Krishnan, N.C., Cook, D.J.: Activity recognition on streaming sensor data. Pervasive Mob. Comput. **10**(Pt B), 138–154 (2014)
35. Krumm, J.: Inference attacks on location tracks. In: LaMarca, A., Langheinrich, M., Truong, K.N. (eds.) Pervasive 2007. LNCS, vol. 4480, pp. 127–143. Springer, Heidelberg (2007). https://doi.org/10.1007/978-3-540-72037-9_8
36. Lane, N.D., et al.: On the feasibility of user de-anonymization from shared mobile sensor data. In: Proceedings of the Third International Workshop on Sensing Applications on Mobile Phones, p. 3. ACM (2012)
37. Lee, H., et al.: Towards unobtrusive emotion recognition for affective social communication. In: Consumer Communications and Networking Conference (CCNC), pp. 260–264. IEEE (2012)

38. Lee, W.-H., Lee, R.: Multi-sensor authentication to improve smartphone security. In: 2015 International Conference on Information Systems Security and Privacy (ICISSP) (2015)
39. Li, S., et al.: Whose move is it anyway? Authenticating smart wearable devices using unique head movement patterns. In: Pervasive Computing and Communications (PerCom), pp. 1–9. IEEE (2016)
40. Maiti, A., et al.: Smartwatch-based keystroke inference attacks and context-aware protection mechanisms. In: Proceedings of the 11th ACM on Asia Conference on Computer and Communications Security, pp. 795–806. ACM, New York (2016)
41. Matsuo, Y., et al.: Inferring long-term user properties based on users' location history. In: IJCAI, pp. 2159–2165 (2007)
42. Michalevsky, Y., et al.: PowerSpy: location tracking using mobile device power analysis. In: USENIX Security Symposium (2015)
43. Mosenia, A., et al.: PinMe: Tracking a Smartphone User around the World. IEEE Trans. Multi-Scale Comput. Syst. **4**(3), 420–435 (2018)
44. Naeini, P.E., et al.: Privacy expectations and preferences in an IoT world. In: Thirteenth Symposium on Usable Privacy and Security (SOUPS) (2017)
45. Nannuru, S., et al.: Radio-frequency tomography for passive indoor multitarget tracking. IEEE Trans. Mob. Comput. **12**(12), 2322–2333 (2013)
46. Narayanan, A., Felten, E.W.: No silver bullet: de-identification still doesn't work. http://randomwalker.info/publications/no-silver-bullet-de-identification.pdf
47. Nef, T., et al.: Evaluation of three state-of-the-art classifiers for recognition of activities of daily living from smart home ambient data. Sensors **15**(5), 11725–11740 (2015)
48. Notra, S., et al.: An experimental study of security and privacy risks with emerging household appliances. In: Communications and Network Security (CNS), pp. 79–84. IEEE (2014)
49. Owusu, E., et al.: ACCessory: password inference using accelerometers on smartphones. In: Proceedings of the Twelfth Workshop on Mobile Computing Systems & Applications, p. 9. ACM (2012)
50. Parate, A.: Designing Efficient and Accurate Behavior-Aware Mobile Systems. University of Massachusetts Amherst (2014)
51. Shen, Y.-L., Shin, C.: Distributed sensing floor for an intelligent environment. Sens. J. IEEE. **9**, 1673–1678 (2010)
52. Shukri, S., Kamarudin, L.M.: Device free localization technology for human detection and counting with RF sensor networks: a review. J. Netw. Comput. Appl. **97**, 157–174 (2017)
53. Spreitzer, R.: PIN skimming: exploiting the ambient-light sensor in mobile devices. In: Proceedings of the 4th ACM Workshop on Security and Privacy in Smartphones & Mobile Devices. ACM, New York (2014)
54. Tang, Q.: Automated detection of puffing and smoking with wrist accelerometers. Northeastern University Boston (2014)
55. Thomaz, E., et al.: A practical approach for recognizing eating moments with wrist-mounted inertial sensing. In: Proceedings of the ACM International Conference on Ubiquitous Computing, pp. 1029–1040. ACM Press (2015)
56. Wang, H., et al.: MoLe: motion leaks through smartwatch sensors. In: Proceedings of the 21st Annual International Conference on Mobile Computing and Networking, pp. 155–166. ACM Press (2015)
57. Xu, Z., Zhu, S.: SemaDroid: a privacy-aware sensor management framework for smartphones. In: Proceedings of the 5th ACM Conference on Data and Application Security and Privacy, pp. 61–72. ACM Press (2015)

58. Yang, J., et al.: MotionAuth: motion-based authentication for wrist worn smart devices. In: Pervasive Computing and Communication Workshops (PerCom Workshops), pp. 550–555. IEEE (2015)
59. Yang, L., et al.: Inferring occupancy from opportunistically available sensor data. In: Pervasive Computing and Communications (PerCom), pp. 60–68. IEEE (2014)
60. Ziegeldorf, J.H., et al.: Privacy in the internet of things: threats and challenges. Secur. Commun. Netw. **7**(12), 2728–2742 (2014)

Issues in Implementing a Data Integration Platform for Electric Vehicles Using the Internet of Things

Martin Smuts(✉), Brenda Scholtz, and Janet Wesson

Nelson Mandela University, Port Elizabeth, South Africa
{s210035447,Brenda.Scholtz,
Janet.Wesson}@mandela.ac.za

Abstract. The emergence of the Internet of Things (IoT) has brought new improvement and development opportunities to the automotive industry, such as electric vehicles (EVs). EVs are well-known for their short ranges and many studies have reported on the challenges of trip planning and accurate remaining driving range (RDR) estimation. While the demand for connected vehicle applications and its enabling technology has progressed significantly in recent years, there are several constraints for connected and collaborative vehicle application deployments. Data integration issues are currently hindering the development of effective trip planning and RDR estimation solutions for drivers of EVs. Additional constraints have been identified in developing countries, including lack of charging station networks, EV data sources, and software applications. The purpose of this paper is to report on some of the main issues hindering EV data integration, as well as to report on an implementation in South Africa of a Data Integration Platform for EV data using the IoT. The findings show that data integration issues primarily relate to data availability, data quality, and interoperability between devices, IoT platforms, and EV service providers. The paper also identifies enabling technologies, drivers, and future directions for researchers in the IoT and EV domains.

Keywords: Internet of Things · Internet of Vehicles · Connected vehicles · Electric Vehicles · Trip planning · Telematics · Vehicular networks

1 Introduction

The Internet of Things (IoT) presents a range of potential opportunities for the improvement and development of Electric Vehicles (EVs). The emergence of the IoT has brought sensor-based "intelligent" technologies, high bandwidth networking systems, and cheaper memory to EVs, which has enabled more detailed travel/traffic data exchanges between transport infrastructure, mobile phones, and navigation systems [1]. Sensing devices transmit data on a massive scale and, in some cases, adapt and react to changes in the driving environment automatically as infrastructures, cloud computing models, and machine learning algorithms can manage real-time streams of EV and smart grid data [2]. Service providers and auto manufacturers, however, struggle to access all the required data as it differs in accuracy, resolution and structure [3], and

L. Strous and V. G. Cerf (Eds.): IFIPIoT 2018, IFIP AICT 548, pp. 160–177, 2019.
https://doi.org/10.1007/978-3-030-15651-0_14

they haven't mastered the technologies needed to capture and analyze the valuable data at their disposal [2]. A need exists for higher investments in vehicular technologies and infrastructure. The need for accurate trip planning applications is growing since their usage can reduce drivers' range anxiety [3–6].

One issue with EVs is the inaccuracy of the Remaining Driving Range (RDR) in on-board displays [3, 7]. The RDR is the distance an EV can cover with the energy stored in the battery at any given time, whether fully charged or not. RDR displays are important as they can help drivers with "trip planning", but are insufficient by themselves as the battery's residual energy can be utilized in many ways. Other issues relate to limited battery capacity, availability of public charging stations, and long charging cycles [8]. Existing on-board RDR calculations only consider a limited number of factors, and often ignore the effects that driving behaviour, weather, traffic, and terrain have on future trips [3, 7]. EVs also suffer from a lack of suitable data integration technologies within the EV infrastructure [4, 9]. A lack of standards and methodologies has led to a proliferation of proprietary systems and data formats, with limited interoperability [4, 10]. These systems are tailored to work only within specific scenarios, e.g. in a given geographic area with specific target users or EV models [4]. Many connected platforms are not supported in all countries and/or lack consistency and reliable information [11]. For example, when charging station applications are not updated with the latest locations of chargers, drivers could potentially avoid taking a trip, as they fear they will not reach their destination. Drivers require a "trip plan" that assists them to drive in the most efficient way to obtain a desired range and trip time [4].

The lack of connectivity between EVs and software platforms cause these systems to remain unintegrated and force drivers to use several software products simultaneously. Drivers are forced to develop their own coping mechanisms such as finding charging possibilities during the day, plan detours, or use alternative transport modes [12]. These problems require an extension of traditional in-vehicle dashboard displays and navigation systems to consider EV limitations and drivers' preferences [1, 11]. Integrating EVs and the IoT can benefit from the virtually unlimited capabilities and resources of cloud computing to compensate for EVs' technological constraints (e.g., storage, processing, communication) [13]. Cloud technologies provide the ideal solution to manage various data sources in a distributed and dynamic manner. The above mentioned issues are worsened in developing countries such as South Africa, as limited infrastructure and EV management software is available [14].

The purpose of this paper is to address the gap in the literature related to data integration issues for EVs using the IoT. The paper reports on a literature review of data integration challenges related to EVs, with a particular focus on 'connected vehicles' and the IoT. The main goal of the paper is to propose a Data Integration Platform to successfully integrate EV data that can be used as a foundation to develop trip planning and RDR estimation applications. The research reported on in this paper forms part of a larger study that aims to develop a solution to estimate the RDR based on various factors (weather, route typology, traffic, and driver behaviour) to display useful information to drivers about all aspects necessary for trip planning and EV management. A case study methodology was adopted in conjunction with the Design

Science Research methodology. The case study was an e-mobility research organization in South Africa. For purposes of anonymity the organization is referred to as Emobi.

The paper is structured to present the main contributions in chronological order: A short introduction to the IoT is provided to help readers understand the complex data integration and data management issues with EVs and the IoT (Sect. 2). A real-world South African case study is presented of an electric mobility (e-mobility) organization (Sect. 3). A Data Integration Platform is proposed that uses cost effective and easily available resources such as smartphones, plug-in devices, cloud computing, the IoT and data services for EVs (Sect. 4). The data integration issues encountered and lessons learned from the case study are related to security, availability, quality and interoperability, and confirmed some of those from literature (Sect. 5). Finally, the paper concludes with remarks and future research directions (Sect. 6).

2 Background: Internet of Things and Connected Vehicles

2.1 Connected Vehicles: A Subset of the Internet of Things

The development of enabling technologies in modern vehicles does not only provide computation capabilities via embedded chips and remote clouds, but also support by mobile and complex networks [15, 16]. These networks are capable of sensing, wide-area connectivity, inference, and action consisting of up to 70 electronic control units (ECUs) capturing more than 2500 signals for the chassis, powertrain, user interfaces and safety networks [9]. The unity of the underlying technologies enable 'Connected Vehicles' or Vehicular Communication Networks (VCN), which fall into a category known as the Internet of Vehicles (IoV), a subset and indispensable member of the IoT paradigm [2, 15, 16]. The IoV allows for an environment where vehicles are equipped with dedicated on-board units (OBUs), capable of communicating with other vehicles, Vehicle-to-Vehicle (V2V) connections, and receiving data services from infrastructure (e.g. smart grids, road side units), cellular base stations, and Wi-Fi access points regarded as Vehicle-to Infrastructure (V2I) communications [15, 16]. The IoV relates to the scenario where drivers, passengers, and pedestrians can enjoy services provided through the Internet.

2.2 Enabling Technologies

For an EV to have an integrated data platform five types of technologies should form part of the connected vehicle environment [9]. These are: *Sensing*, *Intravehicular Connectivity*, *Intervehicle Connectivity*, *Inference*, and *Action and Feedback.*

Sensing. Electronic Control Units (ECUs) consist of various control modules, such as Engine Control Module or Brake Control Modules. The ECUs are typically embedded with software and sensors that monitor the internal systems of the vehicles. Vehicle sensors and systems fall into two categories: internal sensor systems and external sensor systems [17]. Internal sensors monitor the performance of vehicles such as wheel speed, yaw rate, steering inputs, driver inputs, powertrain outputs, or hydraulic braking [17]. Other internal sensors, specifically for EVs, can monitor battery state of charge (SoC), battery temperature, and battery current and voltage from the Battery Management System (BMS) [7]. External sensor systems have grown exponentially in recent years and are focused on enhancing driver safety, perception and autonomous navigation. These systems include a combination of camera, GPS, RADAR, LIDAR, Ultrasonic, and Dedicated Shortrange Communications [17, 18].

Intravehicle Connectivity. Intravehicle networks, or internal networks, are purposely built to share data among the different sub-systems, ECUs, sensors, and actuators to facilitate the operation of a single vehicle [9, 19]. Standardized intravehicle networks, such as the Controller Area Network (CAN), Local Interconnect Network (LIN), FlexRay, and Media Oriented Systems Transport (MOST) are well documented and allow different technologies to communicate with each other [19, 20]. The purpose of these networks is to ensure that On Board Diagnostics (OBD) services are readily available for drivers and technicians to monitor vehicle performance and health by offering fault tolerance, determinism, and flexibility [9]. Although the sensors and networks are proprietary to original vehicle manufacturers, these technologies typically follow standards that allow for vehicle diagnostics and future connected applications via interfaces, allowing external technologies from the vehicle network to communicate with the vehicle [19].

Intervehicle Connectivity. Intervehicle connectivity relates to networking approaches that allow data to move from within the vehicle to remote computing devices and other cloud computing infrastructures [9]. While local applications are contained within the vehicle, remote applications may make use of the vehicle data and combine it with data from external sources, such as traffic or weather data. Advancements in data collection and wireless transmission via telematics units or plug-in devices use cellular networks to share data among vehicles and infrastructures to facilitate data collection and optimization. Numerous competing IoT and intervehicle network standards and protocols exist, which can be a problem when considering interoperability and integration between vehicle and infrastructures [10]. Although a detailed discussion of different intervehicle networks are beyond the scope of this paper, popular networking communications found in connected vehicles are either categorised as mesh networks or cellular networks [8, 9].

Cellular networks are ideal for machine-to-machine (M2M) connectivity as they are commoditized and ubiquitous [21]. They also offer benefits of being robust, long range, and are capable of sharing data as parallelized streams when traffic density is sparse [8, 13]. As cellular networking technologies such as 4G/5G and LTE expand and costs fall, vehicles may rely on cellular technologies to facilitate connectivity for critical applications and often connect to users' personal devices [8, 15, 21].

Indirect cellular connectivity can refer to Bluetooth, Wi-Fi, and other vehicle interfacing hardware devices or visualization tools [15]. The signals from most sensors and systems flow through the CAN and can be captured through the OBD interface/port using either a wireless dongle [18] or wired equipment [22]. The dongles are usually equipped with Bluetooth or Wi-Fi functions that are able to interface with smartphones or computers, allowing data to be extracted over HTTP(S) [13, 22].

Inference. The combination of sensors and connectivity in EVs is producing massive amounts of valuable data. The advancements in in-vehicle and cloud computing power, as well as scalable data handling platforms, has made aggregation and synthesis easier in recent years. Cloud computing poses the perfect supplement for scalable server-side processing to transfer in-vehicle processing to remote locations [13]. Analyzing EV data with other vast datasets for insights can provide critical new services for EVs and their drivers. By applying big data and machine learning tools, applications can assess, learn, and adjust EV operations, and serve as a foundation for larger applications to make informed decisions. For example, to use live GPS and EV performance data and combine it with third-party devices like smartphone apps to predict or predict driving behaviour [18]. While in-vehicle analytics demonstrates the value of data in controlling EV functions in real-time, remote analytics demonstrates the potential to apply large-scale connectivity, computation and distributed information toward improving vehicle efficiency, reliability, and performance [9].

Action and Feedback. The data insights and intelligence of 'inference' technologies will enable data-informed control over the connected vehicle to attain maximum impact on the IoV environment. The control can either be a direct or an indirect approach [9]. A direct approach relies on ECU controllers and networked data to manipulate the vehicle functions. For example, light sensors will switch on the vehicles headlights automatically if daylight diminishes. An indirect approach uses the data from the sensors and other sources to provide feedback to a human operator on an in-vehicle display, or a second-screen interface to provide occupant feedback [9]. Examples of in-vehicle displays are used to monitor and improve energy economy at a glance. Second-screen feedback displays are typically found on smartphones, tablets, and more recently, smart watches, to increase the level of interactivity drivers have with their vehicles and allow applications to run on upgradable hardware [4, 8, 23].

2.3 Drivers, Platforms, and Applications of the IoT for Electric Vehicles

The evolving market of IoT is expected to offer promising solutions to transform transportation systems and automobile services [13]. In the context of EVs, solutions are needed to better communicate with their users, charging stations, and utilities to effectively manage energy resources [8]. Applications and platforms that connect EVs, users and infrastructure have been created to address this need. Telematics applications have been developed to integrate EVs into the IoT environment to provide applications such as roadside assistance, remote door unlocking, charging activity feedback, navigation services and collision notifications [9]. Many automobile manufactures allow drivers to check the status of their EVs and remotely control their charging through mobile apps [8]. Some examples of smart charging software applications are ChargePoint, PlugShare, and BMW iDrive [8]. Other researchers have combined IoT and cloud computing with machine learning approaches to identify driving behaviour [18], estimate the RDR and battery SoC [3], V2I applications and charge recommendations [16], predict cost of charging [6], trip planning decision support and navigation suggestions [4], and calculation of CO^2 emissions [22].

3 Research Methods and Contributions

The research reported on in this paper adopted the Design Science Research (DSR) methodology of Johannesson and Perjons [24]. A case study approach was used in conjunction with DSR and the case study was an e-mobility organization in South Africa, which for anonymity purposes is referred to as Emobi. The case study illustrates the application of the IoT in the EV domain and provides a real-world context for implementing the proposed EV Data Integration Platform using the IoT to support a solution for integrating EV data. An interview was conducted with a senior engineer at Emobi to establish an overview of their EV environment and the data integration issues faced. Emobi owns a fleet of three Nissan Leaf model vehicles, which are used for general transport activities and experimentation activities. Emobi needs to collect data from the EVs to better manage their driving experience and improve their energy usage. Prior to this study, Emobi had no data integration platform. Staff at Emobi stated that they have no sophisticated navigation or trip planning system to help them deal with the limited range issues inherent to EVs. Staff keep track of drivers and trips by entering driver details and EV parameters manually in a logbook. These records are then given to a receptionist to type manually into a spreadsheet and to perform manual summary statistics, e.g. distance travelled.

To collect and store data, a GPS was installed into the EVs by a service provider (called LogCo). The available data was generated with a logger device recording the CAN bus signals of a 2015 Nissan Leaf (24 kWh Li-Ion battery, 80 kW electric motor, 1700 kg vehicle mass). The logger registered the battery's current and voltage, the SoC, the GPS coordinates, and the timestamp for a period of seven months. The data can be retrieved using a Simple Object Access Protocol (SOAP) API provided by LogCo in either a summarized format (e.g. duration, distance, energy used, path, date etc.) or in finer granularity that records data directly from the CAN bus (e.g. time stamp, latitude, longitude, speed).

Several novel contributions are made by this study when compared to existing literature. Prior studies do not consider all factors when estimating the energy consumption. This study considers five main factors as summarized in the authors' prior paper to estimate energy consumption [25]: weather (wind direction and temperature), route typology (highway vs urban routes, traffic), battery parameters (voltage, state of health, and SoC), as well as historic driving behaviour. Most studies focus on efficient routing algorithms based on graph-theory concepts to navigate drivers to destinations or chargers. This study proposes to integrate existing services and technologies (e.g. Google Roads API, ChargeNow API). To the best of the authors' knowledge, this is the first study that has proposed a Data Integration Platform based on a case study situated in a developing country, such as South Africa. Further, many studies are evaluated in simulated EV environments, whereas this study worked with a real-life e-mobility company to analyze challenges when implementing an EV data management platform.

4 Data Integration Platform for Electric Vehicles Using the Internet of Things

The main, high-level objective of the EV Data Integration Platform is to provide EV drivers the tools to manage EV data and to receive services such as RDR estimations as part of a trip planning solution. The RDR estimations and trip planning services, such as charge recommendations, are enhanced by using machine learning algorithms to learn driver behaviour patterns. Deploying machine learning algorithms is important as energy consumption is heavily dependent on the driver behaviour. The platform will allow the driver to plan an EV itinerary considering spatial (route typology and length), temporal (duration of charging and route) and costing issues (cost of charging).

4.1 Overview and Requirements

The EV Data Integration Platform had three main requirements: (1) allow for data interoperability, (2) allow for service expandability, and (3) allow for device heterogeneity. In order to meet these three requirements, the platform incorporates the Microsoft Azure IoT and the HDInsight suite [26]. One reason for selecting the Azure IoT suite was that it provided various configuration and interconnected services to build large scale data analytics applications. Furthermore, Azure offered scalable and flexible services, such as facilitating a central IoT gateway hub, stream analytics engine, distributed databases, and configurable machine learning algorithms in the cloud. The Azure suite was critical for data integration and extensibility for developing trip planning services.

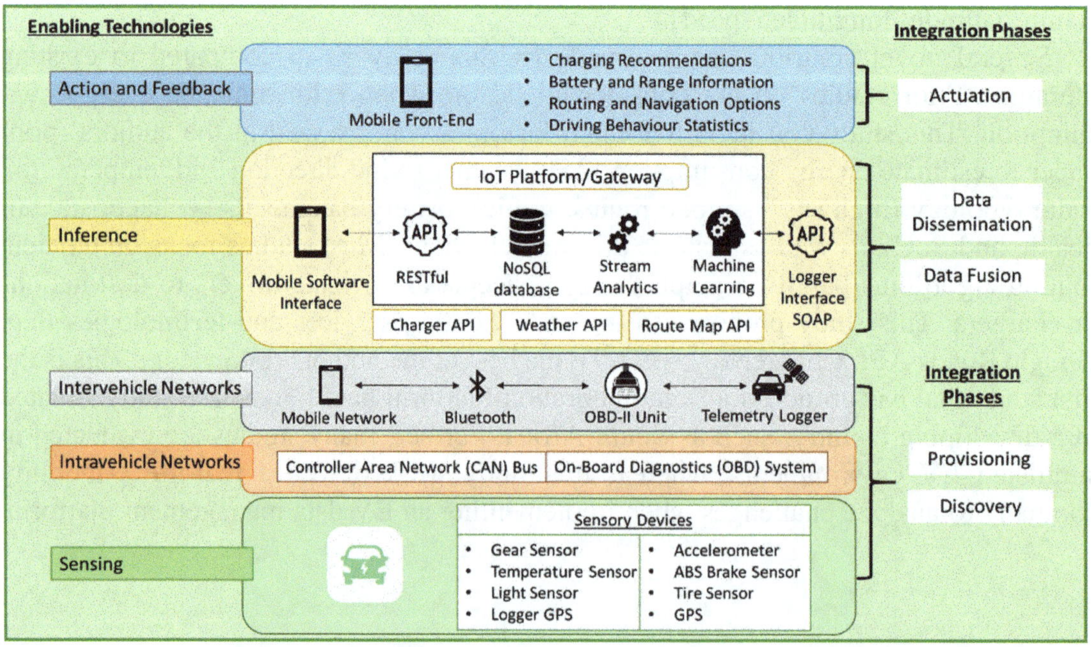

Fig. 1. Proposed Data Integration Platform for EVs using the IoT (constructed by author).

The proposed Data Integration Platform for EVs using the IoT (Fig. 1) is based on the five categories of enabling technologies (Sect. 2.2) and the five integration phases for integrating connected vehicles in the IoT ecosystem [10]. The platform describes the flow of data from the EV, the IoT, and cloud technologies through the five phases proposed in [10]: from the Resource Discovery phase, the Provisioning phase, to the Data Fusion, Data Dissemination and Actuation phases.

4.2 Resource Discovery Phase and Provisioning Phase

The Resource Discovery phase includes the configuration and uniform descriptions of available resources such as sensors, actuators and other associated OBUs that form part of the EV and its infrastructure. The platform mostly relies on the sensors installed in the Nissan Leaf EV, such as temperature, tyre pressure, light, rain, ABS braking, speedometer, and gear sensors. Third-party sensors are also considered such as the GPS installed via the logger unit and the smartphone accelerometer and GPS sensors. The measurements from these sensors are communicated via the CAN as raw data that need to be interpreted. This phase also includes the discovery of other sensors such as the GPS and accelerometers in the smartphone used, and the GPS from LogCo.

While the Resource Discovery phase retrieves a set of available sensors to provide raw data, the Provisioning phase monitors the rules, ontologies, protocols, and semantic reasoning for data to be transmitted via the networks. For example, the CAN coordinates the data that is transmitted from various sensors in the EV and enforces the permissions to prevent unauthorised devices to retrieve data from the network.

When adopting the platform in the case study of Emobi, two popular methods for extracting raw data were used as described in Wang et al. [18] and Tseng et al. [22]. The first method used a GPS logger installed by LogCo to extract data from the CAN. This approach is like the 'sniffing tool' approach where CAN message traffic is observed and requires knowledge of CAN protocols to program firmware to record and extract the CAN packets [22]. The second method, and an easier way to extract data, is to use an OBD dongle, which plugs into an OBD-II port generally situated in the cabin of the EV. The OBD dongle is programmed to interpret the CAN message traffic and parses them to return human readable parameters based on OBD conversion rules. The data were logged at a 5 Hz frequency as in Wang et al. [18] and De Cauwer et al. [12].

4.3 Data Fusion Phase

The Data Fusion phase acts as a distributed knowledge base within the EV and IoT ecosystem. Data interoperability is important in this phase. It is worth noting that service providers (e.g. charging station providers) are responsible for their own data management platforms, which are characterised by their own data representation formats [4]. As mentioned before, the Data Integration Platform does not aim to replace existing systems but is rather aimed at serving as a data collector or integrated repository for EV data management. Raw data originating from the EV and other smart devices (smartphone GPS sensors) are integrated or 'fused' to attain a higher level of intelligence.

When adopting the platform at Emobi, the technical complexities of retrieving data from the CAN had to be considered. The choice was made to use a mobile application called LeafSpy, which has gained popularity in the EV community, to monitor Nissan Leaf diagnostics from a smartphone using an OBD dongle. LeafSpy has a large support community, allows a large variety of EV parameters to be traced from the CAN, and supports configuration settings to send data in JSON (JavaScript Object Notation) format to a server using a cellular network. This allowed for quick access to EV data. Although LeafSpy allows additional configuration to setup a server, a RESTful (representational state transfer) API had to be developed to divert the streamed data to the Azure IoT gateway server. This API was developed using the Node.js programming language, which is invoked when the data is sent from the smartphone.

Despite the cloud's scalability and relative low cost of operation, increasing computing power does not address data management challenges [9]. Traditional databases cannot handle real-time requests and require technologies that use distributed storage and parallel computing. For this reason, the data is streamed from the smartphone and is stored in a MongoDB instance (NoSQL database) hosted in Azure, which allows for quicker access. Due to popular issues with telematics devices being intermittent [13], the platform collects EV data from both the OBD dongle and the tracking unit (LogCo) as a backup for potential data loss. The benefits and challenges of having both devices are compared in Table 1. Nine criteria were used to perform this comparison: the graphical user interface, supported APIs for data access, data governance, flexibility, cost, mobile connectivity, data backup and driver identification. Effort refers to the amount of effort to configure the data collection approach [27]. Graphical User Interface refers to information displays about the EV or driver performance [28]. API support relates to additional web services that allow data to exchange between the EV and a server to either render data to an end-user device or another server for storage or processing purposes [4, 13]. Data governance is the extent to which a service provider, or EV owner, is responsible for the installation, processing, and safeguarding of the data retrieved from the EV [9, 27]. The cost relates to the installation cost and ongoing costs to retrieve and maintain the data [28]. Flexibility refers to the ability to manipulate the approach to collect, transform and use data for applications [19, 22]. Data transport protocol refers to the protocol that is used to transport data from the EV to an end-user device or storage device. Driver identification relates to the ability to identify the driver [18].

The EV Data Integration Platform relies on web services from third parties to collect and integrate data for the five factors influencing RDR. Data sources were selected based on their ability to provide data on each of the following five factors: *Weather (W)*, *Route and Terrain (RT)*, *Vehicle Model (VM)*, *Battery Model (BM)*, and *Driving Behavior (DB)*. The available data sources were mapped to the data attributes that they contribute to as inputs to the machine learning and prediction algorithms (Table 2). The data sources for some of these factors, are webservice APIs available through RESTful formats (JSON). Other APIs that were used are the AccuWeather API and the Google API, which provided both XML and JSON data formats, as per Table 2. A smartphone application, called the Trip Planner App (TP-App) was developed as a user interface to consume services from the Data Integration Platform and perform trip planning activities (e.g. input destination and driver ID).

Table 1. Comparison between LeafSpy OBD approach and LogCo tracking services.

Criteria	LogCo (Telematics CAN-based)	LeafSpy (OBD-based)
Effort [27]	Once-off	On-going
Graphical user interface [28]	None	Live monitoring of EV data
APIs support [4, 13]	SOAP/XML (Provided)	RESTful/JSON (self-managed)
Data governance [9, 27]	Service provider (web service provided)	Self-managed (own server and database)
Cost [28]	Monthly subscription Initial installation	Mobile data costs Once-off
Flexibility [19, 22]	Limited to technical knowledge and service level agreement	Limited to software
Cost [27]	Installation fee + monthly subscription	Initial purchase fee for equipment + cellular network
Data transport protocol [13, 22]	Satellite-based (GPS/GSM)	Cellular network-based/HTTP
Driver identification [18]	None	None

AccuWeather. Weather data from hourly forecasts based on the location's coordinates was obtained from the AccuWeather API [29]. The coordinates can be provided from the Google Maps API for the current location and segments of the planned route, if the destination is known. Data can be retrieved for all *Weather* data needs, such as temperature, wind speed and direction, visibility, cloud cover and precipitation. Of particular importance is the head on wind speeds that create additional forces on the EV, and possible rain that will cause the EV to use its headlight and windscreen wipers.

Google APIs provide a variety of services that satisfy the data needs for the *Route and Terrain*, and *Driving Behaviour* factors [30]. These APIs make use of a smartphone's GPS and mobile network to communicate with cell towers and Wi-Fi nodes to provide real-time trip data. Support is provided for collecting and retrieving data on points of interests, travel times, live traffic alerts, directions, elevation data, and offers geocoding services to track full-length trips.

Charging APIs such as PlugShare [31], Google Places, and ChargeNow [32] were used to supplement missing data related to the other factors. PlugShare was selected as it supported the most charging stations in South Africa at the time of this study. Data can be retrieved in a JSON format, which allows developers to integrate details for listed charging stations across all three platforms based on location information. Data can be retrieved related to charging stations, such as connecter type, charging station type, operating hours, cost, and location. Google maps can select the most suitable route based on charging station availability and route.

Table 2. Comparison of available data attributes for each factor from sources.

	Data attributes	LeafSpy	LogCo	Accu-Weather	TP-App	Google maps	Plug-Share
RT	Latitude and longitude	✓	✓	x	✓	x	x
	Elevation	✓	x	x	x	✓	x
	GPS heading	x	✓	x	x	x	x
	Time stamp	✓	✓	x	✓	x	x
	Distance	x	x	x	x	x	✓
	Gradient and terrain	x	x	x	x	✓	x
	Speed limit	x	x	x	x	✓	x
	Traffic	x	x	x	x	✓	x
	Charging location	x	x	x	x	✓	✓
W	Wind speed/direction	x	x	✓	x	x	x
	Ambient temperature	✓	x	✓	x	x	x
VM	Speed	✓	✓	x	x	x	x
	Braking	✓	x	x	x	x	x
	Tyre pressure	✓	x	x	x	x	x
	Auxiliary items	✓	x	x	x	x	x
	Acceleration	✓	x	x	x	x	x
	Odometer	✓	✓	x	x	x	x
BM	SoC	✓	✓	x	x	x	x
	Battery health	✓	x	x	x	x	x
	Voltage and current	✓	✓	x	x	x	x
	Battery temperature	✓	x	x	x	x	x
DM	Driver ID	x	x	x	✓	x	x
	Driver score	x	x	x	✓	x	x

4.4 Data Dissemination Phase

Future applications of EVs will provide powerful analytical and machine learning services to drivers, thus requiring heterogeneous data collected in the Data Fusion phase. In the Data Dissemination phase, two analytical components are included: The Batch Processing Layer and the Streaming Layer.

Batch Processing Layer. This layer is concerned with data from persistent or long-term storage, such as those large datasets found in the NoSQL database (MongoDB). Machine learning algorithms are executed here in regular time intervals to adapt to changes in patterns in data. The main machine learning algorithms applied here are for detecting patterns in driving behaviour and scoring drivers according to aggressive, normal or calm categories. Once drivers are classified, analytics are performed based on energy usage per route segment (e.g. highway, urban, mixed). Azure allows for configurable machine learning algorithms and scripts through a drag-and-drop interface. This enabled easy configuration for cleaning and aggregating datasets, feature selection and training, and evaluating and publishing of results in the Azure IoT platform. Two important processing steps were applied, namely pre-processing and model training.

Pre-processing required a number of Python scripts to process the raw data in order to obtain a list of features that is suitable for applying the machine learning model. For raw sensor data, this typically included further sub-stages such as a sampling stage, data cleaning, feature extraction and noise filtering [33]. The first Python script that was written handled the cleaning of the trip data to ensure that there are no missing or incomplete values. Once cleaning was complete, specific data attributes had to be derived that provide a suitable input to the machine learning model. For example, energy consumed, distanced travelled, trip number (ID), acceleration, elevation, and gradient. Other APIs that were used were Google's Roads and Elevation APIs, and the AccuWeather API to understand the route segment, traffic, and weather conditions at recorded GPS coordinates and timestamps. By doing this, driving behaviour and energy consumption patterns could be determined.

Streaming Layer. The purpose of the streaming layer is to analyze the incoming EV streams in real-time and combine them with the data from other sources required for the trip ahead. The data is also pre-processed in this step using the same pre-processing step as for the Batch Layer.

Azure's IoT Hub was used with its Stream Analytics job functionality to aggregate, filter, and compute data streamed from a smartphone. Once again, the data was combined with other APIs from other service providers, based on the user inputs. For example, the driver would input his/her identification and the planned destination in the TP-App. The input data was important when considering retrieving the driver category (aggressive, calm, normal), as the energy consumption estimation algorithm would adapt its calculations accordingly. Data was also retrieved from Google Roads and AccuWeather APIs to retrieve route and weather inputs for the specified route. This was mainly used to estimate energy consumed over the planned route and to provide charging recommendations. Azure's publish/subscribe approach was incorporated, where machine learning and stream analytics functionality can be published as a series of web services; thus, allowing for the results of the Stream Processing and Batch Processing learning layers to be published to a front-end application using HTTP RESTful interfaces.

4.5 Actuation Phase

During the Actuation Phase, the smart mobile devices of passengers and/or the on-board ECUs can take decisions and send commands to actuators allowing the EVs to react to the environment [10]. The developed mobile application (TP-App) subscribed to the RESTful services hosted on the Azure suite. An example of the smartphone's use is where the driver can view the estimated energy usage for a trip or view charging opportunities along the path to the inserted destination. If the driver chooses a new destination, the route and energy requirements are recalculated based on the machine learning model and a check is performed to know if enough energy is stored in the battery to reach the destination. The driver is informed of the amount of energy required to recharge the EV to reach the next destination. If no destination is entered, the model relies on historical driving cycle data, driver category, and real-time GPS data to predict driving routes.

5 Issues Identified and Lessons Learned

5.1 Data Availability and Governance

Despite the heterogeneity of data sources that are required for effective data integration in EVs, one of the major challenges is the lack of publicly available real-world data for EVs and their charging infrastructures [23]. The reasons are partially due to privacy issues of driver, non-disclosure agreements set with telematics service providers, or unsupported data sharing formats (e.g. poorly developed APIs) [4, 13]. Some of these issues were experienced when attempting to connect to the LogCo APIs, which were often unavailable and inflexible in terms of upscaling the frequency of logging equipment and the number of parameters recorded. EV data and characteristics were often aggregated (e.g. trip summaries instead of logged data), which made simulation of real-life environments and the evaluation of predictive models difficult [23].

A strategy to protect EVs from security and privacy breaches is to shield network components using gateway devices and software to monitor network interceptions [20]. The retrieval of data from sensors is difficult to attain as the utility of sensors are governed to mask raw data in the EV [9, 22]. A thorough understanding of CANs is required to extend the scope of data parameters.

5.2 Heterogeneity and Interoperability

IoT platforms need to support data interoperability, service-level expandability, and device heterogeneity in connected vehicles as a way to communicate effectively and efficiently [4]. The heterogeneity of existing sensing hardware, end-user devices (e.g. smartphones), and vehicle characteristics often differ in vehicular M2M communication [8, 10]. Cloud-based IoT platforms and services depend heavily on RESTful webservices and IP technologies to provide interoperability and ease development [10]. For this reason, third-party apps that interpret OBD readings from CAN were purchased. Often these configurations are prone to cause higher latency and quality of service [10], whereas the ideal solution would be to send the data directly from the EV network to the cloud.

5.3 Security, Privacy, and Authentication

Security controls are required for EV data management and backup data storage facilities as sensitive information can be exposed to attacks [20]. Challenges were encountered when attempting to send data to Azure from the TP-App as well as to connect to the RESTful (MongoDB) and SOAP APIs (LogCo). This issue was due to computers that were not provisioned in the Azure suite, as well as computers trying to access the databases from unauthorized IP addresses. Additional programming was required to pass a Globally Unique Identifier (GUID) from the smartphone to Azure to establish a secure connection.

5.4 Accuracy, Reliability and Completeness

Data accuracy and reliability is critical for connected applications in the context of EVs [9, 13]. During test runs with the EV, the telematics solution and cellular network for the smartphone were often intermittent and suffered from imprecision and signal loss. Some of the logs were incomplete and missing data could be averaged by following a similar approach as in [12]. For example, speed values were missing from the GPS logs. If the speed was monotonically increasing (positive acceleration) or decreasing (negative acceleration) over multiple measurement points, the acceleration was averaged up to a maximum of four measurement points (4 s). Although averaging is a workaround method for incomplete data, this method negatively affects the accuracy of data. Another issue was that the telematics logger often became intermittent, impacting its reliability. The logger often indicated that the EV was moving, but did not show changes in SoC measurements. In this case, if the SoC readings could not be recovered from the alternative LeafSpy logs, the trips had to be disregarded as the energy usage could not be determined and would skew the training results of the machine learning model. Another issue was that LeafSpy user interface often stopped, but still logged the data to the server during a trip. The issue was overcome by purchasing a newer version of LeafSpy.

5.5 Training and Human Error

Using the OBD dongle and smartphone equipment for each trip relies on people, which means that improper configuration or forgetting to charge the gateway smartphone can cause a data loss [9]. Although the issue never occurred, it was a challenge to install preventative measures such as training drivers to use the OBD and smartphone app. Reminders were placed inside the EV to charge the smartphone, check that the phone was connected to the OBD dongle, and to power the phone off after each trip to save battery consumption.

5.6 Timeliness and Temporal Issues

The timeliness of data is often impacted by unpredictable issues, which causes real-time applications to experience poor performance. While a significant challenge exists to attain stable, acceptable network performance between devices and cloud resources, it is often difficult to ensure timeliness of data. IoT applications that require quick reactivity for provisioning and authentication often suffer due to delays in network traffic, which negatively impacts performance, usability, and user experience. One issue experienced after analyzing the logged data was that often trips are recorded for short periods where the EV is either idle or travelling short distances (under 1 km). This issue related to Emobi drivers switching on the EV to check the SoC or odometer readings, or moving the EV from one parking lot to another. These trips are insignificant for the broader RDR estimation problem and its consequences caused outliers in the analyzed data. It was important to automate the cleaning of such trips in the data set. A similar approach was taken to clean data as described in Sect. 5.4.

6 Conclusions and Future Directions

This paper forms part of a larger study and extends the work on enhanced RDR estimation models to support drivers in efficient trip planning for EVs. The main theoretical contribution of this paper is a Data Integration Platform for EVs using the IoT and several enabling technologies found in modern EVs. The platform was implemented at an e-mobility organization in South Africa to demonstrate the practicality of the proposed platform. A second contribution is the data integration issues identified in a real-world case study in South Africa. These issues verified some of those reported in other literature, but additional issues were also reported. Furthermore, this paper highlights some of the main drivers and applications for connecting EVs using the IoT. A comparison was derived between investing in data retrieval services (e.g. telematics provider) and self-managed data retrieval techniques (OBD and smartphone).

The Data Integration Platform can support drivers to accurately estimate the RDR and to plan their trips. To fully benefit from the platform and its overall design, associated enabling technologies and IoT platforms need to support a variety of data sources and analytical techniques. Data should be collected from heterogeneous charging management software, weather websites, telematics devices (OBD and tracker unit) for live EV modelling and battery modelling data, as well as route and terrain data from mapping packages such as Google Maps. The issues and lessons learned can provide guidance to other researchers to avoid similar data integration pitfalls. Practitioners can use the platform for designing EV systems, thereby reducing development costs and supporting the creation of innovative services in the IoT and EV domain. The limitations of this study were that it could not evaluate big data methods as the size of the data was still manageable with traditional data analytical techniques. Another limitation was that a full evaluation of the Data Integration Platform remains to be completed.

Future work will report on the results of automating driving behavior analysis to predict energy consumption based on driver style, as well as to make driver identification automatic. The evaluation of RDR estimation accuracy will also be investigated using the proposed platform. Lastly, user experience and user interface techniques will be evaluated based on the usefulness and helpfulness of information presented to drivers to plan trips more effectively.

Acknowledgements. The financial assistance of the National Research Foundation (NRF) and the Telkom Centre of Excellence (CoE) towards this research is hereby acknowledged. Opinions expressed, and conclusions arrived at, are those of the author and are not necessarily to be attributed to the NRF or Telkom.

References

1. Gambuti, R., Canale, S., Facchinei, F., Lanna, A., Di Giorgio, A.: Electric vehicle trip planning integrating range constraints and charging facilities. In: 23rd Proceedings on Mediterranean Conference on Control Automation, pp. 472–479 (2015)
2. Lee, C., Wu, C.: Collecting and mining big data for electric vehicle systems using battery modeling data. In: 12th International Proceedings on Information Technology - New Generations, pp. 626–631. IEEE (2015)
3. Rahimi-Eichi, A., Chow, M.Y.: Big-data framework for electric vehicle range estimation. In: 40th International Proceedings on Annual Conference of the IEEE Industrial Electronics Society, IECON, pp. 5628–5634. IEEE (2014)
4. Bedogni, L., Bononi, L., Di Felice, M., D'Elia, A., Cinotti, T.S.: A route planner service with recharging reservation: electric itinerary with a click. IEEE Intel. Transp. Syst. Mag. **8** (3), 75–84 (2016)
5. Sarrafan, K., Sutanto, D., Muttaqi, K.M., Town, G.: Accurate range estimation for an electric vehicle including changing environmental conditions and traction system efficiency. Electr. Syst. Transp. **7**(2), 117–124 (2017)
6. Ferreira, J., Monteiro, V., Afonso, J.: Dynamic range prediction for an electric vehicle. In: 27th Proceedings on World Electric Vehicle Symposium and Exhibition (EVS27), pp. 1–11 (2014)
7. Sarrafin, K., Muttaqi, M., Town, G.: An intelligent driver alerting system for real-time range indicator embedded in electric vehicles. Proc. 2016 IEEE Ind. Appl. Soc. Annu. Meet. **53**(3), 1751–1760 (2016)
8. Mahmud, K., Town, G.E., Morsalin, S., Hossain, M.J.: Integration of electric vehicles and management in the internet of energy. Renew. Sustain. Energy Rev. **82**, 1–25 (2017)
9. Siegel, J.E., Erb, D.C., Sarma, S.E.: A survey of the connected vehicle landscape, architectures, enabling technologies, applications, and development areas. IEEE Trans. Intell. Transp. Syst. **19**, 1–16 (2017)
10. Datta, S.K., Da Costa, R.P.F., Harri, J., Bonnet, C.: Integrating connected vehicles in Internet of Things ecosystems: challenges and solutions. In: Proceedings of 17th International Symposium on a World of Wireless, Mobile and Multimedia Network (WoWMoM), pp. 1–6 (2016)
11. Monigatti, P., Apperley, M., Rogers, B.: Smart energy interfaces for electric vehicles. In: Proceedings of International Working Conference on Advanced Visual Interfaces (AVI), pp. 413–416 (2014)
12. De Cauwer, C., Van Mierlo, J., Coosemans, T.: Energy consumption prediction for electric vehicles based on real-world data. Energies **8**(1), 8573–8593 (2015). https://doi.org/10.3390/en8088573
13. Botta, A., De Donato, W., Persico, V., Pescapé, A.: Integration of cloud computing and Internet of Things: a survey. Future Gener. Comput. Syst. **56**, 684–700 (2016)
14. EVIA: Unity in sustainable mobility: roadmap towards building a unified electro mobility industry in South Africa (2016). http://www.evia.org.za/EVIA2016Booklet.pdf. Accessed 01 Nov 2018
15. Chen, J., Zhou, H., Zhang, N., Yang, P., Gui, L., Shen, X.: Software defined internet of vehicles: architecture, challenges and solutions. Commun. Inf. Netw. **1**(1), 14–26 (2016)
16. Cao, Y., Song, H., Kaiwartya, O., Lei, A., Wang, Y., Putrus, G.: Electric vehicle charging recommendation and enabling ICT technologies: recent advances and future directions. IEEE COMSOC MMTC Commun. Front. **11**(2), 1–10 (2016)

17. Varghese, J.Z., Boone, R.G.: Overview of autonomous vehicle sensors and systems. In: Proceedings of 2015 International Conference on Operations Excellence and Service Engineering, pp. 178–191 (2015)
18. Wang, B., Panigrahi, S., Narsude, M., Mohanty, A.: Driver identification using vehicle telematics data. In: Proceedings of WCX™ 17: SAE World Congress Experience, pp. 1–8 (2017)
19. Hank, P., Muller, S., Vermesan, O., Van Den Keybus, J.: Automotive ethernet: in-vehicle networking and smart mobility. In: Design, Automation Test in Europe Conference Exhibition (DATE), pp. 1735–1739 (2013)
20. Parkinson, S., Ward, P., Wilson, K., Miller, J.: Cyber threats facing autonomous and connected vehicles: future challenges. IEEE Trans. Intell. Transp. Syst. **18**(11), 2898–2915 (2017)
21. Shladover, S.E.: Connected and automated vehicle systems: introduction and overview. J. Intell. Transp. Syst. **22**(3), 190–200 (2018). https://doi.org/10.1080/15472450.2017.1336053
22. Tseng, C.M., Zhou, W., Al Hashmi, M., Chau, C.K., Song, S.G., Wilhelm, E.: Data extraction from electric vehicles through OBD and application of carbon footprint evaluation. In: Proceedings on Electric Vehicle Systems, Data, and Applications (EV-SYS), pp. 1–6 (2016)
23. Li, B., Kisacikoglu, M.C., Liu, C., Singh, N., Erol-Kantarci, M.: Big data analytics for electric vehicle integration in green smart cities. IEEE Commun. Mag. **55**(11), 19–25 (2017)
24. Johannesson, P., Perjons, E.: An Introduction to Design Science. Springer, Cham (2014). https://doi.org/10.1007/978-3-319-10632-8
25. Smuts, M., Scholtz, B., Wesson, J.: A critical review of factors influencing the remaining driving range of electric vehicles. In: Proceedings of 1st International Conference on Next Generation Computing Applications (NextComp), pp. 1–6 (2017)
26. Microsoft Azure Homepage. https://azure.microsoft.com/en-us/services/hdinsight/. Accessed 01 Nov 2018
27. Kolarova, V., Kuhnimhof, T., Trommer, S.: Assessment of real-world vehicle data from electric vehicles – potentials and challenges. In: Proceedings of 11th International Conference on Transport Survey Methods (ISCTSC), pp. 1–11 (2017)
28. Castignani, G., Derrmann, T., Frank, R., Engel, T.: Driver behavior profiling using smartphones: a low-cost platform for driver monitoring. Intell. Transp. Syst. Mag. **7**(1), 91–102 (2015)
29. AccuWeather Homepage. https://developer.accuweather.com/apis. Accessed 01 Nov 2018
30. Google Maps Homepage. https://cloud.google.com/maps-platform/. Accessed 01 Nov 2018
31. PlugShare Homepage. http://developer.plugshare.com/. Accessed 01 Nov 2018
32. ChargeNow Global Homepage. https://www.chargenow.com/web/chargenow-global. Accessed 01 Nov 2018
33. Strohbach, M., Ziekow, H., Gazis, V., Akiva, N.: Towards a big data analytics framework for IoT and smart city applications. In: Xhafa, F., Barolli, L., Barolli, A., Papajorgji, P. (eds.) Modeling and Processing for Next-Generation Big-Data Technologies. MOST, vol. 4, pp. 257–282. Springer, Cham (2015). https://doi.org/10.1007/978-3-319-09177-8_11

Working with IoT – A Case Study Detailing Workplace Digitalization Through IoT System Adoption

Viktor Mähler(✉) and Ulrika Holmström Westergren(✉)

Department of Informatics, Umeå University, 90187 Umeå, Sweden
{viktor.mahler,ulrika.westergren}@umu.se

Abstract. As the Internet of Things (IoT) continues to grow in scope it is bound to pervade an increasing number of firms. To that end it becomes important to understand the challenges and opportunities associated with introducing IoT in the workplace. By studying IoT implementation and usage from the perspective of three different stakeholders cooperating around the same IoT system, we explore how the introduction of IoT in the workplace presents unique opportunities and challenges for both management and individual workers. We conclude that the identified opportunities expressed by the different stakeholders were increased productivity, the ability to monitor performance, and improved customer relations. Challenges encountered were increased stress among some workers and forming a shared understanding of the IoT system's capabilities amongst different stakeholders.

Keywords: Internet of Things · Digitalization · Building maintenance

1 Introduction

The digital transformation of the workplace is an ongoing process for firms that are striving to stay relevant within today's business environment. Moving towards a digital profile is to some extent inevitable, as information technology (IT) pervades all types of branches and sectors. Thus, the real question lies within how this transformation is imagined and implemented both from a management perspective as well as by individual workers. Previous research has highlighted the need for a processual and contextual understanding of the role of IT within the workplace [18] in order to capture, for example, the situated use of IT [17, 28], IT value [13, 15], IT usage and communities of practice [7], and effects on demands for skilled labor [2]. However, as IT is constantly evolving, there is need for more research that takes into account the new solutions and offerings that are currently on the market, impacting workplaces in new ways.

This paper targets the Internet of Things (IoT) as an emerging technological paradigm. Current estimates say that in 2020 there will be 20 billion connected products globally, and numbers are expected to rise. Naturally a large number of these products and solutions will be implemented within workplace environments, where the

L. Strous and V. G. Cerf (Eds.): IFIPIoT 2018, IFIP AICT 548, pp. 178–193, 2019.
https://doi.org/10.1007/978-3-030-15651-0_15

capture, transmission and analysis of contextual data will be used to increase efficiency, transparency and effectiveness [8]. As we are only in the first stages of the IoT, most of the research so far has focused on technological, architectural and infrastructural requirements in order to set up a functioning IoT-network [31]. Although there is an emerging stream of research that focuses on organizational impacts of IoT, for example IoT business models and on IoT ecosystems [20, 21, 25, 26], there are few empirical studies about how the introduction of IoT in the workplace will affect organizational strategy, worker conditions, and possibilities for value creation [33].

In this study we follow the digitalization of building maintenance in the form of an IoT system designed for efficient cleaning services and ask the question: *What are the challenges and opportunities associated with introducing IoT in the workplace?* By studying IoT implementation and usage from the perspective of three different stakeholders: the building/operations management of the firm, the IoT system provider, and the cleaning services provider, we aim to show how the introduction of IoT in the workplace has implications on professional life. By conducting interviews with key personnel, reviewing existing research and analyzing our case through the Technological Frames framework [19], we capture people's understanding of the IoT, thereby contributing to the discourse on IT in organizations in general and IoT in the workplace in particular. We conclude that the identified opportunities expressed by the different stakeholders were increased productivity, the ability to monitor performance, and improved customer relations. Challenges encountered were increased stress among some workers and forming a shared understanding of the IoT system's capabilities amongst different stakeholders.

The paper proceeds as follows: In the next section we give an overview of related research regarding the digital workplace and the IoT. In Sect. 3 we introduce our theoretical framework, followed by methodology and results in Sects. 4 and 5. We end the paper with a discussion of the results and conclusions and provide suggestions for further research.

2 Related Research

2.1 The Digital Workplace

Ever since technology was first introduced in the workplace in the 1950s, scholars have attempted to understand and explain the social and organizational consequences of information technology [11, 23, 24, 30]. Earlier research shows, for example, how IT has been linked to worker productivity, by reducing the cost of information exchange and providing access to knowledge needed for project multitasking [1]. In addition, it has been shown that employees' adoption of IT is strongly influenced by co-workers' attitudes, pinning social factors as one of the most important adoption factors, along with training and management support [7], and the involvement of affected parties within an organization to facilitate a successful implementation of IT [4]. Furthermore, it has made possible the extensive electronic monitoring of employees, adding layers of legal, ethical and privacy aspects to the mix [16]. As IT has evolved and continues to pervade professional life, the concept of the digital workplace has emerged in information systems research, denoting a context where workers are exposed to a multitude of digital tools that allow for both collaboration and mobility, but also require a certain compliance and may lead to undesirable outcomes in terms of stress and overload [12].

In order to become a digital workplace, the organization must actively engage in a process of digitalization. As devices and networks start to be able to communicate and process information amongst one another they achieve *convergence*, which – when reaching a certain point – will allow for the social infrastructures to converge and change to fit the technology. This may change the way the business itself operates, combining several different aspects to achieve a new way of working, and providing a pervasive system that garners support and increases likelihood of being used [29, 34]. A current example of the entanglement of digital technology and organizational infrastructure is seen in the organizational adoption of IoT, which imposes new opportunities and challenges for the digital workplace.

2.2 The Internet of Things

The IoT denotes a technological paradigm where physical and digital systems melt together to form cyber-physical systems [3]. The common theme is a non-separable combination of physical hardware and digital software along with sensors, data storage and remote connectivity. The ongoing and rapid expansion of an affordable IT-infrastructure together with new technological developments driving miniaturization of components, has driven the costs of hardware ever downward [5], virtually removing the threshold for adding connectivity to everyday consumer products. In addition, there has been an ongoing strive for platforms and application programming interfaces to permit interoperability, which is crucial if IoT systems are going to be able to scale [27].

The IoT has so far mostly been studied from a technological, architectural and infrastructural perspective and less is known about the organizational implications of IoT [31, 33]. However, as the IoT is expected to grow in scope, many firms are seeing opportunities for value creation through the capture and analysis of data. For some firms this means moving from selling products to selling services, for others the IoT can provide new markets where already existing services are enhanced by the provision of contextual data. For yet others, the IoT offers new opportunities to apply existing skill sets, for example in data analysis or interface design [26]. In addition, the IoT is expected to be developed by ecosystems of firms, where one firm might deliver the technology, another the implementation context, and a third provide the services based on the captured data [20, 25]. Such a collaborative environment presumes overlapping ambitions and mutual goals, but different stakeholders might have divergent perspectives on both value creation and organizational implications of IoT implementation.

Furthermore, the IoT offers unprecedented access to data about products, processes and people. Data that is generated and captured can be analyzed to distinguish employee work patterns as well as customer behaviors and organizations. Firms therefore need to make strategic choices about data management [20] as well as strive to create a balance between trust, security and privacy concerns [6]. In sum, in order to explore the implications of introducing the IoT in the workplace, one must consider not only the IoT system and its service offerings, but also the perspectives of the ecosystem stakeholders and their respective notions of IoT value production and capture.

3 Theoretical Framework

In order to capture and understand the perspectives of different IoT ecosystem stakeholders we use the Technological Frames framework developed by Orlikowski and Gash [19]. The concept or technological frames is that there exists underlying assumptions, interpretations, and expectations of a system; *technological frames* – and these frames might widely differ between different groups in an organization; such as those in a managerial position, workers and technicians. Technological frames may have a powerful effect on the adoption of new technology as they will strongly influence the choices that are made; in regards to the design and the use of the technologies when presented to workers [19].

If the expectations and the assumptions made by the various groups are running along similar lines then *congruence* is achieved – meaning that the view of the system is shared in its intended functionality. If the viewpoints, on the other hand, are *incongruent*, it means that the frames do not match between the groups – for example a manager expecting a system to deliver something entirely different than what the workers are expecting. The end result of *frame incongruence* had been observed as the eventual cancelation of the project in which it was identified, and that it can have severe negative impacts where it is prevalent [9, 19].

The *Technological Frames framework* contains three main concepts; *Nature of technology,* representing the understanding of the functionality and potential of technology. *Technology Strategy,* meaning the view of what technology might add to the organization and the reason for its implementation. And *Technology-in-use;* being the everyday use of the technology and the consequences deriving from its usage [19]. By using this framework, we are able to highlight different views and perspectives and detect both congruent and incongruent frames in regards to IoT adoption.

4 Research Methodology

We chose to perform a qualitative case study [10, 32] in order to gain an insight into the personal thoughts and reasons presented by key personnel amongst the three stakeholders, being the cleaning service provider, the building manager and the system provider. The main method of data collection was through semi-structured interviews [14], where the rationale behind the IoT system implementation, viewpoints, challenges and positive effects were discussed at length in order to create an understanding for both the technology and the technological frames present within the three stakeholder groups.

By examining key actors' taken-for-granted notions of technology, we were able to draw insights into the development, usage and implications of introducing IoT within the workplace.

4.1 Research Context

The three actors related to this are – *BuildingCo*, a sporting facility owning a large building complex featuring recreational activities, with roughly 4000 visitors every week, *CleanCo,* a large organization offering cleaning services; where this is one of their contracts (with an assigned cleaning crew), and a *SystemCo*; delivering both the IoT system and cleaning products (with the IoT system being our primary focus).

BuildingCo had moved towards implementing a new system when the old cleaning company that had been working for them was fired due to complaints and inadequate performance output. BuildingCo, together with the new cleaning provider, CleanCo, aimed to provide a better service and through that reduce complaints. Along came SystemCo, offering BuildingCo a chance to install their brand new IoT system.

The IoT system was a complete service purchased from SystemCo; which already sold the cleaning products used by BuildingCo; such as paper towels, toilet paper, soap and various other supplies. In installing this IoT system, the soap- and paper dispensers were outfitted with sensors measuring the volume dispensed by the containers, as well as visitor counters, counting the number of people that frequented critical areas; such as toilets and shower facilities.

Data that is gathered through the various sensors is wirelessly transmitted to wall-mounted receivers placed throughout the building. These receivers have a vastly larger bandwidth and processing power than individual sensors. The receivers then transmit the aforementioned data to a cloud based service where statistics are measured and organized in a graphical user interface accessible to the building/operations manager for BuildingCo, team-leaders of CleanCo, and SystemCo themselves.

BuildingCo has been using this system for roughly one and a half years, allowing for it to become a daily aspect of their organization, relying upon it for the cleaning being performed, but also serving as a pilot organization for SystemCo.

4.2 Data Collection

The data was collected using snowball sampling where the building manager was first approached. Said manager then referred us to other key actors responsible for the IoT system itself and actors both on the service-side and the operational-side of the organization. The snowball sampling is recommended when dealing with small populations featuring specific characteristics; which in this case was high-level access to the IoT system [22]. From this sampling a total of 14 interviews were performed, featuring personnel from CleanCo, the building manager responsible for the purchase and system as well as personnel from SystemCo. The average interview lasted 50 min with a maximum of 170 min. All interviews were audio-recorded and transcribed (Table 1).

Table 1. A table detailing the interview respondents, their roles and the number of interviews performed with each of the respondents.

Actor role	Person	Role of respondent	No. of interviews
CleanCo	P01	Team-leader, system manager	2
	P02	Team-leader, system manager	1
	P03	Team-leader	1
	P04	Cleaner	1
	P05	Cleaner	1
	P06	Cleaner	1
BuildingCo	B01	Building-/operations manager	2
SystemCo	S01	Customer relations/product owner	2
	S02	Sales representative	2
	S03	Technical manager	1

4.3 Data Analysis

Data was analyzed through the Technological Frames framework [19] and the analysis was performed in two different stages. First, we read through all interviews pertaining to a specific stakeholder firm and coded the data into the three theoretical categories of nature of technology, technology strategy, and technology in use. We have included some sample sentences and their applied codes (see Table 2) to illustrate our coding process. In the second stage, we performed a cross-case analysis searching for both common themes and opposing viewpoints between the different stakeholders. At this point we also looked for congruent and incongruent frames within and between firm groups. The results are presented in the next section. All firm names have been anonymized to protect privacy.

Table 2. Examples of sample sentences and their respective coding.

Sample sentence	Respondent	Coded as
"[…] Now we can see that if it is supposed to give [value] to a customer we have to deliver the big picture, you can't just provide them with a small part – because then we would only have a tiny target audience, and then we would be finished."	S01	Nature of technology "What IoT is and does"
"I would… If I were to guess, I'd say that everything boils down to statistics, but in the end it all becomes an economic issue, being able to see how many visitors, being able to see how much paper and such that is used, in order to make it more effective, and to maximize the income."	P02	Technology Strategy "What IoT adds"
"You can see whether it [the statistics] changes; goes up or goes down, and then you can compare them and see 'Well now the critical time has increased, and why has it done that?'. If I see that the critical time is 7 – that won't tell me anything, but if it used to be 7 and goes to 14, then it tells me something."	B01	Technology-in-use "How IoT will be used"

5 Results

The results section is structured according to the three theoretical concepts and the three stakeholders, discussing the *Nature of technology, Technology strategy* and *Technology-in-use* from the point of view of the different actors. The main findings are then summarized in Table 3. However, we start out with a description of the IoT system and its actual implementation and use.

5.1 An IoT System for Efficient Cleaning Services

System as Used by CleanCo Cleaners. The IoT sensors were connected to an application, that the cleaners accessed via a tablet attached to their respective cleaning carts. A *green* marker indicated a recently filled dispenser or cleaned area; a *yellow* marker (only used by the dispensers) indicated a need for refill (*e.g.* a soap-, toilet paper- or paper towel-dispenser having less than half of its contents left); and a *red* marker that the dispenser was empty or that an area has reached its maximum amount of visits (with an upper limit of 20 selected by the building/operations manager). The area or dispenser corresponding with the sensor moves up on the cleaners' "to-do"-list depending on the status, with red sensors at the top of the list, then yellow and lastly green. The cleaners were expected to address the red and/or yellow markers as they showed up, thus being flexible enough in their work to, when needed, deviate from a pre-set cleaning plan that they would otherwise adhere to.

System as Used by CleanCo Team-Leaders. The team-leaders of the cleaning crew had some added accessibility, for example the ability to add new cleaning-plans detailing how the cleaners should work when not responding to sensors, and to edit existing ones. The system also featured the ability for team-leaders to send out messages to the cleaners, showing up on their tablets and potentially alerting them to certain situations such as broken windows or leaking pipes that would otherwise not be covered by the sensors placed throughout the facility. Team-leaders could also access statistics regarding specific sensors, for example; how long a certain sensor had been red during a particular time-span; or how many visitors there had been in particular zones during certain times. This allowed them to adjust cleaning plans or perform quality assurance on the various areas within the building itself.

System as Used by BuildingCo. The building manager used the statistics provided through the system to monitor overall productiveness, see trends, and identify potential bottlenecks with a significantly higher visitor count or higher usage of supplies. The system and its produced statistics could also serve as a measurement for procurements when it comes to supplies or even as a baseline for labor, should the management choose to hire another company to handle the cleaning service. In this sense the system allowed for both quality assurance, increased negotiating power and also a way to more effectively and accurately monitor the cleaners in their work, and with what speed and detail that various tasks were completed.

System as Used by SystemCo. While SystemCo was less interested in the day-to-day operations, the IoT system and the statistics that it provided, gave an increased understanding of the customer's business and made it possible to tailor sales and other services based on the customer data, for example being able to predict when certain supplies were running out and (hypothetically) pricing the supplies according to the demand for them by the customer. The implementation also facilitated a relationship between the SystemCo and BuildingCo, as continuous coordination benefits both parties – where the building/operations manager receives reports, support and updates that are being produced by SystemCo. Forming a close relationship with the customers can potentially dissuade them from switching to another system provider.

5.2 Nature of Technology

Nature of technology refers to stakeholders' understanding of the IoT system, its functionality, and its possibilities.

CleanCo. When asked about the system itself, it was generally well received by both cleaners and team-leaders (who themselves also did operational work to some extent). The task of cleaning could be split into "need-based" and "frequency-based" cleaning, where the "need-based" cleaning was relying solely on the sensor data, in that cleaning would be performed according to whether system prompts were red or yellow, and the "frequency-based" cleaning was simply following a pre-determined schedule. One of the respondents, who had previously worked frequency-based at a larger building complex, stated that a system such as this would eliminate the uncertainty of whether or not an area had been cleaned comparing it to their previous workplace;

> *"We did not know exactly at which times anybody had been in there [cleaning]. Then you might run over there when somebody had already been there."*

This viewpoint was shared amongst the other respondents, detailing similar stories of previous uncertainty regarding their cleaning schedules. When asked if they were worried about the possibilities of having their work monitored, neither of the respondents reported that this was anything that they were personally worried about. Overall the cleaners themselves held the system in high regard both before and after the implementation process itself.

Building Co. The rationale for adopting the IoT system and digitalizing the cleaning process was mainly due to the fact that a lot of complaints had arisen from customers using the facilities when a previous company provided the cleaning services, with the building/operations manager stating that;

> *"We had a lack of quality, so now we have the same amount of cleaners but we have a significantly better result. That was not the case one and a half, or two, years ago. Back then we had a lot of [complaints]... and most of the complaints were regarding the cleaning".*

As the previous cleaning service was replaced, SystemCo (that was only the supplier of cleaning products at that point) approached the building manager and sold their concept of a digitalized cleaning solution. In the wake of the complaints, that had arisen with the previous cleaning company; being able to monitor the cleaning process and getting an overarching view of the facilities proved to be one of the main motivators for the management team and allowing the procurement of the IoT system, adding an additional level of value, being able to have actual statistics of the work being performed.

SystemCo. When asked about the system, much of the reasoning behind the development was that it would add simplicity for the cleaners themselves. This reasoning was expanded, stating that the addition of the system would give cleaners more freedom, streamlining their work and creating additional value through the aforementioned aspects. Another factor in regards to value creation was that cleaners would feel that someone invested in them by adding technology to enhance their work, something which, according to SystemCo, often gets overlooked or kept at a minimum in most cases in regards to maintenance workers. This would, it was argued, also lead to an increased sense of professional pride amongst the cleaners. One of the system providers argued that;

> *"Well the cleaners think it's a bit fun that their work is seen, [...] All of a sudden they get a tablet and you look at their work – it gives people another status".*

The possibilities for SystemCo themselves were that when moving in on, or approaching, new customers, the strategic benefits of the IoT system could be argued, and that aspect seemed to be, although stated more implicitly, a larger and more important factor than the cleaners' wellbeing. The added benefits, argued to potential customers, would hence be the ability to have a better view of the cleaning process, and an increased quality assurance.

5.3 Technology Strategy

Technology strategy refers to stakeholders' views on what IoT might add to their organization and what the reason is for technology adoption.

CleanCo. The strategic value that the cleaners, and the team-leaders in particular, expressed regarding the system was primarily the ability to centralize the schedules that went out to the various cleaning crews. For instance, in regards to the cleaning of specific areas that required certain chemicals or cleaning agents, the mixtures and compositions could be delivered directly to the cleaners doing their rounds. On the operational level the strategic value was that the system would decrease the amount of check-ups required within different areas, primarily toilets, where the cleaners would not have to open up all the dispensers in order to check the status of toilet paper, paper towels or soap.

This decrease in workload was perceived to be valuable, and from a quality standpoint it would also allow for the cleaners to attend to more areas, creating a better environment in general. When it came to the ability to plan; team-leaders felt that scheduling within the application did not provide them with any benefits, or as one of team-leaders described the hypothetical scheduling for individuals;

> *"[...] If there are a lot of users it would require extensive administration from us, and since we're in-house that would make it very inflexible."*

Because of this, the managing of schedules and planning of individual cleaners was still done outside of the system, using a whiteboard with corresponding times for each of the cleaners.

BuildingCo. For the building/operations manager the primary strategic value was described as the ability to use the statistics provided by the system to monitor the cleaning procedure, gauge differences in time and/or quality, as well as to use the system to get a baseline for future procurements of products, and eventually if hiring a new cleaning company – to be used as a comparison, with the manager stating that;

> *"[It's] on the level that I evaluate if they do a good job, or... we want as little critical time as possible, so I can look at it when I'm going to discuss with their managers, and then we might have others looking at the details in the system".*

In the wake of the complaints that were received with the previous company, much of the arguments for the strategic values revolved around the ability to, in a sense, "control" how the work was being performed, and to deal with it accordingly, and was discussed to roughly the same extent as the quality assurance.

SystemCo. The strategy expressed towards the customers and the cleaners was that the system would increase cleaners' sense of control regarding their work. The digitalization would make running and checking dispensers less of a problem, thus allowing for better planning and use of time. From a SystemCo point of view, the IoT system was a part in helping them transform their business strategy and make the move from product to service provision.

> *"[...] We have become a bit more than only a sanitations product provider. From being a provider, to becoming more like someone that's support... or help... you support [the customer] in a different way – you get a much closer relationship."*

A major reason for moving in that direction was that there could only be so much innovation that could be done with the dispensers themselves analogously, and the products being sold would still have to be at a low price range to make sure that customers would not turn to any competitors. In order to maintain the customer base and attract new customers, the IoT solution was adopted and the dispensers were outfitted with general sensors that could fit within a multitude of dispensers, regardless of their shape.

5.4 Technology-in-Use

CleanCo. While the cleaners were all positive toward the system and stated that it did help them with their day-to-day tasks, one of the team leaders mentioned that they had one of the cleaners approach them and say that the system was leading to a significant increase in stress, and to some extent make them doubt in their ability to do their job. This aspect was to some extent dismissed and it was argued by the team leader that the cleaner in question did not have a "proper mindset" – meaning that the cleaners simply shouldn't let themselves get stressed out from the system, but instead embrace it as a tool, and seeing the "critical-time" more as a guideline than an actual requirement to instantly attend to. One of the team-leaders described it as;

> *"I've had one cleaner telling me that 'I'm bad since I take it too easy, leaving too many areas red, while [another cleaner] manages those cleaning areas off [not red]', and at the same time the cleaner is telling me that they are working too hard and don't know how long they can hold out before something, like, breaks – and that they need more help."*

Very little, if any, blame was given to the system itself, but rather it was somewhat shifted towards the cleaner, where the same team leader as above, was asked about the stress-aspect as a design flaw they stated that;

> *"There's a number of design flaws, however I wouldn't say that the stress aspect is a flaw in the system, instead it has... it's the human factor".*

A similar aspect of "not having the proper mindset" was also expressed in a group meeting that featured both the SystemCo and CleanCo, where the SystemCo seemed to agree that if someone was being stressed by the system it was a question of that person's "mindset". The team leader said that cleaners would occasionally ignore some of the 'critical time', when sensors turned red, and continue working in their own pace – whereas the cleaner that was feeling stressed said that they would run to every area as soon as the sensors turned red.

Further it was also described by another team leader that it was important for them to make sure that the cleaners continuously used the system, as some of the cleaners had been doing their job for so long that they would clean from "muscle memory" rather than the indications from the system itself. The team leader argued that if the cleaners were not continuously exposed to the system, some of them would stop using it and revert back to their old habits and ways of working.

BuildingCo. One of the statistical views that the building/operations manager mentioned as their favorite ones was the 'total critical time', detailing the time within a user-defined time frame that the sensors showed as being 'red'.

As previously described, the IoT system was used by BuildingCo in order to make economic predictions, and as a baseline for price negotiations.

Regarding scheduling it was decided that the cleaners would still work the same hours with the system – mainly using the added time that was saved to be used within their frequency-based cleaning plan in order to maximize productivity. An initial fear that was noted by the building/operations manager was that;

> *"What we were afraid of was that there'd be some kind of 'Big brother is watching you' and those types of things, but it's not... [...] no one that I've heard from has said that there...was... problems, rather it was just cool that they got some new technical [things]."*

From the managerial viewpoint there were no problems related to the surveillance aspect. Neither was it mentioned anything about the cleaner experiencing problems from the system, however it is possible that it had not been relayed to the building/operations manager from the team-leaders of the cleaners. However, overall, the building/operations manager expressed much positivity of the system itself and saw it as a useful tool.

SystemCo. During one of the interviews, two of the system providers described similar stories that many of the customers that had received the system were pleased with it, but that in some instances had been very weary of it initially such as;

> *"[...] We worked in a place where we got comments such as 'I've worked here for twenty years, don't come here and tell my how to clean, I don't want an... an app that tells me how to clean'".*

Respondent S01 also stressed the importance of getting both the cleaning personnel and the maintenance manager on board, in order to successfully market a system such as this – primarily because it could entail a large cost and that they needed employees in the organization ready to sell in the idea to the executive manager, stating that;

> *"What I've learned about the implementation is that you have to push this a lot – they have to be willing to change, and the operations managers have to… you don't just implement a system and hope that it solves itself, you have to work with the system".*

Respondent S03 did note that there had been instances where they had attempted to market the system internationally, sometimes having unions evaluating their products before they could be installed. However, claims that some cleaners became stressed by the system were largely brushed off, and it was argued that the cleaner potentially was "thinking wrong" or simply did not have the correct "mindset".

Table 3 provides a summary of our findings grouped according to the three theoretical constructs and the views expressed by the three stakeholders. These findings are then discussed in the next section where we show how the stakeholders' technological frames influenced their perceptions of both opportunities and challenges with introducing IoT in the workplace.

Table 3. Summary of main findings

Benefits from system	Theoretical construct		
	Nature of technology	Technology strategy	Technology-in-use
	Stakeholder's understanding of IoT, its functionality, and its possibilities	*Stakeholder's views on what IoT might add to their organization and what the reason is for technology adoption*	*Stakeholder's views on how IoT will be used within the organization, and what consequences this will bring*
CleanCo	• Viewed by a majority of the team-leaders as a silver bullet solution • Most personnel believe it is as an improvement over the previous (analogue) method of working	• Useful tool in cleaning, less useful for planning • A way to statistically keep track of work trying to make the business more effective	• Team-leaders state that some cleaners are too stressed because of the system • If the cleaners aren't exposed to the system or "forced" to use it, its usage will diminish
BuildingCo	• Using the data generated to create further value for their own business • Seen as a way to get an overview of the cleaning process	• Using statistics as a means to leverage better contracts with both cleaners and system provider • Noticing discrepancies in the performance of the cleaners themselves	• Being able to monitor cleaning results in real time and identify outliers • Having cleaners work more pro-actively instead of reactively • Changes in prizing from system provider
SystemCo	• Helping businesses with statistical analysis and recommendations to cleaning solutions • Value creation for cleaners through the addition of the technology	• Giving cleaners increased control over their work and duties • Positioning themselves towards a more service-oriented business model • Creating means for co-operation with customers and cleaners	• Important to get cleaners (and possibly the union) to embrace the system • Having team-leaders of the cleaners "sell" the system to the management • If workers feel stressed out, they have to adjust their way of thinking

6 Discussion

For CleanCo and BuildingCo, the implementation of the IoT system started out as what could be characterized as a digitization of operative maintenance work [29]. This was accomplished by moving the previously analogue schedules, cleaning-zone information and messaging in to the IoT system itself. The transmitted sensor data gave the cleaners the opportunity to directly interact with each area, receive real-time information about which action was required and then act upon the given information. This information, combined with data generated from the cleaners' average response time could then be accessed by the building/operations manager, providing them with a statistical overviews on *e.g.* how long it had taken a maintenance worker to clean a certain area, or what the average response time was from the moment that a sensor turned red to when it had been attended to (becoming green). This functionality brought on a form of digital convergence and a symbiotic relationship between technologies and organizational processes, described by [3, 34] as pervasive, meaning that previously physical objects, such as the installed soap dispensers or paper towel dispensers in our case, are incorporated with digital technology.

The IoT system had further changed the way that the building maintenance was being done, where frequency-based maintenance (following a predetermined schedule) in some instances had been completely dropped in favor for a need-based maintenance; a reliance on the IoT system - while also generating less complaints regarding the cleaning when doing so. The cleaners continuous usage further rendered the digital technology to become what is described by [29] as 'infrastructural technology', where a, comparatively, analogue workplace moves in to the digital sphere and moves towards becoming a digital workplace, through the introduction of IoT driving digitalization.

One identified challenge with this type of IoT system is the aspect of monitoring, where this IoT system to some extent, arguably, *was* being used to monitor the process of cleaning, as described by the building manager – even if the cleaners did not express that they felt surveilled. While the user data became anonymized in the application; tying specific times to specific cleaners was something that could be done with relatively little effort, making the IoT system risk being used in a manner that previous research [16] labeled as 'active real-time intrusion' and 'highly intrusive'.

SystemCo stated that the opportunities provided by the IoT system functioned primarily to assist cleaners in their daily routines, so that they could work areas faster and with greater precision. However, it was also stated that the value created for SystemCo was the formation of new relationships with customers and the ability to strengthen the relationships with existing customers. This goes in line with previous research [20, 25], showcasing how connected and smart products allows for the formation of closer relationships between companies and their customer.

SystemCo further noted that a challenge in order to facilitate a successful implementation was that the team-leaders needed to be able to 'sell' the system to the management as a necessity, and also the willingness to work with the system from all participants by involving them and providing them with adequate resources in order to avoid problems, something previous research [4, 7] shows as being of importance.

While the team-leaders for CleanCo had a shared vision about the system decreasing the time it took for the cleaners to attend to connected dispensers, it was evident that some of the cleaners themselves did not experience a simplification of their work, but rather the challenge of an increase in stress. This stress aspect that was not addressed to any major extent by either CleanCo or the SystemCo, and possibly not even known by the operations manager at BuildingCo. This points towards the same frame incongruence as described in the Theoretical Framework section [19] – where different individuals or groups of individuals do not share an understanding of what can be expected of the technology.

Should said frame incongruence persist or increase to the point where the cleaners' understanding and expectations proceed to differ significantly from BuildingCo, SystemCo or even the team-leaders, we argue that it has the potential to severely impact all of the aforementioned challenges and opportunities, as well as hampering a continued successful implementation of IoT within their workplace.

7 Conclusions and Suggestions for Future Research

In this study we set out to explore the question; *What are the challenges and opportunities associated with introducing IoT in the workplace?* Through our interviews with the stakeholders in the case of CleanCo, BuildingCo and SystemCo we have identified several opportunities as well as challenges present to each stakeholder.

One of the opportunities as described by BuildingCo was that the IoT system, allowed them much greater ability to monitor work, and receive detailed performance reports in regards to the cleaning – which could be used in negotiations and as baselines for future hires and identifying outliers in terms of cleaning output.

CleanCo experienced a faster workflow, and a way for the cleaners to work in a more pro-active manner; knowing which areas that needed attention. But the system was also a challenge for some of the cleaners, where they had described an increased level of stress and doubts in regards to their own performance – something that seemed largely brushed off by SystemCo and team-leaders, running the risk of problems arising further down the line.

The opportunity expressed by SystemCo was to form new connections with customers – and a much longer lasting relationship with the ones using the system. But in order to sell the system to new customers, and retain old ones, the challenge described was to get the cleaners on board with the IoT system, desiring to use it and to have them continue doing so throughout the implementation and use of the system.

In order to best meet these opportunities and challenges we argue that it is pivotal for each stakeholder to establish congruent views on what IoT can deliver, how value will be created, and for whom. Incongruent views among the stakeholders can, if not properly addressed, have a detrimental effect on both challenges and opportunities within the implementation and usage.

Through this study we have been able to showcase an empirical example of both challenges and opportunities related to the implementation of an IoT system in a workplace context. We argue that future research should delve deeper into the aspects of increased stress amongst users of similar systems and whether or not IoT-implementations in other successful or failed ventures was preluded by including all the actors to a similar extent in the value creation process.

References

1. Aral, S., Brynjolfsson, E., Van Alstyne, M.: Information, technology, and information worker productivity. Inf. Syst. Res. **23**(3-part-2), 849–867 (2012)
2. Bresnahan, T., Brynjolfsson, E., Hitt, L.: Information technology, workplace organization, and the demand for skilled labor: firm-level evidence. Q. J. Econ. **117**(1), 339–376 (2002). http://www.jstor.org/stable/2696490
3. Borgia, E.: The Internet of Things vision: key features, applications and open issues. Comput. Commun. **54**, 1–31 (2014)
4. Botta-Genoulaz, V., Millet, P.A.: An investigation into the use of ERP systems in the service sector. Int. J. Prod. Econ. **99**(1–2), 202–221 (2006)
5. Brynjolfsson, E., McAfee, A.: The Second Machine Age: Work, Progress, and Prosperity in a Time of Brilliant Technologies. WW Norton & Company, New York City (2014)
6. Eloff, J.H.P., Eloff, M.M., Dlamini, M.T., Zielinski, M.P.: Internet of people, things and services - the convergence of security, trust and privacy. In: Proceedings from 3rd CompanionAble Workshop – IoPTS, Novotel Brussels - Brussels, 2 December 2009
7. Gallivan, M.J., Spitler, V.K., Koufaris, M.: Does information technology training really matter? A social information processing analysis of coworkers' influence on IT usage in the workplace. J. Manag. Inf. Syst. **22**(1), 153–192 (2005)
8. Greengard, S.: The Internet of Things. MIT Press, Cambridge (2015)
9. Hsu, C.W.: Frame misalignment: interpreting the implementation of information systems security certification in an organization. Eur. J. Inf. Syst. **18**(2), 140–150 (2009)
10. Klein, H., Myers, M.D.: A set of principles for conducting and evaluating interpretive field studies in information systems. MIS Q. **23**(1), 67–93 (1999)
11. Kling, R., Jewett, T.: The social design of worklife with computers and networks: a natural systems perspective. In: Yovits, M.C. (ed.) Advances in Computers, pp. 239–293. Academic Press Inc., San Diego (1994)
12. Köffer, S.: Designing the digital workplace of the future–what scholars recommend to practitioners. In: Proceedings of the Thirty-Sixth International Conference on Information Systems, Fort Worth, USA (2015)
13. Kohli, R., Grover, V.: Business value of IT: an essay on expanding research directions to keep up with the times. J. Assoc. Inf. Syst. **9**(1), 23 (2008)
14. Mason, J.: Qualitative Researching. Sage Publications, CA (2002)
15. Melville, N., Kraemer, K., Gurbaxani, V.: Information technology and organizational performance: an integrative model of IT business value. MIS Q. **28**(2), 283–322 (2004)
16. Miller, C., Stuart Wells, F.: Balancing security and privacy in the digital workplace. J. Change Manag. **7**(3–4), 315–328 (2007)
17. Monteiro, E., Rolland, K.H.: Trans-situated use of integrated information systems. Eur. J. Inf. Syst. **21**(6), 608–620 (2012)
18. Orlikowski, W.J., Baroudi, J.J.: Studying information technology in organizations: research approaches and assumptions. Inf. Syst. Res. **2**(1), 1–28 (1991)
19. Orlikowski, W.J., Gash, D.C.: Technological frames: making sense of information technology in organizations. ACM Trans. Inf. Syst. **12**(2), 174–207 (1994)

20. Porter, M.E., Heppelmann, J.E.: How smart, connected products are transforming competition. Harv. Bus. Rev. **92**(11), 64–88 (2014)
21. Porter, M.E., Heppelmann, J.E.: How smart, connected products are transforming companies. Harv. Bus. Rev. **93**(10), 96–114 (2015)
22. Ritchie, J., Lewis, J., Elam, R.G.: Selecting samples. In: Qualitative Research Practice: A Guide for Social Science Students and Researchers, p. 111 (2013)
23. Robey, D.: Computer information systems and organization structure. Commun. ACM **24** (10), 679–687 (1981)
24. Robey, D., Boudreau, M.C.: Accounting for the contradictory organizational consequences of information technology: theoretical directions and methodological implications. Inf. Syst. Res. **10**(2), 167–185 (1999)
25. Saarikko, T., Westergren, U.H., Blomquist, T.: The inter-organizational dynamics of a platform ecosystem: exploring stakeholder boundaries. In: Proceedings from 49th Hawaii International Conference on System Sciences (HICSS), pp. 5167–5176. IEEE (2016)
26. Saarikko, T., Westergren, U.H., Blomquist, T.: The Internet of Things: are you ready for what's coming? Bus. Horiz. **60**(5), 667–676 (2017)
27. Stankovic, J.A.: Research directions for the Internet of Things. IEEE Internet Things J. **1**(1), 3–9 (2014)
28. Suchman, L.A.: Plans and Situated Actions: The Problem of Human-Machine Communication. Cambridge University Press, Cambridge (1987)
29. Tilson, D., Lyytinen, K., Sørensen, C.: Research commentary—digital infrastructures: the missing IS research agenda. Inf. Syst. Res. **21**(4), 748–759 (2010)
30. Truex, D., Baskerville, R., Klein, H.: Growing systems in emergent organizations. Commun. ACM **42**(8), 117–123 (1999)
31. Vermesan, O., Friess, P. (eds.): Internet of Things: Converging Technologies for Smart Environments and Integrated Ecosystems. River Publishers, Aalborg (2013)
32. Walsham, G.: Interpreting Information Systems in Organizations. Wiley, Chichester (1993)
33. Whitmore, A., Agarwal, A., Da Xu, L.: The Internet of Things—a survey of topics and trends. Inf. Syst. Front. **17**(2), 261–274 (2015)
34. Yoo, Y., Boland Jr., R.J., Lyytinen, K., Majchrzak, A.: Organizing for innovation in the digitized world. Organ. Sci. **23**(5), 1398–1408 (2012)

Opportunities for the Internet of Things in the Water, Sanitation and Hygiene Domain

Paula Kotzé[1,2(✉)] and Louis Coetzee[1]

[1] CSIR Meraka Institute, Pretoria, South Africa
paula.kotze@gmail.com, louis.coetzee@csir.co.za
[2] Department of Informatics, University of Pretoria, Pretoria, South Africa

Abstract. This paper analyses the water, sanitation and hygiene (WASH) context in South Africa and presents views regarding the possible use of the Internet of Things (IoT) for WASH in South Africa. The views were informed by an analysis of literature related to the WASH domain nationally and internationally. Example case studies of the use of IoT in the WASH sector in developing countries, and where possible Africa, provided further background. As a triangulation exercise, a survey amongst various stakeholders in the WASH domain was conducted. To contextualise the WASH sector in South Africa, value chains were derived. To identity the opportunities for IoT, the findings of the study were combined with insights acquired on the IoT domain in general, both from literature and our experience and learnings.

Keywords: WASH · Internet of Things · Water · Sanitation · Hygiene · Value chains

1 Introduction

The human rights to water, sanitation and hygiene, collectively known as WASH, are guaranteed under international law as components of the right to an adequate standard of living guaranteed in the International Covenant on Economic, Social and Cultural Rights [1], as well as in many other human rights treaties. Moreover, water, sanitation and hygiene are inextricably linked to a range of other human rights, including the rights to life, health, education and housing [1–5]. Reporting on progress with the United Nations (UN) Millennium Development Goals, UNICEF states that [6]:

- More than 660 million people in 2015 lacked access to safe drinking water sources within a convenient distance from their habitation, 319 million of which lived in Sub-Saharan Africa. A total of 159 million people was dependent on surface water, of which 102 million lived in Sub-Saharan Africa.
- Adequate sanitation facilities, for human excreta disposal in, or close to, peoples' habitation, were not available to 2.4 billion people in 2015, 695 million of which lived in Sub-Saharan Africa.

In South Africa, and many other developing countries, a large number of people still do not have an acceptable toilet and cannot easily access safe water to drink or wash their hands. This leaves significant proportions of young children and vulnerable individuals

L. Strous and V. G. Cerf (Eds.): IFIPIoT 2018, IFIP AICT 548, pp. 194–210, 2019.
https://doi.org/10.1007/978-3-030-15651-0_16

to die of preventable WASH related diseases such as diarrhoea, intestinal nematode infections, lymphatic filariasis, trachoma, schistosomiasis and malaria [7]. This could also contribute to malnutrition and poor school attendance, which could result in cognitive impairment and reduced learning outcomes [8, 9]. It is argued that improvements related to drinking water, sanitation, hygiene, and water resource management could result in the reduction of almost 10% of the total burden of disease worldwide. Access to adequate WASH services is therefore an important mechanism to address risks associated with the burden of disease of any country.

The use of information and communications technologies (ICTs) has been posited as one way to address the burden of disease and improving quality of life for those most at risk. One of the new developments in ICT, the 'Internet of Things' (IoT), allows for the integration of digital and the physical worlds, resulting in the creation of new services that can be deployed for positive impact. In the context of WASH innovative IoT work, including technology development and applications, is being done in relation to WASH services in both the developed and developing world. However, it is unknown to what extent (and if at all) IoT approaches to providing WASH services have been pursued in South Africa.

Following a study conducted for the Water Research Commission of South Africa (WRC) [10], this paper analyses the WASH context in South Africa and presents views regarding the possible use of IoT for WASH services in South Africa. A literature review combined with inputs from a survey was used to collect data for the study.

Section 2 provides background to the WASH domain and IoT in general. Section 3 provides an overview of the findings of our study on the use of IoT in WASH in South Africa. Section 4 contextualises the WASH sector in South Africa using value chains. Section 5 identities benefits and future scenarios for the use of IoT in the WASH sector. Section 6 concludes the paper.

2 Background

2.1 What Is WASH

WASH is the collective term for the associated concepts of safe drinking water, safe sanitation and hygiene [2]. According to the WHO/UNICEF Joint Monitoring Programme for Water Supply and Sanitation (JMP) [11]:

- *Drinking water* services refers to the accessibility, availability and quality of the main source used by households for drinking, cooking, personal hygiene and other domestic uses.
- *Sanitation* is the hygienic means of promoting health through the prevention of human contact with waste as well as the treatment and disposal of waste. Sanitation services refer to management of excreta from the facilities used by individuals, through emptying and transport of excreta for treatment and eventual discharge or reuse. Sanitation can also refer to the maintenance of hygienic conditions through services such as wastewater disposal and garbage collection.

- *Hygiene* refers to the conditions and practices that help maintain health and prevent spread of disease, including handwashing, menstrual hygiene management and food hygiene.

Due to their interdependent nature, these three core issues are grouped together to represent a growing sector, called WASH for short. While each issue can be considered a separate field of work, each of them is dependent on the presence of the other. For example, without clean water, basic hygiene practices are not possible, without toilets, water sources become contaminated, etc. [2]. This paper addresses the WASH concept as defined by the JMP [11], but limiting the hygiene aspect to handwashing.

2.2 Global WASH Context

The UN 2030 Agenda for Sustainable Development [12], comprising 17 Sustainable Development Goals (SDGs) and 169 targets addressing social, economic and environmental aspects of development, seeks to end poverty, protect the planet and ensure prosperity for all. Concerning WASH services, Goals 6, 1.4, 3.9 and 4a [12, 13] apply. In the context of this paper SDGs 6.1 and 6.2 are specifically relevant:

- SDG 6.1: By 2030, achieve universal and equitable access to safe and affordable drinking water for all.
- SDG 6.2: By 2030, achieve access to adequate and equitable sanitation and hygiene for all and end open defecation, paying special attention to the needs of women and girls and those in vulnerable situations.

The UN also identified a number of cross-cutting criteria for good practices in the WASH sector [3]: non-discrimination, participation, accountability, impact and sustainability.

JMP [11] is the custodian of global data on WASH and has derived a normative interpretation for SDG 6.1 and 6.2. JMP also compiled associated service ladders to benchmark and compare service levels across countries and to facilitate enhanced global monitoring of WASH as specified in the SDGs [13]. The JMP ladder for household drinking water services consists of five rungs and also classifies the water resources into four classes [11, 13], as presented in Table 1. Drinking water ladders also exist for schools [13, 14] and healthcare facilities [13]. The JMP service ladder for sanitation for households is presented in Table 2. A service ladder for sanitation in schools also exist [13–15].

The full benefits of improvements in access to sanitation and drinking water cannot be realised without good hygiene. Although there is a distinction between sanitation and hygiene, the two topics are often covered together in literature. Handwashing with soap is considered the main focus for hygiene as it serves as a primary barrier to remove faecal matter from contact with stools and a secondary barrier to prevent pathogens to get into food and fluids consumed by people, allowing pathogens to spread to new hosts [16]. JMP's service ladder for handwashing in households is presented Table 3. Handwashing facilities can consist of a sink with tap water, or other devices that contain, transport or regulate the flow of water [13], for example buckets with taps, tippy-taps [17] and portable basins. JMP also has a handwashing ladder for schools [14].

Table 1. Water service levels and resources [11, 13, 18–21]

Service level	Service criteria	Resource class	Resource	Resource example
Safely managed service	Accessible: on premises Available: when needed Quality: free from faecal and chemical contamination Affordable	Improved	Sources, which by nature of their design and construction have the potential to deliver safe water	Piped water, boreholes or tube wells, protected dug wells or springs, packaged water
Basic service	Improved source does not meet any one of above normative criteria A round trip to collect water ≤ 30 min, including queuing time	Improved		
Limited service	Round trip for water collection >30 min, including queueing time	Improved		
Unimproved		Unimproved	Collected from source	Unprotected dug wells or springs
No service		Surface water	Collected directly from an unprotected resource	Surface water, e.g. lake, river, stream, pond, canals, irrigation ditches

Table 2. JMP service ladder for sanitation in households [13, 15]

Service level	Definition
Safely managed	Use of an improved sanitation facility which is not shared with other households and where excreta are safely disposed in situ or transported and treated off-site
Basic	Use of improved facilities which are not shared with other households
Limited	Use of improved facilities shared between two or more households
Unimproved	Use of pit latrines without a slab or platform, hanging latrines and bucket latrines
Open defecation/no service	No toilets or latrines. Disposal of human faeces in fields, forest, bushes, open bodies of water, beaches or other open spaces or with solid waste

Table 3. JMP service ladder for handwashing in households [14, 15]

Service level	Definition
Advanced	Handwashing facilities available at critical times and accessible to all
Basic	Hand washing facility with soap *and* water in the household
Limited	Handwashing facility without soap *or* water
No facility	No handwashing facility

2.3 What Is IoT

Multiple definitions for the Internet of Things have been proposed in the past [22]. For the purposes of this document, we define IoT as "an ecosystem that integrates the physical and digital via the Internet with associated computing services. Data is ingested from the physical and digital world for sense making, thus enabling the execution of contextual commands" [10: p. 50]. Figure 1 presents the generic IoT process chain. Observations are acquired via a variety of sensors and communicated via the Internet to backend systems (typically cloud infrastructure). A variety of services operate on the data observations. Through the services, value is introduced to society and the environment. Important to note is the bi-directional nature of the process chain. Outputs from services are fed into the processing engines, with those outputs feeding back into the physical world through actuation.

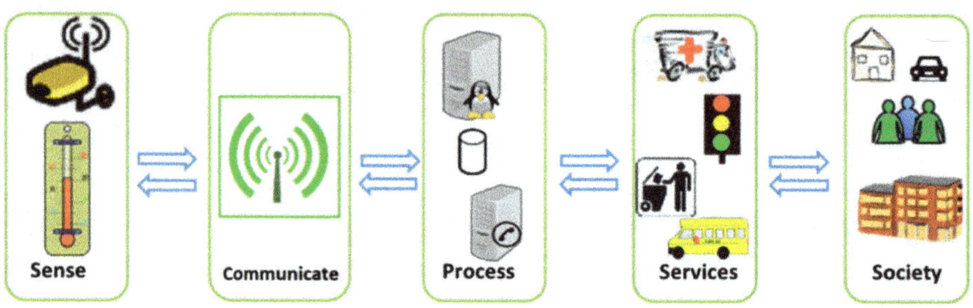

Fig. 1. IoT process chain [10]

IoT is maturing rapidly in the developed world. Many research initiatives at scale have been pursued and commercial solutions are becoming available. There is also an abundance of skilled resources and technologies available. This is not the case in South Africa and the rest of Africa, where the uptake is still in its early stages. This does create a challenge, as it is often believed that the required impact can be obtained by importing a 'canned' solution. Coetzee et al. [23] have shown that canned solutions are not an optimal approach. The drivers quite often differ, thus impacting on the context in which a service needs to be developed.

3 Study to Determine the Status of IoT Use in WASH

The study flowed from a project conducted for the Water Research Commission of South Africa [10]. A literature review combined with inputs from a survey was used to analyse the WASH context in South Africa and present views regarding the possible use of IoT for WASH services in South Africa.

The goal of the literature review was to determine the normative standards applicable to the WASH sector, the WASH context in South Africa and the use, or possible use, of IoT in the WASH sector in South Africa. The review therefore focused on the criteria for WASH related services as set out by the United Nations General Assembly [12] (see Sect. 2.2), WASH value chains and role players, existing IoT technologies, trends and implementations, and existing case studies in IoT or similar domains. In the absence of case studies specific to South Africa, examples from other African countries were included.

The survey amongst stakeholders active in the technical, research, industry and policy domain related to WASH services, aimed to determine the current perception of the WASH sector and the use of IoT in service delivery in the WASH. The survey consisted of open-ended questions addressing the following topics: the WASH and IoT concepts, use of IoT in public sector service delivery (including WASH), what a successful IoT deployment in the public sector means, barriers to the deployment of IoT in the WASH sector, areas in the water/sanitation/hygiene sector service delivery that can benefit from the use of IoT, and any existing or planned South African examples of the use of IoT in the WASH sector or sub-sectors. Online questionnaires were distributed to 47 stakeholders. Only seven responses to the questionnaire were received, resulting in a response rate of 16%. The inputs received were collated, analysed and integrated with those from the literature review.

3.1 WASH Context in South Africa

The literature review found that there is no integrated WASH sector or initiatives in South Africa. Responsibility for WASH services on government level are spread over various national and provincial departments, with overlapping mandates. Internationally, several large bodies, companies and NGOs are active in the WASH sector, some with a focus on the use of ICT. Some of the most prominent of these are the European Commission (e.g. ICT4Water Cluster [24]) and the ITU (e.g. Biggs et al. [25]). Multinationals (e.g. Google [26]), academia (for example, Oxford University [27]) and several NGOs (for example, the Toilet Board Coalition [28]) have a footprint through research, innovation and roll-out initiatives.

From the responses to the survey it appears as if the WASH concept is still not well established. Although three respondents acknowledged the interrelatedness of water, sanitation and hygiene, the remainder only highlighted the water aspect and the management and use of water. Concern was expressed that sanitation and hygiene should not be only a water issue or covered entirely by addressing the availability and quality of water.

3.2 IoT in WASH in South Africa

The literature review found that although IoT are increasingly applied to numerous domains in the context of WASH, overall it is mostly limited to billing purposes and smart water resources management (using smart meters) in the improved water domain in urban areas [24, 29–31]. This also applies to South Africa [32–34] and the rest of Africa [35–37]. There are, however, some examples of other uses of IoT for in-situ monitoring and information collection for rural and developing country contexts. Examples include sensors used by Charity: Water [38] to capture the location, determine the state of wells and if the wells need to be fixed, and accelerometers used in water lever hand pumps to measure utilisation and status of the pumps at specific water points [39]. Other examples are the Akvo [40] applications in Liberia and the Mwater application in Tanzania to measure and communicate the water quality of a water point [36], both which can be used across the water value chain. An example in the basic/limited sanitation domain include the use of sensors to indicate the presence of 'solid waste' in waterless toilets in informal settlements in Kenya [28, 41].

Examples of IoT use in the WASH domain obtained from the stakeholder survey were limited to water and referred to smart metering and automated meter reading *(i.e. safely managed* water). The cross-disciplinary nature of the WASH domain, alongside a lack of IoT knowledge by ordinary people and technical IoT expertise, were listed as barriers to the deployment of IoT in the WASH domain. The issue of appropriate sensors for the harsh environment of the WASH domain, which is mostly submerged or underground and exposed to pollution, was highlighted. Opportunities identified for IoT in the *improved* water sector included measuring the quality and volume of available/used water for smart (hand) pumps, as well as water quality and equitable distribution of rural water supplies. For the sanitation section, the controlled use of chemicals and natural filtering and rehabilitation, was noted as alternative to water.

These examples by no means address the full potential of IoT in the WASH sector in (South) Africa. Most of the available technologies and publications are associated with water resource management, and in most of the cases billing. Sanitation and hygiene have not featured prominently in literature or the stakeholder survey. It is fair assumption that this is most likely due to demanding challenges related to in-situ sensing and communication. For instance, it is challenging to build an able robust sensor that can be installed in the field to accurately measure water quality. This contrasts with a relatively low-tech traditional water consumption meter that is relatively easier to install and maintain.

Overall, the inputs received from the stakeholders concurred with the findings of our literature review. However, a key outcome from both was that it is necessary to understand the context in which WASH services are supplied to determine the role that IoT can play in improving such services.

4 Value Chains for WASH

As a first step we therefore had to map the WASH context in South Africa using the UN and JMP criteria as guidelines. The concept of physical service value chains is one way to depict such context and is used as an example in this paper to depict the WASH context in South Africa. A value chain in the WASH context represents a set of activities or processes that must be performed to deliver coherent WASH services. From the literature review it was found that, in general, the value chains for WASH services in South Africa are similar to the value chains for WASH services in the rest of Africa. The value chains for South Africa would therefore also be applicable to the rest of Africa and most of the developing world beyond Africa.

4.1 Water Value Chain

Several value chains for 'formal' or improved water and sanitation services in South Africa were found during our literature review. In general 'formal' water services is a nonstop sequential delivery process from source-to-tap and from tap-to-source [42, 43]. It involves natural water resources, treatment works (processing), distribution infrastructure and effective operation to deliver potable (drinkable) water and safe sanitation. Rainfall runoff flows into rivers and is captured and stored in dams. Water from dams and other sources, such as groundwater, is purified and treated, and piped to reservoirs for distribution to customers (domestic, business and industrial users). Once the water is consumed, grey water (wastewater from washing, laundry etc.) and sewerage are collected and passed through a network of sewers to a treatment works. The wastewater is purified and treated, after which it is released back into rivers or dams, again becoming a water resource [42, 43]. This formal water and sanitation sector perspective does, however, not provide the complete picture of the water and sanitation sector is South Africa and Africa. As a start, it excludes the 'non-formal' water sources and sanitation services, as it applies to most of the rural domestic inhabitants. It also excludes the agriculture sector not dependent on the 'formal' water supply. Agriculture is the largest user of water globally [30]. In 2015, agriculture in South Africa used 62% of the available water in the country [42]. Water use in agriculture, as a specific focus, is, however not addressed in this paper. It was therefore necessary to augment the existing value chains to represent the complete picture.

Although statistics vary between region and metropolitan areas, the main sources of drinking water in South Africa, according to the 2016 General Household Survey (GHS) [44] and categorised using the JMP ladder, are:

- *Safely managed* water (piped water on premises): Approximately 46.4% of households had access to piped water in their dwellings in 2016 and 26.8% accessed piped water on site.
- *Basic improved* water (piped water not on premises): A further 13.3% of households relied on water from communal taps and 2.4% relied on water from neighbours' taps (called RDP standard in the GHS, provided that the distance to the water source is less than 200 m).

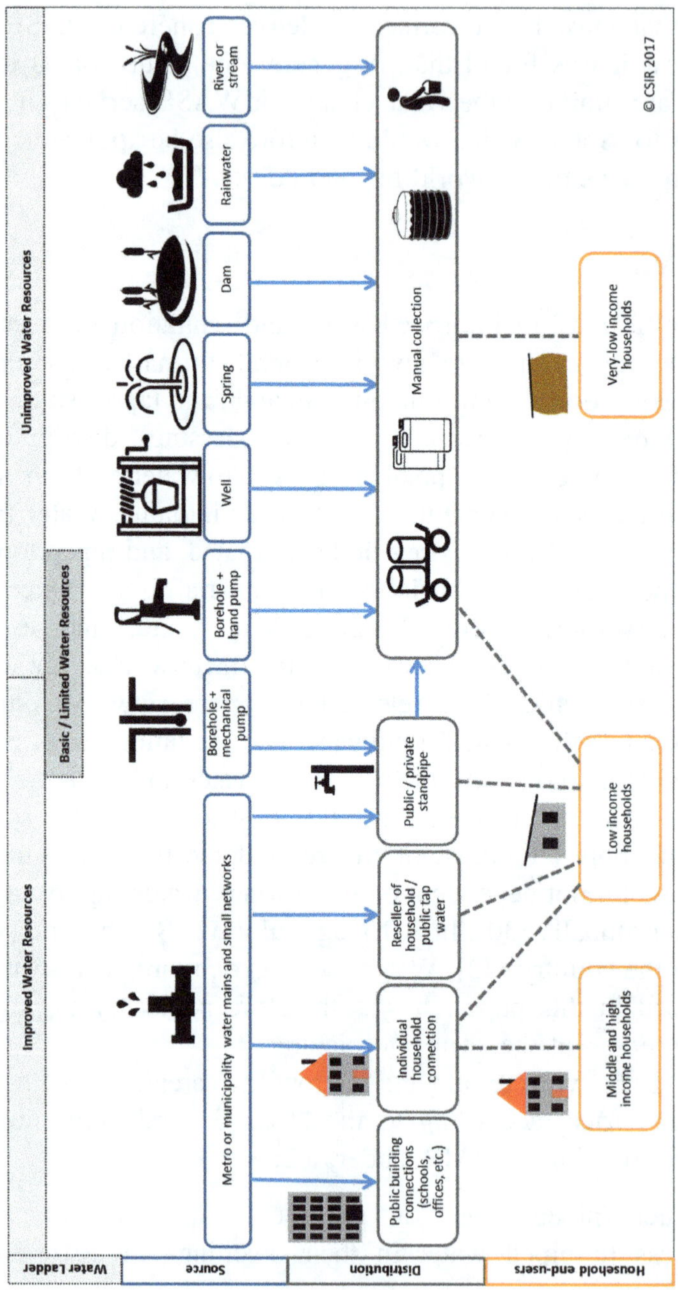

Fig. 2. Value chain for drinking water in South Africa

- *Unimproved* water resources: An estimated 3.7% of households in 2016 still had to fetch water from rivers, streams, stagnant water pools, dams, wells and springs (down from 9.5% in 2002).

Based on analysis of literature on the sources and value chains for drinking water in South Africa and Africa, is a schematic presentation of the sources of water and the diversity of water distribution in South Africa, also applicable to other African countries (see for example [45]). Unlike cities in the United Kingdom, Europe, North America and other industrial nations in the north, where there is often a single source of water serving all residential and most industrial customers, in Africa (urban and rural) there can be a wide variety of water suppliers. Water can be obtained from household wells, neighbours' wells, springs, storing rainwater, water carriers, hand carters, carters using animal traction (unimproved water), standpipes, boreholes with manual pumps (basic/limited water), or even individual connections to the 'formal' city or town water networks (improved water) [42, 45].

4.2 Sanitation Value Chain

Once the water is used/consumed, the sanitation process kicks in. The sanitation value chain is fragmented, characterised by a wide range of stakeholders, businesses, from sole traders to multinationals, the majority responding to limited segments of the chain. Only a few companies/organisations have developed a business model that runs almost entirely across the value chain with the majority concentrating their core activities at either end of the value chain [46]. No specified value chain for sanitation for South Africa could be found in literature, but the general value chain for sanitation is also applicable to South Africa. The general sanitation value chain includes six phases [47, 48]: capture of sludge, containment of sludge, emptying of sludge, transport of sludge, collection and treatment of sludge, and safe reuse or disposal of treated sanitation waste.

According to the 2016 GHS [44], the majority of households in the City of Johannesburg (95.5%) and Nelson Mandela Bay (92.8%) had access to improved sanitation facilities, while households in the City of Tshwane (82.9%) and eThekwini (83.0%) were the least likely to have access to improved sanitation. Nationally, the percentage of households without sanitation, or who used bucket toilets decreased from 12.3% to 4.2% between 2002 and 2016. Despite the improved access to sanitation facilities in South Africa, the 2016 GHS [44] indicated that many households continue to be without any proper sanitation facilities.

Derived based on an analysis of literature regarding the supply sanitation practices in South Africa and Africa, Fig. 3 is a schematic representation of how the overall sanitation market works in South Africa, which is also applicable to other African countries (see for example [45]). Inhabitants adopt one of several basic solutions to the problem of disposing of human waste at the household level. The choice often depends on the physical conditions and on how much money they can spend on construction and periodic cleaning of the sanitation solution/facility. Solutions range from a simple pit or ditch, lined or unlined, with or without a platform slab (*unimproved* sanitation), to a toilet with provision for flushing to a soak pit for the waste water (*basic/limited*

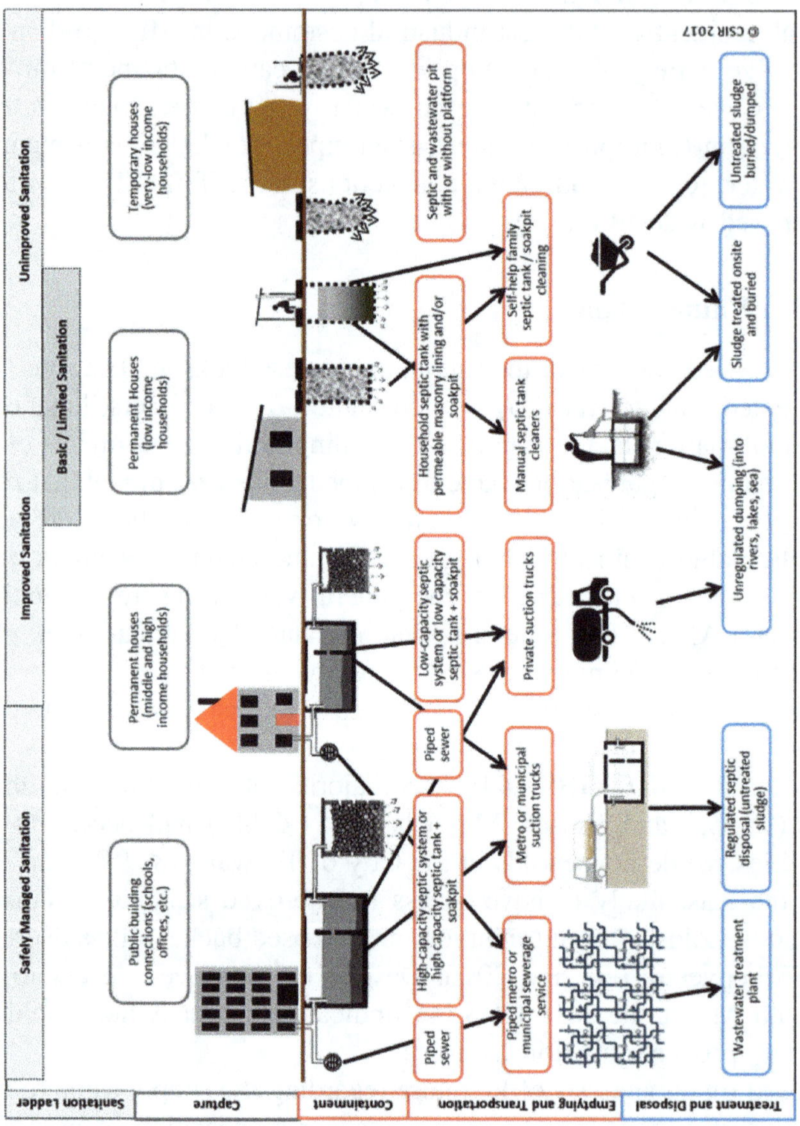

Fig. 3. Sanitation value chain for South Africa

sanitation), or, at the high end of the market, a two-stage lined septic tank and a piped sewerage system (*improved/safely managed* sanitation).

4.3 Hygiene

No value chain specifically for hygiene could be found in literature. There are, however, guidelines on when to wash hands and how to wash hands. In general hands should, for example, be washed [49, 50]: before, during, and after preparing food, before eating food or feeding children, before and after caring for an infected or 'at risk' person, after using the toilet, after changing diapers or cleaning up a child who has used the toilet, after touching an animal, animal feed, or animal waste, after handling pet food or pet treats, after handling money (or using an ATM), etc.

The Centers for Disease Control and Prevention [51] (CDC) recommends a five step process for washing hands when soap and water is available: wet, lather, scrub, rinse and dry. If soap and water are not available, CDC recommends the use an alcohol-based hand sanitiser that contains at least 60% alcohol, although it is said not to be as effective as handwashing when hands are visibly dirty or greasy and cannot eliminate all types of germs and harmful chemicals. If no soap is available or affordable, ash or mud can be used as abrasive, before rinsing [52]. Another alternative in Africa is the use of Moringa oleifera powder [53].

5 Future Scenarios for IoT in WASH

Section 3 presented insights as acquired from numerous reports, publications and a survey on the use of IoT in the WASH context in South Africa. The solutions are patchy, i.e. often only focussing on one aspect within WASH and therefore not utilising the full value cycle of IoT. This section presents a broader view of what IoT can possibly bring to the WASH sector and what should be in place to increase the probability of success. The view is based on our collective learnings from literature and our experience in the WASH and IoT domain.

IoT as ecosystem enables a complete value chain, from data acquisition, processing and finally actuation with the community in the loop at all time (see Fig. 1). IoT is multidisciplinary, spanning competences ranging from device and sensor manufacturing, up to analytics and visualization techniques. However, IoT and its successful utilization span more than just technology. In driving towards a scaled IoT deployment, we therefore argue that the following aspects need to be in place to increase the chances for success in the WASH domain:

- Buy-in from the community.
- Policies for community privacy and security.
- Partnerships linked to research and the local community, vendors. and the various governing structures (e.g. the local water board).
- An established accountable ecosystem that spans technology and community.

An IoT enabled WASH environment that is operating at scale provides access to large quantities of data observations, with opportunities for in areas of big-data and analytics.

The true value of IoT is, however, only manifested when intelligent decisions are being made with the acquired data, resulting in appropriate actions. Furthermore, IoT is entirely dependent on addressing the 'real' challenge which only becomes possible if the community is part of the IoT lifecycle. For a broad IoT deployment, these data observations should ideally be from multiple sensor types (e.g. hand pump utilisation, water quality and flow in the pipe, sanitation pit level, etc.). In such a scaled IoT deployment, the following general benefits can be obtained:

- Better data: Data is associated with the WASH context being directly observed (e.g. water quality). Sensor data can be supplemented through community contributions/ surveys. With better data, 'evidence-based decisions' become possible.
- Better working infrastructure: IoT that enables access to the status of the WASH deployment (e.g. all devices are operational) becomes possible and thus empowers maintenance crews to effectively and rapidly service the infrastructure. Increased access to operational parameters of the devices can realise predictive maintenance.
- The context of a WASH environment will increasingly become better understood: IoT creates an opportunity for the introduction of key performance indicators that will provide insights into the operational efficiencies in WASH environments.
- Community involvement throughout the lifecycle of the WASH deployment: Having the community involved is critical and ensures that the 'real' problem is solved and not the one that appears to be the most attractive (e.g. flashy). Localised business models can be realised, e.g. an empowered local community member can be informed of required maintenance, which would allow for faster turn-around times.

Viewing IoT in relation to the United Nation's crosscutting criteria for WASH [3], several opportunities and benefits can be identified:

- Non-discrimination: Monitoring use through sensors and mobile-based technologies may assist in detecting/reporting denied or restricted access to sanitation facilities and/or water resources.
- Participation: Using mobile-based technologies linked to sensors, communities can contribute to improving their own WASH context.
- Accountability: Armed with the data from the community based IoT solutions, entities responsible for maintenance and planning can make evidence-based decisions.
- Impact: Valid and justifiable choices have a higher probability for impact.
- Sustainability: With the inclusion of communities and the ability to solve that community's specific challenge, the probability of a sustainable intervention is higher.

The benefits above applies to the value of IoT in a fairly broad sense. Using the WASH value chains, as depicted in Figs. 2 and 3, more focused benefits can be identified, some examples of which are listed below:

- Water quality can be measured continuously through in-situ sensors installed permanently or through 'use-once and discard' type of sensors. Data related to taste, colour and odour can be obtained. This allows for early alerting where the water

quality has dropped outside of the required parameters. This approach works for piped water, boreholes, tube and dug wells, springs, and packaged or delivered water. Water treatment plants can be measured before and after the treatment process.
- Indicators related to water distribution can be obtained near real-time. Pressure within pipes can be measured at different locations. Pressure differences can indicate a leak, while a high-pressure point can provide alerts related to possible failures. Smart valves can be used in the distribution system to control the flow of water (e.g. shut off in case of failure, or if the pressure appears to be too high).
- Water availability can be confirmed through sensors that indicate the water level (for instance in a dam or borehole). Trends can be extracted, which in turn can guide the community as well as providers as to the future availability of water.
- Excreta management (sanitation) can be enhanced. Sensors linked to the appropriate back-end systems can provide insights as to when a pit or sanitation tank has reached capacity and needs to be emptied. General (solid) waste management can also be improved with the appropriate sensors and can be enhanced further by optimising the routing of waste trucks and the dispatch of an appropriate truck.
- Handwashing has been highlighted as one of the most important criteria for both hygiene and sanitation. IoT can be used to raise awareness of when hands should be washed. E.g. sensing when a toilet has been flushed, and if the basin has been used directly after the toilet flushing, after which a general reminder can be communicated to the occupant through smart visual aids when leaving the rest room. Also, trends from handwashing can be used as indicators of when and if additional awareness campaigns should be executed.

6 Conclusion

The study found that very limited use is currently made of IoT in the WASH domain in South Africa (and Africa). Currently the only real use of IoT related technology in South Africa is in the smart water (safely managed) management domain, primarily in metropolitan areas, to measure the amount of *improved water* use and payment therefor. No use is made of IoT to improve the livelihood and health of the majority of the South African population, and especially those dependent on basic, limited or unimproved water resources, basic, limited or unimproved sanitation facilities, or basic or limited handwashing facilities. This finding was supported by both the literature review and the inputs received from the stakeholders' responses to the survey.

Apart from the current focus on 'urban' applications of IoT in mainly the water sector, which is also necessary, there are therefore huge opportunities to investigate the use and benefits of IoT in WASH as an integrated and interlinked domain. Vast opportunities also exist for research to determine how IoT technologies can be used to improve the lives and health of the large proportion of the South African population dependent on WASH services that cannot be classified as safely managed, improved or advanced, and to develop suitable technologies to fit such environments.

This paper was positioned to inform policy makers, improve decision-making and shape the design, implementation and commission of IoT-enabled WASH services.

Acknowledgement. The work presented in this paper was jointly funded by the Water Research Commission of South Africa (Grant K5/2779//3), the Meraka Institute of the Council for Scientific and Industrial Research, and the National Research Foundation of South Africa (Grant 115456). The authors specifically wish to acknowledge the support and guidance of Dr Nonhlanhla Kalebaila, WRC Research Manager: Drinking Water Treatment and Quality, during the execution of the project.

References

1. United Nations General Assembly: International Covenant on Economic, Social and Cultural Rights. United Nations (1976)
2. UNICEF: Water, Sanitation and Hygiene. https://www.unicef.org/wash/. Accessed 26 July 2017
3. United Nations General Assembly: Report of the independent expert on the issue of human rights obligations related to access to safe drinking water and sanitation, Catarina de Albuquerque. United Nations (2010)
4. United Nations General Assembly: Report of the Special Rapporteur on the human right to safe drinking water and sanitation, Catarina de Albuquerque: Stigma and the realization of the human rights to water and sanitation. United Nations (2012)
5. United Nations General Assembly: Report of the independent expert on the issue of human rights obligations related to access to safe drinking water and sanitation, Catarina de Albuquerque. United Nations (2009)
6. UNICEF and WHO: Progress on Sanitation and Drinking Water – 2015 update and MDG assessment. WHO Press, Geneva (2015)
7. World Health Organization: Global Health Observatory Data: Mortality and burden of disease from water and sanitation. http://www.who.int/gho/phe/water_sanitation/burden/en/index2.html. Accessed 24 May 2017
8. UNICEF: WASH: Ensuring Safe Water, Sanitation and Hygiene Help Children Survive and Thrive (2017)
9. Department of Health: The National Health Promotion Policy and Strategy 2015–2019. Department of Health, Republic of South Africa, Pretoria (2015)
10. Coetzee, L., Kotzé, P.: The Internet of Things: Opportunities for Water, Sanitation and Hygiene (WASH) Management. Water Research Commission, Pretoria (2018)
11. WHO and UNICEF: JMP. https://washdata.org/. Accessed 26 June 2017
12. United Nations General Assembly: Transforming our world: the 2030 Agenda for Sustainable Development. United Nations (2015)
13. WHO and UNICEF: Safely Managed Drinking Water. World Health Organisation (WHO) and United Nations Children's Fund (UNICEF) (2017)
14. UNICEF and WHO: Progress Core questions and indicators for monitoring WASH in Schools in the Sustainable Development Goals. WHO Press, Geneva (2016)
15. WHO and UNICEF: WASH in the 2030 Agenda. World Health Organisation (WHO) and United Nations Children's Fund (UNICEF) (2017)
16. Curtis, V., Cairncross, S., Yonli, R.: Review: domestic hygiene and diarrhoea – pinpointing the problem. Trop. Med. Int. Health **5**(1), 22–32 (2000)
17. tippytap.org: The tippy tap! http://www.tippytap.org/the-tippy-tap. Accessed 11 Dec 2017

18. United Nations: The World's Woman 2015: Trends and Statistics (E.15.XVII.8). United Nations, Departments of Economic and Social Affairs, Statistics Division (2015)
19. WHO: Guidelines for Drinking-water Quality. World Health Organization, Geneva (2011)
20. United Nations Development Programme: Human Development Report 2006 - Beyond Scarcity: Power, Poverty and the Global Water Crisis. Palgrave Macmillan, New York (2006)
21. Hutton, G.: Monitoring "Affordability" of Water and Sanitation Services after 2015: review of global indicator options. Revised draft United Nations Office of the High Commissioner for Human Rights (2012)
22. Minerva, R., Biru, A., Rotondi, D.: Towards a definition of the Internet of Things (IoT). IEEE Internet Initiat (2015)
23. Coetzee, L., et al.: TRESCIMO: European Union and South African Smart City Contextual Dimensions. In: Proceedings of the 2015 IEEE 2nd World Forum on Internet of Things (WF-IoT) – Enabling Internet Evolution, pp. 770–776. IEEE Computer Society, Washington (2015)
24. ICT4Water Cluster: ict4water.eu. http://www.ict4water.eu/. Accessed 30 Sept 2017
25. Biggs, P., Garrity, J., LaSalle, C., Polomska, A., Pepper, R.: Harnessing the Internet of Things for Global Development. ITU and CISCO, Geneva (2016)
26. Charity: Water: new technology supported by Google. https://blog.charitywater.org/post/143492619882/new-technology-supported-by-google. Accessed 12 Dec 2017
27. Smith School of Enterprise and the Environment: From Rights to Results in Rural Water Services - Evidence from Kyuso, Kenya. University of Oxford (2014)
28. Toilet Board Coalition: The Digitisation of Sanitation (2016)
29. Gemma, P., Sang, Z., McIntosh, A., Ospina, A.V.: Smart Water Management in Cities Telecommunication Standardization Sector of ITU (2014)
30. Department for Business Innovation and Skills: The Smart City Market: Opportunities for the UK. GOV.UK (2013)
31. Glenisson, A., Wojcieszko, G.: Emerging Topics and Technology Roadmap for Information and Communication Technologies for Water Management. EUROPEAN COMMISSION DirectorateGeneral for Communications Networks, Content and Technology Smart Cities and Sustainability Unit (2016)
32. Champanis, M., Rivett, U., Gool, S., Nyemba-Mudenda, M.: ICTs in the water sector – where do we stand? (978-1-4312-0463-2). University of Cape Town (2013)
33. Bridgiot: Bridgiot: Remote Intelligence and Control. https://www.bridgiot.co.za/. Accessed 20 Nov 2017
34. Aguatrip Australia Pty. Ltd.: Aquatrip. www.aquatrip.com. Accessed 6 Dec 2017
35. Ndaw, M.F., Mwangi, P.N.: Unlocking the Potential of Information Communications Technology to Improve Water and Sanitation Services Kenya Case Study. The World Bank Water and Sanitation Program (2015)
36. Ndaw, M.F., Welsien, K.: Unlocking the Potential of Information Communications Technology to Improve Water and Sanitation Services Tanzania Case Study. The World Bank Water and Sanitation Program (2015)
37. Upande: Water Sanitation Hygiene Management Information System (WaSHMIS). http://www.washmis.com/. Accessed 30 Sept 2017
38. Charity: Water: clean water changes everything. https://www.charitywater.org/. Accessed 30 Sept 2017
39. OxWater: OxWater - for sustainable water systems in Africa and Asia. http://www.oxwater.uk/. Accessed 30 Sept 2017
40. Akvo: Akvo.org. http://akvo.org. Accessed 20 Nov 2017

41. SweetSence Inc.: No Village too Remote. http://www.sweetsensors.com/. Accessed 30 Sept 2017
42. Department of Water Affairs: Strategic Overview of the Water Services Sector in South Africa 2015. Department of Water Affairs, Republic of South Africa, Pretoria (2015)
43. Department of Water Affairs: Strategic Overview of the Water Sector in South Africa 2013. Department of Water Affairs, Republic of South Africa, Pretoria (2013)
44. Stats SA: General Household Survey 2016. Statistics South Africa (2017)
45. Collignon, B., Vézina, M.: Independent Water and Sanitation Providers in African Cities: Full Report of a Ten-Country Study. Hydroconseil (2000)
46. Mason, N., Matoso, M., Smith, W.: Private sector and water supply, sanitation and hygiene: driving catalytic engagement. ODI (2015)
47. Bill and Melinda Gates Foundation: Water, Sanitation & Hygiene Fact Sheet. Global Development Program (2010)
48. Sahay, A.: Report of a WASH Dialogue on faecal sludge and septage management Ushering a new era in sanitation value chain management in India. https://www.ircwash.org/blog/ushering-new-era-sanitation-value-chain-management-rajasthan. Accessed 12 Sept 2017
49. Water Sector Trust Fund: Safisan Toolkit. http://www.waterfund.go.ke/safisan/. Accessed 20 Nov 2017
50. Wilkinson, M., du Tout, A., Mashimbye, D., Cooligen, S.: Assessment of Handwashing and Hand Hygiene Behaviour. Water Research Commission, Pretoria (2012)
51. Centers for Disease Control and Prevention: When & How to Wash Your Hands. https://www.cdc.gov/handwashing/when-how-handwashing.html. Accessed 18 Sept 2017
52. McKeever, C.: Handwashing with soap: saving the lives of children in South Sudan and the world. https://www.unicef.org/southsudan/media_15566.html
53. Torondel, B., Opare, D., Brandberg, B., Cobb, E., Cairncross, S.: Efficacy of Moringa oleifera leaf powder as a hand-washing product : a crossover controlled study among healthy volunteers. BMC Complement. Altern. Med. **14**(57), 1–7 (2014)

Internet of Things: The Present Status, Future Impacts and Challenges in Nigerian Agriculture

Funmilayo O. Bamigboye[1(✉)] and Emmanuel O. Ademola[2]

[1] AfeBabalola University, Ado-Ekiti, Nigeria
familade@yahoo.com, bamigboyefo@abuad.edu.ng
[2] Trademark Owner of Power-Age (Management Consulting) Chairman, P-ACC, 2 Edenbridge Close, Orpington, Kent BR5 3SL, UK
ademolaeo@p-acc.co.uk

Abstract. The present study considered the current state of internet of things in Nigeria, future prospects and challenges to the usage of the technology in Nigerian Agriculture. In Nigeria, IoT has been used to dispense feed and water to chicks, virtual fences for monitoring farmlands and forest trees, cashless sales and purchases of farm produce and input, monitoring and management of staff performances on the farm and e-wallet for input, loan and information accessibility on agricultural issues. However, there is room for improvement in the area of security for the animals (animal tracking), weather forecasting and real-time soil monitoring, livestock and crop health surveillance. Challenges faced in the usage of IoT in Nigeria are inadequate/lack of capital, skilled manpower, facilities. In conclusion, IoT has great potentials to move Nigerian agriculture to an enviable position.

Keywords: IoT · Nigerian agriculture · Prospects of IoT · Status of IoT

1 Introduction

Internet of Things (IoT) is a recent technology that is gaining widespread awareness and acceptance in several fields due to its practical relevance in everyday life improvement. IoT has found its utility in transportation, environmental monitoring and forecasting, home and office appliances, agriculture, health, security and energy conservation (Bamigboye and Ademola 2016). In Nigeria, agriculture serves as one of the main resources for income generation for individuals, private and public organisations. However, agriculture in Nigeria as an enterprise and food security outlets for her populace is still backward in the use of IoT. Internet of Things has the potential to improve, enhance and absolutely change the face of Nigerian agriculture to a world-class standard.

Internet of Things (IoT) is the network of physical objects, devices, vehicles, buildings and other items which are embedded with electronics, software, sensors and network connectivity which enables these objects to collect and exchange data (GSI 2015). The Internet of Things allows objects to be sensed and controlled remotely

L. Strous and V. G. Cerf (Eds.): IFIPIoT 2018, IFIP AICT 548, pp. 211–217, 2019.
https://doi.org/10.1007/978-3-030-15651-0_17

across existing network infrastructure, creating opportunities for more direct integration between the physical world and computer-based systems, and resulting in improved efficiency, accuracy and economic benefit. IoT is any object which is capable of identifying, connecting and communicating with other objects (Santucci 2011; LOPEZ Research Series 2013; Reddy 2014).

Agriculture is a profit-driven oriented business; hence, factors that influence the profitability of a farm are of great paramount and interest to the farmer. IoT can be made relevant if it can address the general needs of a locality, be made available and affordable, easy to use and packaged in the local/indigenous languages. With intensification of crop/livestock production systems and increased market demand of animal based products, the importance of information is growing in many developing countries (Morton and Matthewman 1996). Hence, there is need for continual exchange of information and data, decoding and interpretation as well as actions taken to achieve desired success.

(Sasidhar and Sharma 2006) have emphasised that the use of Information and Communication Technology (ICT) has potential to change the economy of livestock, agriculture, and rural artisans in India. (Tiwari *et al.* 2010) argued that the livestock sector should come up with need based, location specific and local language contents in the form of computer software and other electronic material in regards to livestock disease control, dairy herd management, livestock production and for marketing of livestock and livestock produce. ICT based information delivery to livestock sector can significantly improve the quality of decision-making in livestock farming system. In this process of structural change and potential growth in high value products (Gulati *et al.* 2007), ICT based livestock advisory services for knowledge dissemination to the farming communities for better and informed decision-making at the farm level, have become essential.

Nigeria has witnessed a great deal of set-back due to corruption at all levels in every sector; agriculture inclusive. IoT in form of E-wallet was employed to address agricultural inputs and services corruption. Most times, subsidized inputs do not get to the practicing farmers but are rather lost in transit to the rich and influential few that repack and sell at exorbitant prices.

2 Present Status of Internet of Things in Nigerian Agriculture

In Nigeria, the Internet of Things is just becoming popular in all facets of life. However, its usage in agriculture is still backward. Mostly, IoT usage in agriculture is believed to be only profitable to large-scale farmers. But very few farmers in Nigeria practiced large-scale farming. Hence, most farmers have not seen the need for its usage on their farms.

2.1 Mobile Feed and Water Dispensing System

Feeding of poultry birds is a major task that is time-consuming and labour-demanding. Its efficiency also can determine the profitability of a poultry farm. In Nigeria, feed dispensing methods working based on IoT were developed by researchers. In

(Arulogun *et al.* 2010) a mobile intelligent poultry feed dispensing system was developed. The system was able to move, detect and avoid obstructions and dispense solid feed to poultry birds. However, (Olaniyi *et al.* 2014) designed a mobile intelligent poultry feed and water dispensing system; using fuzzy logic control technique.

This unit was responsible for dispensing solid feed to the poultry birds. It comprises of a solid feed trough, a 12 V DC motor connected to a conveyor and a feeder. The solid feed trough is expected to be filled with the appropriate solid feed to be administered to the birds. A feed sensing unit which comprises of a light dependent resistor checks the feed level and in turn determines if there is a need to dispense the feed or not. The microcontroller will then send a signal through the PID controller to the DC motor which will enable it to rotate. The rotation of the DC motor will in turn rotate the conveyor which will result in the dispensing of the solid feed to the feeder. The poultry birds feed from the feeder after feed is dispensed to the feeder for the pre-defined time determined by the microcontroller. A relay circuit is connected between the microcontroller and the DC motor so as to enable proper functionality of the system (Olaniyi *et al.* 2016).

2.2 Virtual Fences

The use of virtual fences to monitor the perimeters of large farmlands and plantations is of tremendous advantage. The most obvious is in terms of cost savings when compared to building high brick fences and employing security personnel to patrol the entire perimeter. With virtual fences, relatively cheap modules can be installed and the entire perimeter monitored remotely (Ajayi and Olaifa 2016).

The Nigerian Satellite Company Limited, has successfully designed, implemented, tested and deployed an RFID-based Staff Attendance and Access Control System (RFID-SAACS). RFID-SAACS is a vital tool for staff management, administration, and monitoring that impacts staff's attitude to work, as time theft by staff is completely eliminated. The logged data can also serve as a means of staff monthly appraisal, while an additional utilisation of the RFID-SAACS system includes integration into the payroll system to facilitate precise salary computation and payment based upon vetting of employees' overall performance (N.C.S.L. 2015). This is used in some automated farms in Nigeria.

Also, the use of point-of-sale (PoS) terminals for the purchase of farm produce to achieve cashless transactions is now common in Nigeria. A PoS terminal is an electronic device that is used for verifying and processing credit/debit card transactions, which transmits data over a standard telephone line or an Internet connection. The Nigeria Interbank Settlement Services (NIBSS) had observed in its recent report that PoS is the most popular non-cash payment channel, preferred among the non-cash payment options by 93.6% of merchants and 35.8% of consumer usage. It described the usage of card and PoS as fair, with an average of three to four out of every 10 customers requesting to pay for transactions by card/PoS (Adeoye 2015). Electronic payment through PoS terminals has risen by 191% to N241 billion in 2014 (Komolafe 2014).

Furthermore, as part of an ambitious strategy to transform agriculture, the Growth Enhancement Support (GES) initiative, introduced in 2012, farmers' cellphones as electronic wallets – distributing vouchers amounting to a 50% subsidy for purchase of fertilizer. Ministry officials say the phones could eventually be used for multiple purposes, from communicating weather and climate information to accessing market data. Experiences in other African countries showed that such uses can deliver higher prices to farmers. Records also show that 1.2 million farmers received their subsidized fertilizer and seeds through cellphone vouchers in 2013, resulting in the addition of 8.1 million metric tons to Nigeria's domestic food supply. As a result, Nigeria reduced its food imports by over 40% by 2013, moving the country closer to self-sufficiency in agriculture (Hultman 2015).

3 Future Prospects of IoT in Nigerian Agriculture

Effective tracking of nomadic cattle-grazing and movements enabled by smart tracking devices would greatly minimize the number of community clashes between nomadic herdsmen and the settled rural farming communities. This would go a long way to help settle the persisting conflict and communal disputes, tensions, which most often degenerate into communal wars between the people (Ume and Haruna 2018). Indiscriminate killings and destruction of properties in the recent time by Fulani cattle herders can be tracked and curbed. Animal theft can be drastically reduced to the minimum.

Since rural communities are sparsely populated, transportation of farm products can be a problem. IoT technologies can empower the transporters by providing them with information of farmers who require transport. Therefore transporters do not need to wait until they have a full truck load of farm products to start off, they can leave any time provided they are aware that there are farmers waiting for transport ahead (Bamigboye and Ademola 2016).

Furthermore, farm workers can receive real-time notifications from farm machinery equipped with wireless sensors as issues arise. The ability to perform preventative maintenance and repair issues immediately could lead to tremendous cost savings in decreasing down time and protecting valuable assets (Farrell 2015). The health of farm animals such as cattle or chicken can be monitored to detect potential signs of disease. This can be linked to a central system which can trigger relevant advice to be sent to farmers, and contribute towards analytics that can be used to identify any outbreaks or trends (Farrell 2015).

Through the use of Near-Field Communications (NFC), the farmers and buyers can benefit from paperless transactions and this helps minimize on theft and fraud. Similarly this is beneficial to rural farmers who have no access to banks within a reasonable distance to deposit cash from purchases or withdraw cash to buy farming inputs. The use of livestock or crop smart health cards which store information related to affected livestock or crops can be beneficial to both the veterinary or agriculture officer and the farmers in Nigeria. This can lead to efficient and effective diagnosis and prescription of medicine since the officer has access to all the historic information of the affected livestock or crop. If satellite transmission is made available in the deep rural area, this has the potential to create jobs for local businesses who could offer low-cost solutions, access and wireless network services cheaper to the communities. Satellite transmission can also enable farmers in rural areas obtain information on markets for their products and prices, government services that they can access, and their rights. The system can also connect to government departments and local and international markets. With the introduction of the mobile internet and low-cost sensors, farmers could interact directly with consumers and cutting off middlemen who usually exploit them. This is beneficial to farmers because they can make better profits on their products (Haas *et al.* 2011).

4 Challenges of IoT in Nigerian Agriculture

Inadequate Skill Manpower
The biggest challenge faced in the usage of IoT solutions in Nigeria is inadequate skilled manpower. Most farmers are found in the rural areas and are mostly unskilled and uninformed in terms of IoT. Adult literacy should be intensified to bring to limelight the usage and usefulness of IoT to rural farmers in Nigeria. Also, training of farmers' children to integrate the household into IoT application usage will further enhance continuity.

Inadequate Facilities
Internet of Things requires a lot of equipment; software and hardware for proper functioning. Without power supply, continual usage of IoT is impaired. However, in the rural area where agriculture is most pronounced and prominent in Nigeria, constant supply of electricity is not guaranteed. Hence, efforts should be made towards the provision of stable and constant power supply. This may be generated from solar, biogas or water which can be obtained even at the rural level.

Insufficient Start-Up Capital
The initial cost of setting up an IoT compliant farm can prove to be a barrier to many small-scale farmers. The cost of importing some of the existing IoT-sensors is still relatively high. Inadequate/lack of access to source of internet has created a great setback for farmers to afford IoT. However, the cost of purchasing mobile data for continuous monitoring and storage either to cloud or remote centres for analysis is also expensive. However, in recent times, Nigerian Communications commission (NCC) is making efforts to improve data rates and supply in Nigeria. The Government also should support the farmers to make internet available even in the remote villages where they are mostly found.

Meager Sponsorships from Corporate Organizations
Most support goes to entertainment- music and comedy rather than education, agricultural research and innovation in Nigeria.

Lack of Collaboration Among Tech Hubs
At present in Nigeria, technology hubs operate solo. As a result of this, innovations developed in one technology hub rarely diffuse to the rest of the country. This is slowing down innovation adoption and circulation in Nigeria. Co-operation and unity should be encouraged among tech hubs.

5 Conclusion

Internet of Things in Nigeria is still at the formative stage. However, future prospects were identified. Nevertheless, the sustainability of IoT in the country is being faced with some challenges.

References

Adeoye, T.: Overcoming challenges of PoS transaction (2015). http://www.ngrguardiannews.com/2015/08/overcoming-challenges-of-pos-transaction

Ajayi, O.O., Olaifa, O.: Detecting intrusion in large farm lands and plantations in Nigeria using virtual fences. In: Conference Proceeding: Transition from Observation to Knowledge to Intelligence 2016, University of Lagos, Lagos, Nigeria pp. 2–11 (2016)

Arulogun, O.T., Olaniyi, O.M., Oke, O.A., Fenwa, D.O.: Development of mobile intelligent poultry feed and water dispensing system. Medwell J. Eng. Appl. Sci. **5**(3), 229–233 (2010)

Bamigboye, F.O., Ademola, O.: Internet of Things (Iot): It's application for sustainable agricultural productivity in Nigeria. In: 6th Proceedings of the iSTEAMS Multidisciplinary Cross-Border Conference, Held at University of Professional Studies, Accra Ghana, 2016, pp. 309–312 (2016)

Farrell, P.: Harvesting the benefits of IoT in agribusiness (2015). https://www.dsiglobal.com/labs/harvesting-the-benefits-of-iot-in-agribusiness/

GSI (Global Standard Initiatives): Internet of things global standards initiative (2015). http://www.itu.int/en/ITU-T/gsi/iot/Pages/default.aspx

Gulati, A., Minot, N., Delgado, C., Bora, S.: Growth in high-value agriculture in Asia and the emergence of vertical links with farmers. In: Swinnen, J.F.M. (ed.) Global Supply Chains, Standards and the Poor: How the Globalization of Food Systems and Standards Affects Rural Development and Poverty, pp. 91–108. CABI, Wallingford (2007)

Haas, S., Plyler, M.G., Nagarajan, G.: Outreach of M-Pesa system in Kenya: emerging trends financial assessment. Financial Service Assessment Project (2011)

Hultman. T.: Cell phones for farmers to cut corruption, deliver services (2015). http://reliefweb.int/report/nigeria/cell-phones-farmers-cut-corruption-deliver-services

Komolafe, B.: PoS transactions rises 191% to N241bn, says NIBSS (2014). http://www.vanguardngr.com/2014/12/pos-transactions-rises-191-n241bn-says-nibss/

LOPEZ Research Series: An introduction to the internet of things (IoT), part 1 (2013). http://www.cisco.com/c/dam/en_us/solutions/trends/iot/introduction_to_IoT_november.pdf

Morton, J., Matthewman, R.: Improving livestock production through extension: information needs institutions and opportunities. ODI Nat. Res. Perspect. **12**, 1–8 (1996)

Nigeria Communications Satellite Ltd (N.C.S.L.): Staff attendance and access control system (2015). http://www.nigcomsat.gov.ng/products.php

Olaniyi, O.M., Folorunso, T.A., Kolo, J.G., Arulogun, O.T., Bala, J.A.: A Mobile Intelligent Poultry Feed Dispensing System Using Particle Swarm Optimized PID Control Technique. In: 6th Proceedings of the iSTEAMS Multidisciplinary Cross-Border Conference, Held at University of Professional Studies, Accra Ghana, 2016, pp. 185–194 (2016)

Olaniyi, O.M., Salami, A.F., Adewumi, O.O., Ajibola, O.S.: Design of an intelligent poultry feed and water dispensing system using fuzzy logic control technique. J. Control Theory Inform. (JCTIS) **4**(9), 61–72 (2014)

Reddy, A.S.: Reaping the benefits of the internet of things. Cognizant report (2014). http://www.cognizant.com/InsightsWhitepapers/Reaping-the-Benefits-of-the-Internet-of-Things.pdf

Santucci, G.: The internet of things: between the revolution of the internet and the metamorphosis of objects (2011). http://cordis.europa.eu/fp7/ict/enet/documents/publications/iot-between-the-internet-revolution.pdf

Sasidhar, P.V.K., Sharma, V.P.: Cyber livestock outreach services in India: a model framework. Livestock Res. Rural Dev. **18**(2) (2006). http://www.lrrd.org/lrrd18/1/sasi18002.htm

Tiwari, R., Shahaji, P., Sharma, M.C.: Status and scope of information and communication technology for livestock and poultry production in India–a review. Indian J. Anim. Sci. **80** (12), 1235–1242 (2010)

Ume, A., Haruna, U.: Smart Agriculture in Nigeria with IoT; a reality. Am. J. Eng. Res. **7**(1), 277–282 (2018)

Check for updates

IoTutor: How Cognitive Computing Can Be Applied to Internet of Things Education

Suejb Memeti[1], Sabri Pllana[1](✉), Mexhid Ferati[2], Arianit Kurti[1,3], and Ilir Jusufi[1]

[1] Department of Computer Science and Media Technology, Linnaeus University, Växjö, Sweden
{suejb.memeti,sabri.pllana,arianit.kurti,ilir.jusufi}@lnu.se
[2] Department of Informatics, Linnaeus University, Växjö, Sweden
mexhid.ferati@lnu.se
[3] RISE Research Institutes of Sweden, Norrköping, Sweden
arianit.kurti@ri.se

Abstract. We present IoTutor that is a cognitive computing solution for education of students in the IoT domain. We implement the IoTutor as a platform-independent web-based application that is able to interact with users via text or speech using natural language. We train the IoTutor with selected scientific publications relevant to the IoT education. To investigate users' experience with the IoTutor, we ask a group of students taking an IoT master level course at the Linnaeus University to use the IoTutor for a period of two weeks. We ask students to express their opinions with respect to the attractiveness, perspicuity, efficiency, stimulation, and novelty of the IoTutor. The evaluation results show a trend that students express an overall positive attitude towards the IoTutor with majority of the aspects rated higher than the neutral value.

Keywords: Internet of Things (IoT) · Education · Cognitive computing · IBM Watson

1 Introduction

Internet of Things (IoT) [17] pertains to networked interactive physical objects (such as, personal devices, connected cars, industrial machines, or household goods) with sensing, processing, communication, and acting capabilities. Evolution of the Internet from a network of computers to the network of things creates opportunities for new services and applications in society [12,21,24] and industry [6,9]. According to Gartner [14], it is expected that by the year 2020 there will be about 20 billion IoT devices worldwide and it is expected that more

This research has received funding from the Swedish Knowledge Foundation under Grants No. 20150088 and No. 20150259.

L. Strous and V. G. Cerf (Eds.): IFIPIoT 2018, IFIP AICT 548, pp. 218–233, 2019.
https://doi.org/10.1007/978-3-030-15651-0_18

than 65% of companies will use IoT solutions. Therefore, adequate education of the future workforce is a precondition for success in the increasingly relevant domain of IoT.

When searching for information about a topic, search engines usually return more results than we can study. For instance, currently Google returns about 35 million results, when we search for *Internet of Things*. Therefore, it is important to have a system that returns succinct information from relevant literature based on a question expressed in natural language.

A cognitive computing [8,19,23] system, such as the IBM Watson [20], relates a text passage (that is a question) with another text passage (that is an anticipated corresponding answer) by using machine learning. Predicting the probable answer involves determining the major features of the question by generating hypothesis and evaluation of possible answers considering the context, and iterative learning from each instance of interaction with the cognitive system. The IBM Watson [13] has been successfully used in many domains [22], such as, the life sciences research [10] or health-care [5]. Goel et al. [15] argue that the IBM Watson has the potential to be used as an educational tool.

In this paper, we propose to use cognitive computing for education of students in the IoT domain. We describe the design and implementation of IoTutor that we use for empirical evaluation of our approach. We have implemented the IoTutor as a platform-independent web-based application using a collection of the IBM Watson cloud services including the discovery service, text-to-speech and speech-to-text services. We trained the IoTutor with selected scientific publications and course books relevant to the IoT education. To investigate users' experience with the IoTutor, we asked a group of students taking an IoT master level course at the Linnaeus University in Sweden to use the IoTutor for a period of two weeks. One of the course assignments was to develop a literature review for the course project. To complete the assignment, they were instructed and encouraged to use IoTutor beside Google Scholar and other digital libraries. Via a user experience questionnaire participants were asked to express their opinions with respect to the attractiveness, perspicuity, efficiency, stimulation, and novelty of the IoTutor. The results show a trend that participants expressed an overall positive attitude towards the tool. The majority of aspects were rated higher than the neutral value, while the rest were slightly lower than the neutral value. We observed that for some questions IoTutor showed sub-optimal answers, which may be a consequence of using a relatively small number of training questions and papers.

Major contributions of this paper include,

1. a development of IoTutor, which is a cognitive computing tool able to interact with users through text and voice using natural language,
2. a training of IoTutor for education of students in the IoT domain,
3. an evaluation of IoTutor with the help of a group of students at Linnaeus University.

The rest of the paper is organized as follows. In Sect. 2 we discuss the related work. Section 3 describes the design and implementation of IoTutor. In Sect. 4

we first demonstrate the use of IoTutor, and thereafter we discuss the results of the user experience questionnaire. We conclude our paper and provide future research directions in Sect. 5.

2 Related Work

In this section we first provide examples of related work and thereafter we contrast the work presented in this paper with the related work.

Goel et al. [15] used different Watson services to develop six diverse applications that aim at understanding the functionality and capabilities of Watson and enhancing the human-computer co-creativity. By developing these diverse applications the authors argue that Watson has potential to be used in different domains, and has large range of opportunities to be used as an educational tool.

Achilleas et al. [4] propose to use social networks and media for increasing motivation of students for STEM education and careers. They developed a social media aware platform and evaluated it in the context of a pan-European contest in STEM disciplines. More than 700 pre-university students participated in the contest and via a user-experience questionnaire they had the opportunity to express their opinion. Results of the questionnaire suggest that the contest using social media had positive influence on learning and motivation of participants.

Chen et al. [10] investigate the use of IBM Watson for accelerating the life sciences research. The authors trained Watson using large amounts of data including pharmacological data, genomics data, patents, and literature in life sciences. Watson is able to recognize concepts and their synonyms when they appear as an image or text in literature. For instance, Watson was able to generate in real-time relationships between the multiple sclerosis and any gene using data from more than 26 million MEDLINE abstracts.

Witte et al. [26] uses natural language processing to bring new levels of support to software developers. A plug-in that is integrated in the Eclipse IDE is developed, which provides quality analysis of the comments found in source code and version control commits. The aim of this project is to help software developers reduce the effort required to analyze their code by extracting useful information that might be valuable to understand the functionality of the application that is not always obvious by looking at the source code only.

Chozas et al. [11] study the use of cognitive computing for assisting novice programmers in avoiding the commonly made mistakes in parallel programming with OpenMP. They use the dialogue service of the IBM Watson for implementation of their solution that enables a dialog-based interaction with a programmer in English and Spanish during the process of parallel programming.

Harms [18] proposes an approach that is able to monitor and understand the programming skill level of the developer and adaptively suggest code examples that may help to learn new programming concepts found within the suggested examples. The author argues that this approach avoids overwhelming the memory of novice programmers by considering the previous knowledge of the programmer and carefully suggesting examples that contain new information.

In contrast to the related work, we use the cognitive computing technology to develop the IoTutor that assists students to learn about the domain of Internet of Things.

3 Design and Implementation

In this section, first we describe the design of our solution, thereafter we highlight implementation details.

3.1 Design

The goal of IoTutor is to provide means for communication (related to the area of Internet of Things) between the user and the computer through natural language in a similar fashion as personal assistants like Apple Siri, Google Now, and Microsoft Cortana. While these personal assistants are incorporated in the operating system, and can be used only within a selected operating system, we aim at developing a web based platform that is independent from the operating system and device. IoTutor allows users to interact with it, that is ask questions related to Internet of Things, through a dialog-based interface.

A high-level architecture overview of our system is depicted in Fig. 1. The main components of the system are the front-end, the back-end, and the Watson Cloud Services. The user interacts with the front-end. The front-end forwards requests from the user to the back-end, and returns responses from the back-end to the user. The back-end is connected to Watson Cloud services, which are used to extract knowledge from a corpus of data (in this case scientific publications), and enhance IoTutor with speech capabilities (that is text-to-speech and speech-to-text).

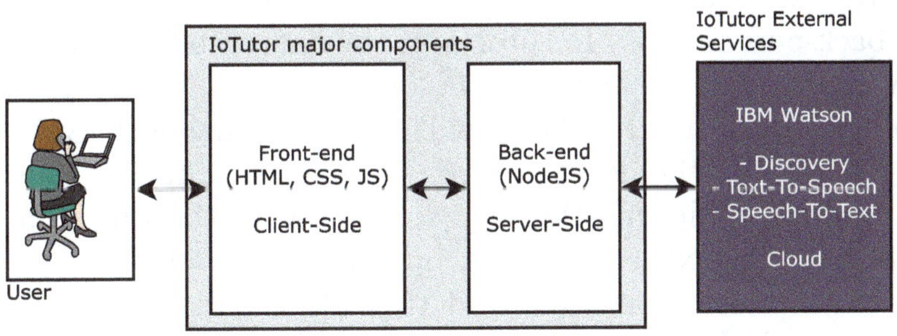

Fig. 1. A high-level overview of IoTutor architecture. The front-end provides means for interaction with the user, and the back-end interacts with the IBM Watson cloud services. The front-end is a web based dialog view that can be accessed with any internet browser.

Figure 2 depicts the flowchart with the major events of the IoTutor. When the tool starts, the page is rendered and a welcome message is displayed. Then

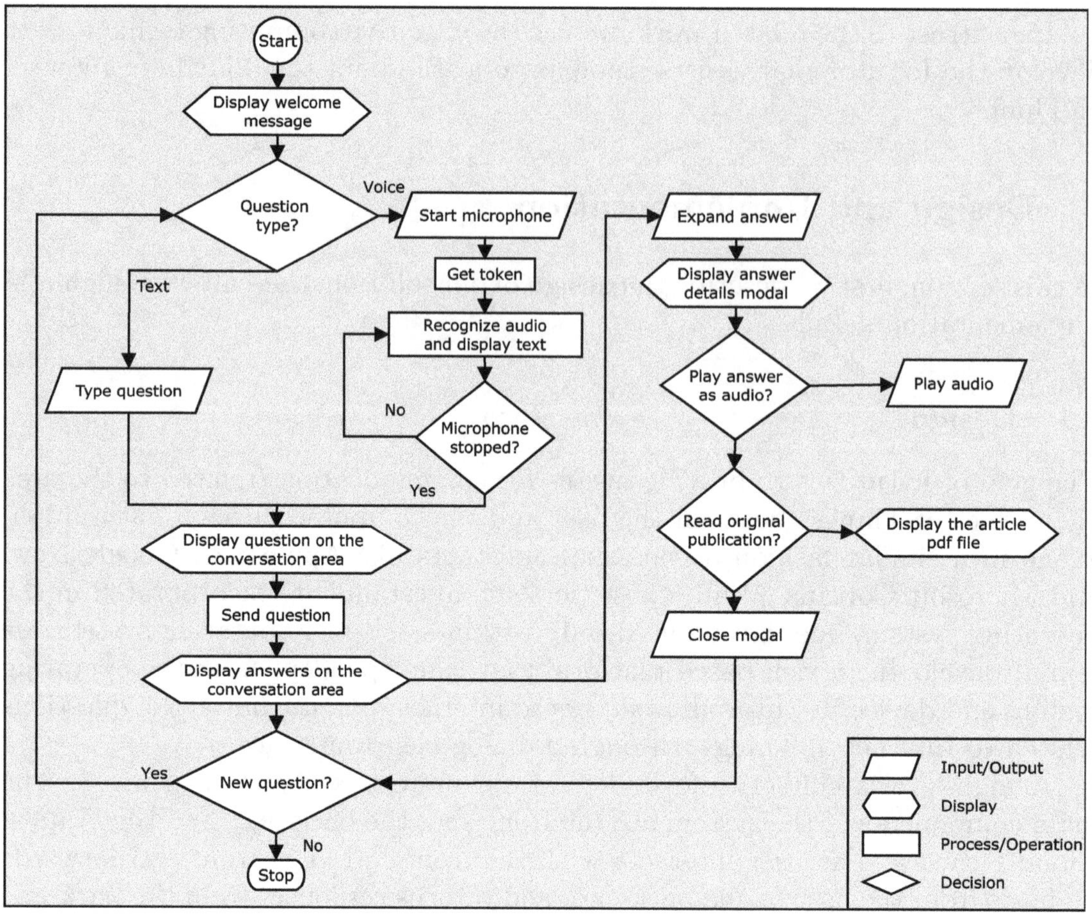

Fig. 2. A flowchart of user interaction with the IoTutor.

depending on how the user wants to interact with IoTutor, that is voice or text, the following steps are performed. If the user wants to use voice commands, then the microphone button should be pressed, which will establish a stream through the back-end between IoTutor and the speech-to-text Watson, and the recognized words will be displayed in the question box. Unless the user toggles the microphone from on to off, IoTutor will keep recognizing the voice commands and display the text on the question box. Otherwise, if the user decides to use text to ask questions, the question can be typed on the question box. When the microphone is stopped, or the send button is pressed, the question will be displayed in the conversation area, and then it will be sent to the back-end. When the list of relevant answers is retrieved, those will be displayed in the conversation area. Passages of answers are displayed first, which the user may click to expand and then the answer will appear in a modal (pop-up) window with more details. Those details include a link to the full article and an option to let IoTutor read the full text to the user. Once the button to read the text is pressed, an audio player will be shown and IoTutor will start reading the text. If the link to the full article is pressed, the user will be redirected to the full pdf file. When the close button is clicked, the modal window will be closed, and the user may either choose to expand another answer, or ask a new question.

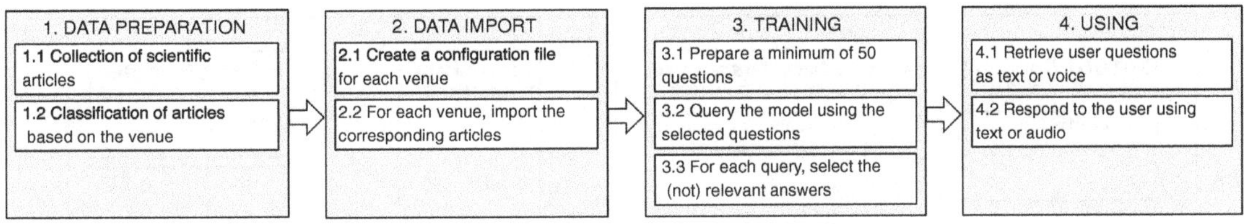

Fig. 3. IoTutor development process. Major steps include data preparation, data importing, IoTutor training, IoTutor using.

A high-level overview of the development process of IoTutor is depicted in Fig. 3. There are four main activities, including data preparation, data import, training of the model, and using the model. In what follows we describe each activity.

Data Preparation (activity 1): Scientific articles related to Internet of Things were collected from different electronic databases, including ACM, Spring-er, IEEE Explore, and Elsevier (activity 1.1). They were classified in respective folders, where each folder corresponds to an electronic database. The scientific articles were further classified by the venue, such as a conference, journal, or a magazine (activity 1.2).

Data Import (activity 2): To be able to split the scientific publications in subsections, which is useful to correctly identify all relevant sections of the manuscript, a separate configuration file was created for each database and venue. For example, a configuration file, named *Springer-conference-configuration.json*, was used to identify sections of Springer conference scientific articles (activity 2.1). These configuration files were used to import the data into the Watson Discovery service. The corresponding configuration files were used to import the scientific articles collected from each venue of a digital library (activity 2.2).

Training (activity 3): According to the Watson Discovery Service documentation [1], a minimum of 49 queries should be used to train the Watson Discovery service. We used minimal resources and have defined 50 questions to train the model (activity 3.1). For each question, we have added a natural language query to the Watson Discovery service for training (activity 3.2). For each question, Watson suggests a set of answers, which need to be marked as relevant or not-relevant (activity 3.3). We went through 15 answers for each question and marked their relevance. Since the training process is a one-time activity, we have used the Watson Discovery Tooling interface, rather than using the API to implement the same functionality. In total, we fed Watson with 50 paper and 2 books in the topics of Internet of Things. The training process took 6–7 h excluding the time to find the articles and preparing the questions.

Using the Service (activity 4): Once the Discovery service was trained, the tool was ready to accept various questions related to Internet of Things (activity 4.1). A set of relevant answers are provided by Watson, and displayed to the user (activity 4.2).

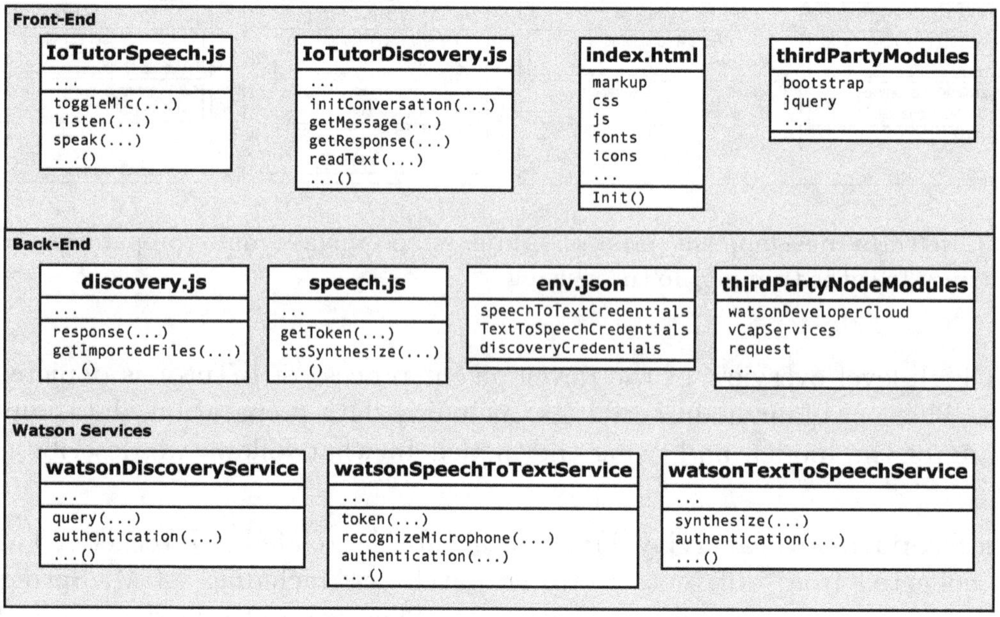

Fig. 4. An overview of components used to implement our solution.

3.2 Implementation Details

Figure 4 shows an overview of components used to implement our solution. There are three layers of the architecture, the front-end, the back-end, and the Watson Cloud Services.

Front-End. The major components of the front-end include the *IoTutorSpeech*, *IoTutorDiscovery*, and *index.*

The *IoTutorSpeech* component has three main functions, *toggleMic()* used to turn the microphone on and off, *listen()* used to initiate the process of streaming data to the corresponding Watson services when the microphone is on, and *speak()* will start reading the corresponding answer when the user clicks the play button.

The *IoTutorDiscovery* component has four main functions, *initConversation()* used to initiate the conversation, which basically says the welcome message and some instructions on how to use IoTutor. The *getMessage()* is triggered when the user asks a question, it displays the question on the conversation area, and sends it to the corresponding Watson services. The *getResponse()* is triggered when the back-end has found a response and it displays it on the conversation area. The *readText()* will simply call the *speak()* function from the *IoTutorSpeech* component with the corresponding parameters.

The *index* component is a simple file which includes the html markup, the style-sheets, java-scripts, fonts, and icons. It also has an *init()* function which is used as a constructor to set the variables. Third party libraries such as bootstrap and jQuery were used to implement the front-end.

Back-End. The major components of the back-end include the *discovery*, *speech*, and *env*. Third party NodeJS modules, such as Watson Developer Cloud SDK, vCapServices and request, were used in our implementation. For design and security reasons, the front-end communicates with the Watson services through the back-end. The back-end has the environment file (*env.json*) that contains the credentials (such as, username, password, url, workspace, version, collection_id, configuration_id, and environment_id) for each of the Watson Cloud services, including discovery, text-to-speech, and speech-to-text.

The *discovery* component is a simple application program interface (API), which accepts requests (in this case questions) from the front-end and sends it to the Watson Cloud Discovery service. The API needs to authenticate first using the information found in the *env.json* file. When a response is received from the Watson Discovery service, the back-end forwards the response to the front-end. Additionally, the back-end has a database of files that were imported in the Watson Discovery service, and it can easily map a response to an actual scientific publication, such that if the user wants to read more, the front-end can provide a link to the paper.

The *speech* component is an API, which handles requests and responses for speech-to-text and text-to-speech services. It can basically establish a stream that can listen to the user's microphone and display the recognized text in the input box of the IoTutor GUI, as well as can generate an audio file corresponding to a given input text. Similar to the *discovery* component, it first authenticates to the text-to-speech or speech-to-text service using the information provided by the *env.json* file, and then it can send specific requests to the Watson Cloud text-to-speech or speech-to-text services.

Watson Cloud Services. Watson provides different cloud services, such as speech-to-text, text-to-speech, discovery, conversation, and natural language understanding. To achieve the goals of our paper, we have used only three of them, *discovery*, *text-to-speech*, and *speech-to-text*.

The *discovery* service allowed us to extract useful information from various scientific publications related to Internet of Things, such that when the user asks a question, we can query the service and retrieve a list of ranked responses (publications, sections of publications, or a specific sentence or paragraph in such articles) that are relevant to the question being asked.

The *speech-to-text* service allowed us to enhance the IoTutor with voice recognition, such that the user may use their microphone to ask questions. This service will listen to the microphone and as a response will provide a stream of recognized text.

The *text-to-speech* service allowed us to enhance the IoTutor with the possibility to read the provided answers for users. This service accepts a text input and provides an audio file which can be played on demand by the user. The combination of the *speech-to-text* and *text-to-speech* services enabled us to provide an interaction between the user and IoTutor, similar to personal assistants like Apple's Siri [7] or Google's Now [16].

Environmental Details. To implement our application, we have used HTML5, CSS, and JS in front-end, whereas NodeJS [2] is used in the back-end. Among others, in the back-end we used the Watson Node SDK [3] to access the IBM Watson Developer Cloud services. The application was deployed on an Ubuntu v14.04 server with Apache v2.4 and node v6.11 installed. For the voice commands to work on the front-end, which requires data to be encrypted, we enabled the Hyper Text Transfer Protocol Secure (HTTPS) on our server (Table 1).

Table 1. Key software components of IoTutor server

Software component	Version
Operating System	Ubuntu 14.04 x64
Web Server	Apache 2.4
Runtime Platform	NodeJS 6.11
Libraries and Packages	Watson Node SDK 2.4, Unirest 0.51, Bootstrap 3.3.7

4 Evaluation

In this section, we first demonstrate the functionality of IoTutor and how users can interact with IoTutor to ask questions related to Internet of Things. Thereafter, we describe the evaluation method and results of our evaluation.

4.1 Demonstration

Figure 5 shows the graphical user interface of IoTutor and demonstrates a use case scenario when a user asks an IoT related question, and IoTutor provides a list of relevant answers. When IoTutor is loaded, the welcome message is displayed (see Fig. 5a) and waits for the user to either press the microphone button and talk, or type a question on the question box. The question will appear in the conversation area together with the list of relevant answers. IoTutor provides up to 10 relevant answers, out of which the first two will appear first, and the rest can be accessed using the navigation links. To help users quickly find a desired answer, the list of answers shows only excerpts of the full answer, which can be displayed when the user clicks the *View Document* button.

The *Expanded answer view* is depicted in Fig. 5b, and it contains information related to the scientific publication that contains the answer, including article title, authors, and publication year, as well as a link to the full article. The text shown in this view provides the complete information, which sometimes was lengthy, and to help the user focus on the most important parts, we highlight the passages in a light blue color. Instead of reading the text, the user may choose to let IoTutor read the text. In that case, an audio player will be shown containing the controls to play, pause, or move forward and backwards through the audio stream.

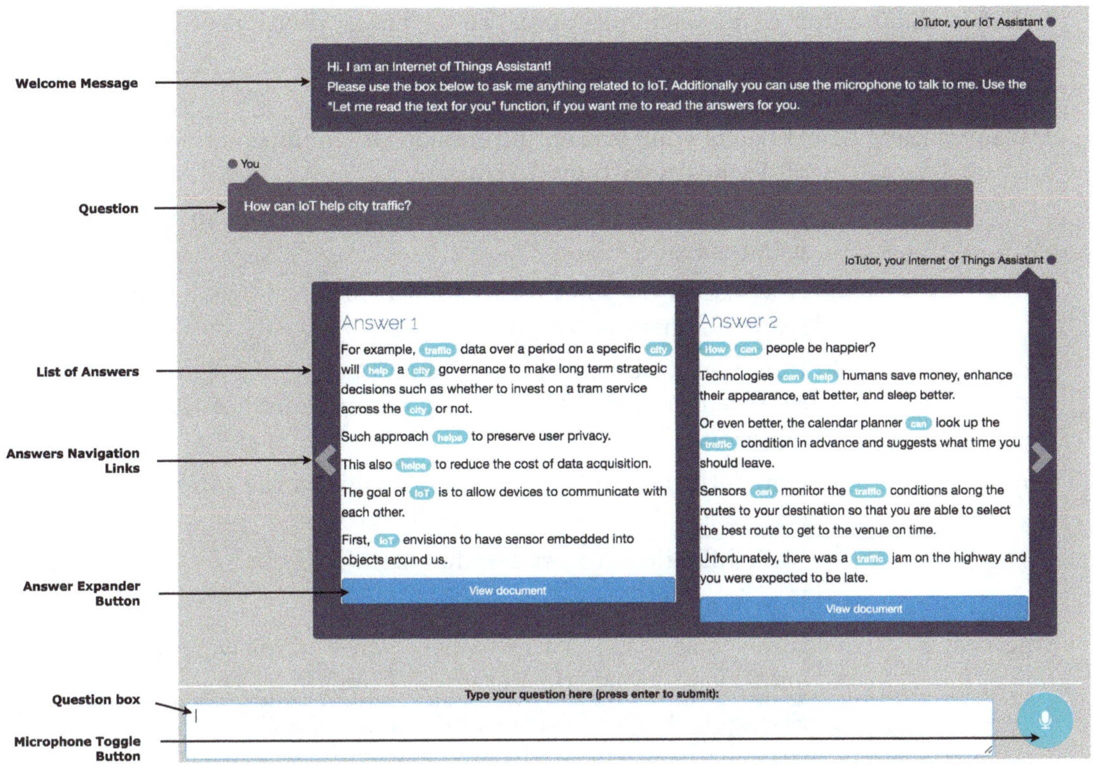

(a) The conversation area view, including the greeting message, questions, list of answers, question box, and microphone toggle button.

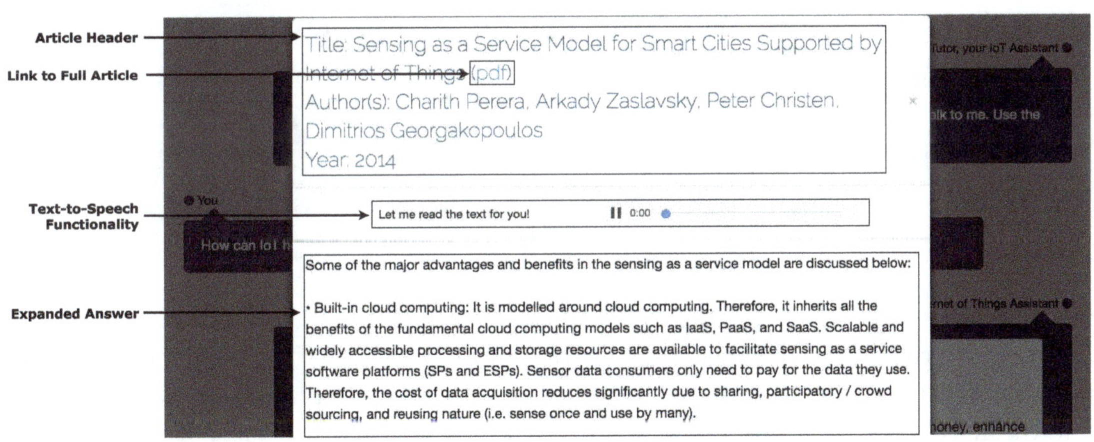

(b) The expanded answer view, including the article information (title, authors, year), the text-to-speech functionality, and expanded answer.

Fig. 5. Demonstration of a case where the user: (1) asks a question and IoTutor shows a list of answers (a); and (2) clicks the *View Document* button to expand the answer (b).

4.2 Evaluation Method and Results

To understand users' interaction and experience with the IoTutor, we conducted an evaluation of the tool. The IoTutor was initially presented to participants and

Table 2. The user experience questionnaire for the evaluation of IoTutor.

Aspect	Id	Question
Attractiveness	a1	What is your overall impression of our interactive Internet of Things Assistant (IoTutor)?
	a2	How useful do you find the possibility to ask questions using voice?
	a3	How useful do you find the feature that allows IoTutor to read the answers for you?
	a4	How useful do you find the functionality of IoTutor that returns research articles as answers to some of the questions?
Perspicuity	p1	How intuitive and easy to understand is the GUI (Graphical User Interface) of IoTutor?
	p2	How difficult is to get familiar with IoTutor?
	p3	How easy it is to use IoTutor?
Efficiency	e1	How efficient is IoTutor to help you find answers for questions related to Internet of Things?
	e2	How quickly did IoTutor find the answers?
Stimulation	s1	How valuable is to use IoTutor for the assignment?
	s2	How exciting is to use IoTutor for the assignment?
	s3	How interesting is to use IoTutor for the assignment?
	s4	How much does IoTutor motivate you to learn about the Internet of Things?
Novelty	n1	Dull/creative
	n2	Conventional/inventive
	n3	Usual/leading edge
	n4	Conservative/innovative

then they were given two weeks period to explore it. Most of the participants were students taking an Internet of Things master level course at Linnaeus University. One of the course assignments was to develop a literature review for the course project. To complete the assignment, they were instructed and encouraged to use IoTutor beside Google Scholar and other scientific libraries. After they had used IoTutor, participants were instructed to answer questions (see Table 2) of a User Experience Questionnaire (UEQ), which was adopted from [25]. The questionnaire measured six dimensions: *attractiveness* (four questions), *perspicuity* (three questions), *efficiency* (two questions), *stimulation* (four questions), and *novelty* (four questions). Questions were represented in a five-scale semantic differentials, where 1 indicates the most negative answer, 5 indicates the most positive answer, and 3 indicates a neutral answer. Ten participants consented and answered the questionnaire.

The results of the UEQ show a trend that participants expressed an overall positive attitude towards the tool. Most of the aspects/dimensions (12 out of 17) were rated higher than the neutral value, while the rest were slightly lower than the neutral value (see Fig. 6). However, the highest average rating was 3.8, which is an indication that although positive, these results are still not convincing.

When looking cumulatively at each of the five aspects/dimensions, all ratings appear over the neutral value (see Fig. 7). Considering that the aspects of *perspicuity* and *efficiency* measure the usability of the tool, and the aspects of *simulation* and *novelty* measure the user experience, the indication is that both show similar ratings. Slightly higher ratings were shown for *perspicuity* and *novelty*, which is an indication that participants had no difficulty to familiarize themselves with using the tool, and participants had recognized the innovativeness and creativeness of the tool.

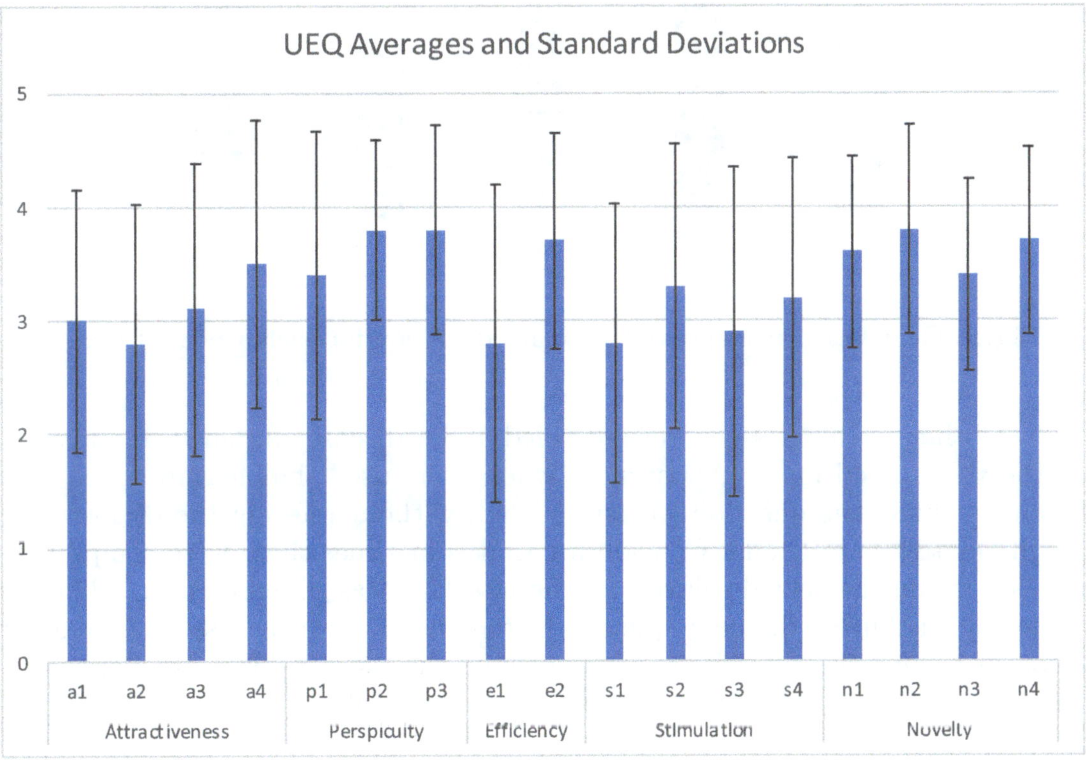

Fig. 6. The average and standard deviation for each of the answers in the user experience questionnaire.

Besides the UEQ results, we had an opportunity to briefly discuss the tool with two participants after they have used the tool and provided their UEQ answers. One major concern expressed was that the tool provided keyword-based answers, which was not expected considering that the interface tool was accepting natural questions. Participants' expectation was that an interface that is based on Watson should provide more natural and comprehensive answers.

Indeed, such interface behavior was also noted by the researchers. Because this seemed inappropriate, we did contact IBM and inquire whether the service was working correctly or if training process and resources fed to Watson were with omission. Their reply confirmed that the procedure we followed was correct. It remains to speculate that perhaps in order to get better results, Watson should be trained with more content and more questions than what we had provided (described in activity 3).

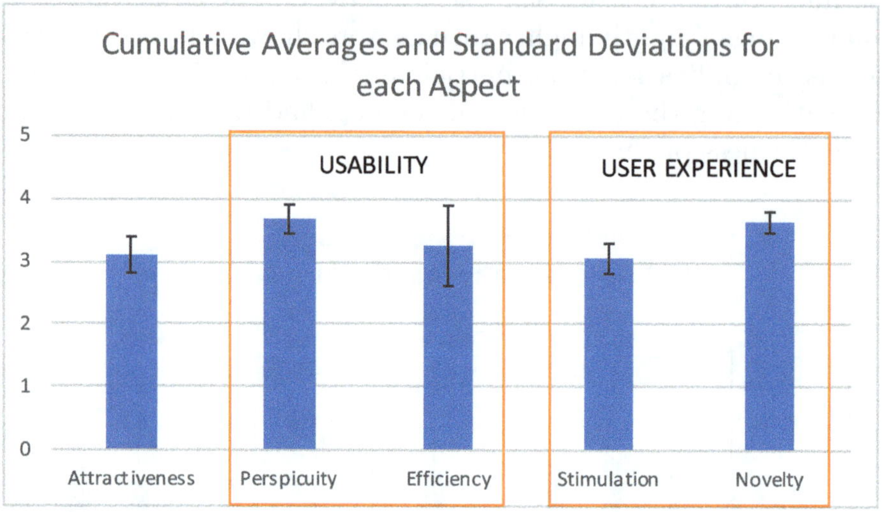

Fig. 7. Cumulative averages and standard deviation for each aspect of UEQ.

Two other usability issues were revealed in our discussion. One was considering the voice-based input. Apparently, when users used that feature, once they stopped talking, the question was submitted, without offering the opportunity to edit the text beforehand. Considering that sometimes there were comprehension issues and the text displayed by the interface was different from what the participant had uttered, being able to edit the question was necessary. The other issue was the interface feature to read out loud the excerpts from the paper provided as an answer. This feature was actually possible only when participants expanded the initial answer and viewed an extended excerpt from the source paper. Participants expected that the interface would read even the initial brief answer provided. This was an interface omission to clearly communicate when that feature is availability.

5 Conclusions and Future Work

With above 20 billion IoT devices expected to be used in the near future, adequate education of skilled work-force is a priority. Considering the recent success of cognitive computing solutions in health or financial domains, and the increasing volume of IoT literature in various formats, we have proposed in this paper the application of cognitive computing to IoT education.

We have described the design and implementation of IoTutor, which is a platform-independent web-based application that enables dialog-based interaction with users that want to learn about IoT. The interaction in text or speech form is done using natural language. We have investigated the usefulness of IoTutor by asking a group of students at the Linnaeus University to use the IoTutor for a period of two weeks. Participants have expressed their opinions with respect to the attractiveness, perspicuity, efficiency, stimulation, and novelty of the IoTutor. The majority of aspects were rated higher than the neutral value, while the rest were slightly lower than the neutral value.

We have observed that using a relatively small number of training questions and papers may result with sub-optimal answers from IoTutor. Our intention with this study was to see the quality of answers that IoTutor would provide with minimal training resources. In the future, we plan to use a larger digital library of scientific publications during the training process of IoTutor to measure its impact in the increase of the quality of the answers provided by the tool.

References

1. IBM Cloud Docs: Discovery - improving result relevance with the tooling. https://console.bluemix.net/docs/services/discovery/index.html. Accessed 17 Apr 2018
2. Node.js: Node.js Foundation. https://nodejs.org/en/. Accessed 4 Mar 2018
3. Watson Developer Cloud Node.js SDK: IBM Open Source at GitHub. https://github.com/watson-developer-cloud/node-sdk. Accessed 15 Feb 2018
4. Achilleos, A., et al.: SciChallenge: a social media aware platform for contest-based STEM education and motivation of young students. IEEE Trans. Learn. Technol. (2018). https://doi.org/10.1109/TLT.2018.2810879
5. Ahmed, M.N., Toor, A.S., O'Neil, K., Friedland, D.: Cognitive computing and the future of health care cognitive computing and the future of healthcare: the cognitive power of IBM Watson has the potential to transform global personalized medicine. IEEE Pulse **8**(3), 4–9 (2017)
6. Alsouda, Y., Pllana, S., Kurti, A.: A machine learning driven IoT solution for noise classification in smart cities. In: Proceedings of the Machine Learning Driven Technologies and Architectures for Intelligent Internet of Things (ML-IoT), pp. 4–9. ML-IoT, Euromicro (2018)
7. Apple Inc.: iOS - Siri - Apple. http://www.apple.com/ios/siri/ (2017). Accessed 9 Feb 2018
8. Cer, D., et al.: Universal Sentence Encoder. arXiv e-prints, March 2018
9. Cerf, V., Senges, M.: Taking the internet to the next physical level. Computer **49**(2), 80–86 (2016). https://doi.org/10.1109/MC.2016.51
10. Chen, Y., Argentinis, J.E., Weber, G.: IBM Watson: how cognitive computing can be applied to big data challenges in life sciences research. Clin. Ther. **38**(4), 688–701 (2016)
11. Chozas, A.C., Memeti, S., Pllana, S.: Using cognitive computing for learning parallel programming: an IBM Watson solution. Procedia Comput. Sci. **108**(Suppl. C), 2121–2130 (2017)
12. Ferati, M., Kurti, A., Vogel, B., Raufi, B.: Augmenting requirements gathering for people with special needs using IoT: a position paper. In: Proceedings of the 9th International Workshop on Cooperative and Human Aspects of Software Engineering, CHASE 2016, pp. 48–51. ACM, New York (2016)

13. Ferrucci, D.A.: Introduction to "This is Watson". IBM J. Res. Devel. **56(3.4)**, 1:1–1:15 (2012)
14. Gartner: Internet of Things. https://www.gartner.com/technology/research/internet-of-things/. Accessed 3 Mar 2018
15. Goel, A., Creeden, B., Kumble, M., Salunke, S., Shetty, A., Wiltgen, B.: Using Watson for enhancing human-computer co-creativity. In: 2015 AAAI Fall Symposium Series (2015)
16. Google Inc.: Google Now (2017). https://support.google.com/websearch/answer/4541722. Accessed 9 Feb 2018
17. Gubbi, J., Buyya, R., Marusic, S., Palaniswami, M.: Internet of Things (IoT): a vision, architectural elements, and future directions. Future Gener. Comput. Syst. **29**(7), 1645–1660 (2013)
18. Harms, K.J.: Towards a programming environment that adaptively suggests examples and corresponding puzzles based on programmer skill. In: 2014 IEEE Symposium on Visual Languages and Human-Centric Computing (VL/HCC), pp. 185–186, July 2014. https://doi.org/10.1109/VLHCC.2014.6883047
19. Henderson, M., et al.: Efficient natural language response suggestion for smart reply. arXiv e-prints, May 2017
20. High, R.: The era of cognitive systems: an inside look at IBM Watson and how it works. REDP-4955-00, 12 December 2012. http://www.redbooks.ibm.com/redpapers/pdfs/redp4955.pdf. Accessed 3 Mar 2018
21. Memedi, M., Tshering, G., Fogelberg, M., Jusufi, I., Kolkowska, E., Klein, G.: An interface for IoT: feeding back health-related data to Parkinson's disease patients. J. Sens. Actuator Netw. **7**(1), 14 (2018)
22. Mercer, C.: 16 innovative businesses using IBM Watson: which companies are using Watson's big data and analytics to power their business? (2017). http://www.computerworlduk.com/galleries/it-vendors/16-innovative-ways-companies-are-using-ibm-watson-3585847/. Accessed 12 Mar 2018
23. Modha, D.S., Ananthanarayanan, R., Esser, S.K., Ndirango, A., Sherbondy, A.J., Singh, R.: Cognitive computing. Commun. ACM **54**(8), 62–71 (2011)
24. Perez, D., Memeti, S., Pllana, S.: A simulation study of a smart living IoT solution for remote elderly care. In: 2018 Third International Conference on Fog and Mobile Edge Computing (FMEC), pp. 227–232, April 2018
25. Schrepp, M.: User Experience Questionnaire Handbook. All you need to know to apply the UEQ successfully in your project (2015)
26. Witte, R., Sateli, B., Khamis, N., Rilling, J.: Intelligent software development environments: integrating natural language processing with the eclipse platform. In: Butz, C., Lingras, P. (eds.) AI 2011. LNCS (LNAI), vol. 6657, pp. 408–419. Springer, Heidelberg (2011). https://doi.org/10.1007/978-3-642-21043-3_49

Author Index

www.ingramcontent.com/pod-product-compliance
Lightning Source LLC
LaVergne TN
LVHW082158200926
848484LV00008B/2176

* 9 7 8 1 0 1 3 2 7 3 4 9 0 *